# MEET ME ON THE
# MIDWAY

# MEET ME ON THE
# MIDWAY

## A HISTORY OF WISCONSIN FAIRS

JERRY APPS

Wisconsin Historical Society Press

Published by the Wisconsin Historical Society Press
*Publishers since 1855*

The Wisconsin Historical Society helps people connect to the past by collecting, preserving, and sharing stories. Founded in 1846, the Society is one of the nation's finest historical institutions.
*Join the Wisconsin Historical Society:* wisconsinhistory.org/membership

Publication of this book was made possible in part by grants from the Alice E. Smith fellowship fund and the Amy Louise Hunter fellowship fund.

Photographs identified with WHi or WHS are from the Society's collections; address requests to reproduce these photos to the Visual Materials Archivist at the Wisconsin Historical Society, 816 State Street, Madison, WI 53706.

Front cover image credits: prize-winning steer at the Rock County Fair, courtesy of Mary Check, Rock County 4-H Fair; teacup ride at the Wisconsin State Fair, courtesy of Travel Wisconsin; cream puffs, courtesy of Travel Wisconsin; Grant County Fair midway at night, courtesy of Amy Olson, Director, Grant County Fair. Back cover image credits: child with cow, photo by Shelly Holmes Portraiture; 1915 Wisconsin State Fair stamp, WHi Image ID 33247. Spine photo of pig by Steve Apps

Frontmatter photo credits: page ii: Alice in Dairyland Marjean Czerwinski rides in the official Alice car during the Army Day Parade at the 1951 Wisconsin State Fair, WHi Image ID 25430; page v: a flower exhibit at the Waukesha County Fair, photo by Lacey Olson, used with permission by UW–Madison Division of Extension; pages vi–vii: Grant County Fair midway at night, photo courtesy of Amy Olson, Director, Grant County Fair; page viii: Herman Apps's collection of fair ribbons, photo by Steve Apps; page ix: carnival rides at the Wisconsin State Fair, photo courtesy of Travel Wisconsin

Part-opener photo credits: Part I, pages XII–1: view of the Wisconsin State Fair midway, circa 1920, WHi Image ID 33325; Part II, pages 20–21: Columbia County Fair, photo courtesy of Travel Wisconsin; Part III, pages 70–71: Dodge County Fair postcard, circa 1910, WHi Image ID 31530; Part IV, pages 192–193: Dane County Fair, photo courtesy of Travel Wisconsin

Printed in Canada
Designed by Brian Donahue / www.bedesigninc.com

26 25 24 23 22    1 2 3 4 5

Library of Congress Cataloging-in-Publication Data
Names: Apps, Jerold W., 1934– author.
Title: Meet me on the midway : a history of Wisconsin fairs / Jerry Apps.
Description: Madison, WI : Wisconsin Historical Society Press, [2022] |
   Includes bibliographical references and index.
Identifiers: LCCN 2021043903 (print) | LCCN 2021043904 (e-book) |
   ISBN 9780870209833 (paperback) | ISBN 9780870209840 (epub)
Subjects: LCSH: Agricultural exhibitions—Wisconsin—History. |
   Fairs—Wisconsin—History.
Classification: LCC S555.W6 A66 2022 (print) | LCC S555.W6 (e-book) | DDC
   630.7409775—dc23/eng/20220103
LC record available at https://lccn.loc.gov/2021043903
LC ebook record available at https://lccn.loc.gov/2021043904

# CONTENTS

# INTRODUCTION

My dad loved fairs. I don't know how old he was when he attended his first, but he often told stories about showing cattle at the Waushara County Fair in 1927 and 1928, when he was in his mid-twenties. He and my mother had recently become established at the home farm and had a small herd of Holstein cattle: a dozen or so milk cows and a few calves and young stock.

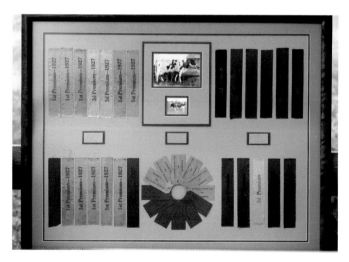

The home farm is about eight miles from Wautoma, which is both the county seat for Waushara County and the location of the fairgrounds. The challenge for Pa was getting his herd of cattle, along with the hay to feed them, to the fairgrounds. "Easy," Pa said when I asked him how he did it, "I drove them." Pa piled hay on the hay wagon, hitched up the team, turned the cows loose, and walked them to Wautoma. "Nothin' to it," he said. "Some of them needed a little encouragement because they wanted to stop and eat grass along the way, but the horses and I kept them going."

After arriving at the fairgrounds, Pa found stalls for the cattle and the team. "Where did you sleep?" I asked. Smiling, Pa told me, "I slept on the load of hay—never slept better."

He showed his cattle in several classes and won a few ribbons. He also showed his team of draft horses. In those days, horses did all the heavy work on farms, and farmers were proud to show them off. "Those were great times," Pa

recalled. He knew most of the farmers he competed against. "We had a good time, swapping stories and trying to best each other. I learned a lot, too, like the characteristics of a first-prize cow. Sometimes you gotta get away from home to do that."

Pa was right. For some folks, especially youngsters, the fair was a rare opportunity to be away from home. I attended my first county fair when I was just four years old. On a hot August day in 1938, in the depths of the Great Depression, I stood near my dad next to the fence that encircled the show ring. We watched boys and girls not much older than I was as they led their calves around the ring. The judge stood in the center, carefully eyeing each animal. I know it was a hot day because Pa bought me a five-cent chocolate candy bar, and I recall it melting in my hand as we stood there.

The kids in the ring belonged to 4-H—a club I would not be eligible for until age ten. Not only were the animals on their best behavior in the show ring, they were also meticulously washed and brushed so not a hint of dirt could be seen. I was impressed. After watching the judging for a while, we walked through the barns to look at the cattle. Dad stopped now and again to chat with a farmer helping his 4-H son or daughter prepare their calves for the show ring. The smells were familiar to me, the same smells as at home in our barn. Next we walked through the sheep barn. We had no sheep at home, so this was new to me. Then on to the hog barn, the horse barn, and the shed that housed the chickens, ducks, and turkeys, all quacking, gobbling, and crowing. I don't remember walking down the midway, but I heard the music and roar of the gasoline engines that powered the various rides. I caught the smell of hamburgers and onions cooking, but I knew Pa wouldn't be buying any—we had no money to indulge in fair food and had brought our lunch from home.

By late afternoon, evening chores beckoned, and we headed for home. I didn't know at the time how important the county fair would be in my life in later years as a 4-H leader, county Extension agent, and fair judge. But the experience had made an indelible impression on me, and I never forgot my first trip to the fair.

On these pages, we will take a trip to the fair, starting with the earliest incarnations as livestock exhibitions to today's multitudes of exhibits and demonstrations, grandstand entertainment, games and rides, and competitions of all sorts. We will stroll down the midway, hop on the Ferris wheel, visit the cattle barns and exhibits, and sample favorite fair food. We'll look behind the scenes to learn about the experiences of judges, fair managers, and carnival ride attendants. We'll explore concise histories of Wisconsin's county and district fairs and the state fair. And we'll meet people who have stories to tell about the fair and its importance in their lives.

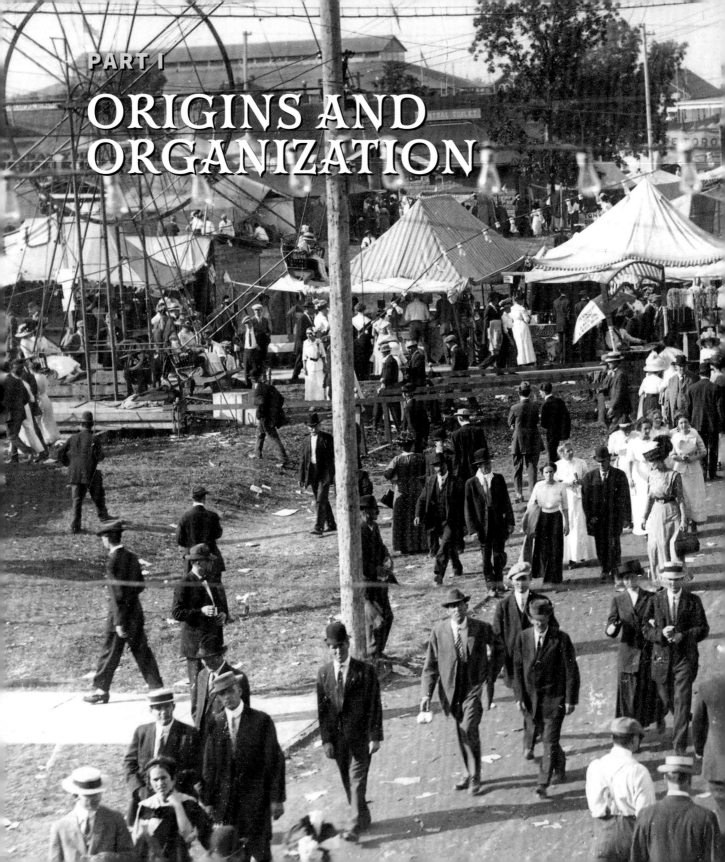

# PART I

# ORIGINS AND ORGANIZATION

# 1

# THE FIRST FAIRS

The source of the word *fair* is believed to be the Latin word *feria*, meaning "free day" or "holy day."[1] The *Encyclopaedia Britannica* defines *fair* as a "temporary market where buyers and sellers gather to transact business," noting further that a fair "is held at regular intervals, generally at the same location and time of year, and it usually lasts for several days or even weeks. Its primary function is the promotion of trade."[2] Early fairs essentially fit that definition but, along with buying and selling, also included religious celebrations. Fairs are mentioned in the Bible (Ezekiel 27:12, Authorized [King James] Version): "they traded in thy fairs."), and some took place as early as 500 BCE.[3]

The Romans introduced fairs to northern Europe to encourage trade after conquering that territory beginning in 200 BCE. By the seventh century CE, a large fair at Saint-Denis near Paris had emerged. In the eleventh century, Easter fairs became popular in Cologne, Germany. For several hundred years, beginning in the mid-1100s, fairs at Champagne, France, were the largest and most prominent in Europe. They mostly consisted of religious celebrations along with the buying and selling of a variety of products, ranging from Russian furs, to spices from East Asia, to linens from southern Germany. Fairs also took place in other parts of the world, including China and Mexico. One legend says that the Spanish conquistadors found a great Aztec fair on the site of present-day Mexico City. For hundreds of years, European commerce was based on fairs. With the coming of the industrial revolution, religious fairs and those based solely on the buying and selling of products began to disappear.[4] Some, however, morphed into agricultural fairs. European settlers brought their tradition of fairs with them to the Americas. The first known agricultural fair in the New World took place in Nova Scotia in 1765.[5]

Entrée triomphale de la Lieuse MAC CORMICK

A L'EXPOSITION UNIVERSELLE

Lithograph of a
McCormick reaper at
the 1900 World's Fair
in Paris

WHI IMAGE ID 51274

# THE ROOTS OF AMERICAN FAIRS

Unlike most other business owners, who held tight to their trade secrets, farmers traditionally shared their successes and failures with one another for the improvement of farming practices. One way they did so was by organizing agricultural societies. In 1785, twenty-three merchants, businessmen, and landowners in the Philadelphia area organized the Philadelphia Society for Promoting Agriculture, the first of its kind in the United States. These farmers and tradespeople recognized that current farming practices resulted in soil erosion, that their farm animals lacked quality, and, most important, that "the wealth and prosperity of the country was dependent on agriculture."[6] Soon other agricultural societies sprung up in New England, and eventually the idea moved west with the pioneers.

Elkanah Watson of Pittsfield, Massachusetts, is credited with starting the first agricultural fair in the United States. In 1807, Watson displayed two of his prize Merino sheep in the Pittsfield town square. Merino sheep were new to the area, and a curious crowd gathered. People marveled at the quality of the Merino's soft wool—and the first American agricultural fair was born. Watson believed that by exhibiting his animals and sharing information about them, agriculture could be improved. Watson soon helped to organize the Berkshire Agricultural Society, which sponsored its first fair in 1811. The event was billed as a "cattle show" and included 383 sheep, 109 oxen, 7 bulls, 9 cows, and 3 heifers.[7]

The Berkshire Agricultural Society, always looking to improve its fairs, introduced a plowing contest in 1818, likely the first held in the country. The Berkshire group also incorporated a competition, with prize money going to best oxen, cattle, swine, and sheep. Watson would go on to help other New England communities organize their own agricultural societies and fairs.[8]

In the early days of white settlement, most people in the United States lived on farms. As settlers moved west, they organized agricultural societies at both the county and state levels. To help farmers learn from one another—and recognizing the motivation sparked by the opportunity to compete for ribbons and prizes—the agricultural societies began sponsoring fairs.

Certificate awarded by the Waupaca County Agricultural Society in 1881

PHOTO COURTESY OF RICHARD LUEDKE

Doing so was no small feat. For example, when Calumet County mounted its first fair, in 1856, it "was a time of dirt roads, oxen teams, Indian villages and wild animals. . . . Portland [later named Brant] was a thriving community composed of a church, blacksmith shop, saloon, general store, stage depot, and post office. The stage made three trips a week from Chilton to Portland, to Stockbridge, then on to Fond du Lac, and was the only link to the outside world. Calumet County was the edge of the wilderness."[9]

## WORLD'S FAIRS

The first modern "world's fair" was held at London's Hyde Park in 1851. Called the Great Exhibition of the Works of Industry of All Nations, or sometimes simply the Crystal Palace Exhibition, its purpose was to showcase Great Britain to an international audience and enhance sales of British goods abroad. The fair featured scientific and technological exhibits along with exhibitions of art and craftsmanship from several countries. Some six million people attended, earning the fair a substantial profit.

The Hyde Park fair's success set off a flurry of other world's fairs, held in such far-flung places as Australia, Tasmania, Guatemala, and Hanoi. In 1853–1854, inspired by these world's fairs, the United States held an Exhibition of the Industry of All Nations in New York. That endeavor lost money, and it would be more than twenty years before the United States held another world's fair, this one in Philadelphia in 1876.

Of the several world's fairs held in the United States, arguably the most successful was the Columbian Exposition, held in Chicago in 1893. Even though the country was in the midst of a recession, several million people attended the fair. For many, it was the first time they saw electric lights. The fair also introduced attendees to the idea of a midway, a place set apart from the exhibits and offering rides and other attractions now common at county and state fairs. The Chicago World's Fair even offered rides on the first-ever Ferris wheel. (See chapter 6 for more on the Ferris wheel.)

NOTE

John Findling, "World's Fair," *Encyclopaedia Britannica*, www.britannica.com/topic/worlds-fair.

## WISCONSIN'S FIRST COUNTY FAIRS

The first Wisconsin county fair opened in Waukesha in 1842, six years before Wisconsin became a state. At that time, Milwaukee County included what is now Waukesha County. The fair, operated under the auspices of the Milwaukee County Agricultural Society, awarded prizes in four departments: cattle (which included a prize for the best yoke of oxen), horses, sheep, and hogs. The fair also held a plowing contest. The Waukesha County Fair did not operate for the next eight years. In 1849, the Walworth County Fair opened in East Troy, and in 1859 the Kenosha Agricultural Society held a one-day fair. During the next five years, agricultural associations in Columbia, Fond du Lac, Grant, Green, Jefferson, Sauk, Sheboygan, Washington, and Waukesha Counties held annual fairs. As a writer for the *Wisconsin State Journal* later stated, "These [fairs] were the pioneers

The midway at the Lafayette County Fair, early 1900s
LAFAYETTE COUNTY HISTORICAL SOCIETY

in the county fair movement. Unaided by state money, and much critized, they blazed the trail for others to follow."[10]

The interest and wide-ranging support of these agricultural society–sponsored fairs did not go unnoticed by Wisconsin's lawmakers. Indeed, agricultural society members encouraged their representatives to vote to provide monetary support for these annual events.

During its 1856 session, the Wisconsin Legislature passed "An Act for the encouragement and promotion of Agriculture," legislation that would have far-reaching effects on the future of fairs in the state. In section 1, the legislature made official the agricultural societies that were springing up around the state, stating that: "It shall be lawful for any number of persons in any county in this state, to associate together and form a county society, to encourage and promote agriculture, domestic manufactures and the mechanic arts therein."[11]

The legislation included details for the organization and operations of agricultural societies. Section 2 stated: "Such societies shall be formed by written articles of association, subscribed by the member thereof, specifying the objects of the Society." Section 3 described leadership requirements: "Such societies, not exceeding one in each county, shall be organized by appointing a president, vice president, secretary and treasurer, and such other officers as they may deem proper, to be chosen annually."[12]

Most important for county fair operations, the state authorized funds for the operation of fairs in the amount of one hundred dollars for each agricultural association. The money was to be used for "paying the necessary incidental expenses of such societies and "be annually paid out for premiums awarded by such societies. . . . [for] live animals, articles of production and agricultural implements and tools, domestic manufactures, mechanical improvement and productions as are of the growth and manufacture of the county, and also all such experiments and discoveries, or attainments in scientific or practical agriculture as are made within the county where such societies are respectively organized."[13]

## AGRICULTURAL SOCIETIES AND THE CIVIL WAR

The Civil War years of 1861 to 1865 caused considerable havoc for the agricultural societies as the public's interest was diverted to the war and governments cut financial support to the societies. According to economic historian Frederick Merk, in 1861 the Wisconsin legislature eliminated funding for the Wisconsin State Agricultural Society. The work of the state society was "practically suspended" for a time, and the county societies suffered as well. "Of the thirty-seven county agricultural societies active at the beginning of the war, only eighteen survived the year, and not until the end of the decade did the number again reach it former proportions."

Prior to the war, the Wisconsin State Agricultural Society had held the annual state fair in Madison, but in 1861 the society turned over its fairgrounds to Governor Randall for use as a military training camp. From Camp Randall, as the former fairgrounds were now called, about two-thirds of Wisconsin Civil War soldiers were trained for battle. The state fair was

The 1879 Wisconsin State Fair, held at Camp Randall
WHI IMAGE ID 27141

cancelled for 1861, 1862, and 1863. Those agricultural societies that survived the first year of the Civil War continued to hold their annual fairs, but interest dwindled. By 1864, the agricultural societies and fairs saw a revival, and the State Agricultural Society reinstated its state fair in that year.

NOTES

Frederick Merk, *Economic History of Wisconsin During the Civil War Decade* (Madison, WI: Wisconsin Historical Society, 1916), pp. 50–51.

# FAIRS AND LIVESTOCK IMPROVEMENT

In his 1922 *History of Agriculture in Wisconsin*, historian Joseph Schafer explained that Wisconsin's state and county fairs were largely designed to promote interest in the improvement of livestock breeds. "Good cattle, sheep, pigs, horses and poultry really made the fairs," he wrote.[14]

Cattle judging at the Langlade County Fair, 1915

WHI IMAGE ID 123160

The cattle department was the most lively and influential feature of those early fairs. The first cattle exhibited were Devons and Durhams. At the 1880 Green County Fair, one Ayrshire cow was exhibited. And in 1883, at the Racine County Fair, Herefords, a beef breed, first appeared. A few years later, dairy breeds, including Brown Swiss and Jerseys, appeared at county fairs. It wasn't until 1889 that the now ubiquitous Holsteins were exhibited.

A 1922 *Wisconsin State Journal* article credited those early county fairs with developing the state as a dairy powerhouse, the writer noting, "It was in the cattle department that our Wisconsin farmers received their first lessons in dairying. It sowed the seed from which grew the great dairy industry as we now know it."[15]

No horses were exhibited during Wisconsin's first fairs, as oxen did the heavy work on the farms during the early settlement days. But by 1860, nearly every fair had a horse department. The Morgan breed, developed in Vermont, was one of the first to be featured. By the start of the Civil War, most Wisconsin farmers had turned their trusty oxen out to pasture and replaced them with the heavier draft horse breeds, such as Clydesdales, Belgians, and Percherons. By 1875, the horse department was a popular attraction, and imported breeds of draft horses filled the fairs' horse barns.

Horse racing competitions grew out of the growing interest in horses, with the lighter carriage and saddle horses prevailing. Earliest racing fans were interested only in the speed of each horse, not how horses competed against one another: the horse with the best time was declared the winner. It wasn't until 1859, at the Racine County Fair, that a horse race as they're known today took place, with horses competing against one another on a racetrack.[16]

For a time, cattle and horses overshadowed other livestock species. But because wool was a popular item on Wisconsin's frontier, sheep exhibits emerged at the county fairs, with classes for both long- and short-wool breeds. Early breeds exhibited included Southdowns, Merinos, and Hampshires, soon followed by Shropshires, Oxfords, and Cheviots. Purebred hogs were the last livestock to appear, not arriving on the fair scene until the 1850s, and even then described as "nondescript breeds." The earliest hog breeds to be shown at county fairs, Polands and Duroc Jerseys, made their appearance around that time.

# THE DOMESTIC ARTS

Early Wisconsin county fairs were devoted primarily to farm animals. But farm women felt they had something to contribute that was just as important as the improvement of livestock. Referred to as the *domestic arts*—later *home economics*, and still later *family living*—this department grew in prominence at all county fairs. Soon prizes were awarded for cooking and baking, sewing, "fancy work," canning, artwork, floral arranging, and many other skilled endeavors.

Judges examine dresses entered in a Wisconsin State Fair sewing competition.
WHI IMAGE ID 33343

By 1884, fifty-four fairs operated in Wisconsin, roughly one for each county at that time. Fair organizers continued to add events and attractions that would not only educate but also entertain fairgoers: "By the mid-eighties the county fair was taking on more of a carnival atmosphere with harness racing and even beer tents."[17] And by the turn of the twentieth century, nearly every state hosted one or more agricultural fairs. To succeed and to grow year by year, fairs required careful management and organization.

# 2

# FAIR MANAGEMENT

The University of Wisconsin, organized in 1848, initially showed only slight interest in the education of Wisconsin's farmers—and no interest in fairs. The university made few changes in its basic curriculum—focused on geography, Latin, Greek, and English grammar—until President Lincoln signed the Morrill Act in 1862. Commonly called the Land-Grant Act, the Morrill Act made federally owned lands available to the states. The states could use the proceeds from the sale of those lands to establish college programs in agriculture and engineering.[1]

In 1868, the University of Wisconsin hired William W. Daniells as its first professor of agriculture. Daniells created an agriculture major, but the program differed little from the bachelor of arts major already on campus, and essentially no one enrolled. By the 1870s, Wisconsin farmers were increasingly unhappy with the university's lack of interest in their struggle to move from wheat growing to other agricultural enterprises, and in 1878 the Wisconsin Agricultural Society convinced the governor to appoint a farmer, Hiram Smith, to the university's board of regents. Smith urged university officials to add a second full-time professor of agriculture, which they did in 1880 when they hired William A. Henry. In 1889, the university combined all of its agriculture programs in a new College of Agriculture, with Henry as its dean. During these years, the university launched farmers' institutes, held all across the state, and began offering the farm short course during winters on the Madison campus. But no one was yet making a connection between what the university was doing to educate farmers and what the agricultural societies were doing through their fairs.[2]

For more than fifty years, Wisconsin's county fairs had been managed by local agricultural societies. But after the University of Wisconsin established the

Students enrolled in the University of Wisconsin College of Agriculture farm short course examine corn samples, 1916.

WHI IMAGE ID 122661

Agricultural Extension Service (later called Cooperative Extension) within the College of Agriculture in 1914, Extension agents took over much of the management of county fairs. Two years earlier, the university had already hired its first county agricultural agent, E. L. Luther, based in Rhinelander.[3] The passage of the Smith-Lever Act by Congress in 1914 created the Cooperative Extension Service, funded by federal, state, and county governments. The Cooperative Extension Service became the delivery system for taking the research of the land grant colleges and agricultural experiment stations to farm families.[4] Soon all of the state's northern counties had an Extension agent in place, with the central and southern counties close behind. These county-based university staff almost immediately recognized fairs as one important way to reach farmers.

Around this same time, a national program to engage young people in farm education had begun to take shape; eventually formalized under the name 4-H, the organization would grow to involve thousands (and eventually millions) of children who would influence fairs for generations to come. In Wisconsin, youth corn-growing clubs were among the early forerunners of 4-H. (For more on 4-H and other boys' and girls' clubs, see chapter 3.)

With Extension agents now working across the state, and with 4-H members ready to exhibit their projects at their local fairs, Wisconsin's fairs changed dramatically. Not only did the number of exhibits expand with 4-H member

Sawyer County 4-H members display their chickens, 1930.

WHI IMAGE ID 87353

participation, but now local Extension agents became involved in the operation of the fairs, along with the fair boards that had often been in place for years. Most fair boards consisted of volunteers who supervised the operation of the local fairs. The relationship between Cooperative Extension and the local fair boards did not always work smoothly. Even many years after extension agents began working with a fair, lingering disagreements between old-time fair boards and the Cooperative Extension Service sometimes continued. Nancy Franz, a longtime Cooperative Extension agent, recalled:

> My first fair as a county 4-H agent (1981) was at the Head of the Lakes Fair in Superior. I attended some fair association meetings representing 4-H interests. The relationship between the fair board and the 4-H leaders was often strained. I sometimes got caught in the middle. The fair board wanted to make money, and the 4-H leaders wanted the fair to appropriately recognize the educational and life skill achievements

As a 4-H and livestock agent for Brown County, author Jerry Apps (at center) taught 4-H members how to judge dairy calves.
PHOTO COURTESY OF JERRY APPS

of youth. One year during the fair, emotions were running high between these groups. I arranged a meeting with the county board member who served on the fair board and two 4-H leaders who wanted to share their concerns about the lack of support for 4-H at the fair. The meeting started well, but the county board member made a comment about 4-H being allowed to be at the fair as a gift to 4-H and that the fair could easily run without 4-H. I saw one of the leaders lift her fist toward the county board member just as the other leader caught her hand and led her away to cool off. I quickly ended the meeting and told the county board member he had probably lost some votes from 4-H leaders in his district (he wasn't reelected, by the way). The only thing that improved the 4-H relationship with the fair board was when a 4-H leader was hired to serve as the fair director. Even so, the Head of the Lakes Fair never gave 4-H or other educational exhibitors full support at that time.[5]

Fair board members also have stories to tell. Guy Dutcher, Waushara County Circuit Court judge, has served on the Waushara County Fair Board for twenty-eight years. He recalled a time in the mid-1990s when he was both Waushara County district attorney and a member of the fair board. As he pointed out, "These roles were not always entirely compatible during Fair Week because I would basically attempt to be simultaneously present at the courthouse and the fairgrounds while performing tasks that lacked symmetry with one another." He continued,

I had arrived at the fairgrounds early Friday morning to open the gates and determine whether the dairy superintendents needed any assistance with last minute details for the 8 a.m. show. Arrival at the dairy barn revealed a crisis. One of the cherubs participating in the "Tykes in Training" program had lost control of his calf and it was running loose about the south end of the fairgrounds. While others consoled the dismayed kindergartner, I was recruited to join the search and recover mission that was quickly formed to locate and capture the wayward exhibit before she exited the fairgrounds and began strolling about the city of Wautoma. The only difficulty with my participation in this venture was that I was dressed in slacks, a tie, and a neatly pressed white shirt that were appropriate for my pending appearances in a courtroom rather than as a dairy exhibitor.

The mission to locate the misguided quarry was soon successful. Almost immediately, she was observed casually jogging about the vacant parking area adjacent to the livestock buildings. Unfortunately, the capture portion of this enterprise would be far more prolonged. Invigorated by her newly achieved freedom and undiscovered environment, the young calf resisted the valiant efforts that her detractors were making to pursue and control. The sight of a half dozen young, athletic humans exhausting themselves during pursuit of a delinquent, three-month-old calf likely provided far better entertainment to the early morning fair attendees than any paid, scheduled grandstand act could ever have given.

Ultimately, this game of seek and conquer concluded when the calf cornered herself at the far southeast corner of the fairgrounds. There was one final scene to this comedy that would rival any Shakespearean masterpiece. The district attorney, the public official who would have undoubtedly brought charges against the offending critter were the Model Penal Code applicable to bovines, unwisely attempted to seize the tail of the calf in an attempt to steer her along the two-hundred-yard journey to her proper domain. The predictable response to this effort was for the conquered beast to defiantly wave her tail, striking her well-clad pursuer across the chest of his pressed white dress shirt fifteen minutes before his first scheduled court appearance.[6]

By the second half of the 2000s, with Extension agents involved in their county fair's management, it was not uncommon for the agent's entire family to help in running the fair. Barbara Rogan recalled that she assisted her father, Bill Rogan, who was county agricultural agent for Waukesha County during the 1970s and who did much of the administrative work for the fair at that time. "We used a three-car garage as the fair office," she explained, continuing,

> I worked my regular job during the day on Thursday and Friday of fair week and worked at the fairgrounds until closing. On Saturday and Sunday, I worked afternoons and evenings. Prior to the fair opening, my dad would bring home boxes of entries, and my younger sisters and I would write the tags for the entries. Once the fair opened and the judging started, I assisted in transferring the results from the judges' sheets to the entry cards. At that time, the fair ran from Thursday to Sunday. Along with the clerical work, I was there to answer questions, help direct people to the different areas of the fair, and take care of the lost children brought to the fair office. . . . On Sunday, the last day of the fair, my mother brought dinner out for whoever was working. She always brought chicken, German potato salad, fruit, and a dessert.
>
> When the new fair building opened, the office was switched to a corner area and we had more interaction with the fairgoers. My duties were still the same but it was more fun being closer to the exhibitors and the visitors. On Friday nights when the animal auction took place, my dad would be in the crowd working to get the bids up, and if he thought the bidding wasn't going high enough, he would put a bid in to get it higher. That worked most of the time, but he got stuck with

a lamb one year, so he stopped doing that. There were fireworks on Friday and Saturday nights, and I remember one year when we were sitting in the office area waiting for them to finish, someone came in and said the embers were coming down on top of some of the tents. I think that was the first time I ever saw my dad run off in a panic, afraid that a tent would start on fire. Luckily, it didn't happen. . . .

Dad was a member of the local Kiwanis club, which had a food booth at the fair. They offered a pancake breakfast on Saturday mornings. I can still remember getting home around 11 or 11:30 on Friday night and then getting up at four on Saturday morning so I could help set up and serve coffee and clear tables when they opened at five."[7]

Lester Van Loon served as Waushara County Extension agricultural agent for twenty-eight years, retiring from that position in 1979 but continuing to serve as fair secretary until 1991. He was involved in everything that needed to be done before, during, and after the fair. One of his tasks was to count the money from the day's beer stand sales. Half of the money went to the organization sponsoring the beer stand, and the other half went to the fair association. Van Loon recalled that the money was often wet, so he would take it home and put it in the clothes dryer before he counted it. In the years he was fair secretary, he did everything from booking the grandstand entertainment to organizing saddle horse racing and setting off the fireworks in front of the grandstand.[8]

By the late 1980s, Extension agents' involvement in the administration and operation of fairs began changing. Nancy Franz, who worked as a 4-H agent in several Wisconsin counties during the 1980s and 1990s, noted that the roles and responsibilities of agents varied based on tradition and on the skills and interests of the agent. However, she explained, the Extension administrators in Madison thought agents' roles at the fairs should be focused on education, not on service. "Home economists/family living agents were discouraged from leading family life departments or assisting with food booths," she said. "Agricultural agents were expected to visit only a few hours each day and provide some support for market animal sales. 4-H agents were encouraged to turn over leadership roles to volunteers or paid fair staff and focus just on youth development." According to Franz, this sounded good in theory as a way to lessen the agent's stress and time commitment. But in practice, the philosophy often put agents in conflict with local traditions and expectations. "As an agent," she explained, "I found it

wise to please my local county board (including the county fair board) first and my out-of-county supervisors second. This meant finding a middle ground—including a strong fair volunteer development process. My philosophy was that everything related to the fair should be able to run without the 4-H agent in case something prevented the agent from being present. I feel we were able to get to that point in Bayfield County and luckily never tested it with an absent agent."[9]

Much of the management of fairs has long depended on volunteers. Abigail Martin, Wisconsin's 2019 Alice in Dairyland, called volunteers the backbone of local, county, and district fairs. She noted,

Young volunteers register 4-H members for the Dane County Junior Fair, 1959.

WHI IMAGE ID 102649

Throughout the year, members of fair boards spend hours booking entertainment, contracting food vendors, and brainstorming new activities to engage fair attendees. . . . No matter which part of the fair you visit, you will find a volunteer not far away. Project superintendents, 4-H club leaders, and FFA chapter advisors can be seen supporting youth in all corners of the fair. . . . These special people spend their free time teaching youth how to sew, how to can pickles, or how to wash a chicken. Yes, you have to wash a chicken before the fair. . . . Dedicated volunteers are an integral part of youth development at the fair. Their devotion sparks new passions, teaches patience, and encourages teamwork.[10]

In response to the changing relationship between Cooperative Extension and fair boards, particularly in terms of roles and responsibilities, at least one county in Wisconsin has taken steps to ensure continued positive working relationships. The Lincoln County 4-H Leaders' Association and the Lincoln County Fair Association, Inc., in 2012 created a formal memorandum of

# GUIDELINES FOR EXTENSION'S ROLE

In 2017, the University of Wisconsin Board of Regents restructured Cooperative Extension as a division of University of Wisconsin–Madison. The new Extension division released "Guidelines on the Educational Roles of County Extension Educators at County Fairs" in 2019 to clearly describe Extension staff's role in county fairs. These guidelines represented a significant shift in how county agents had long participated in fairs, including me. (I remember well those years that I helped scrub down the cupboards that would hold 4-H exhibits, prepared the exhibit barns, and took care of a host of other tasks before, throughout, and after the fair.) The guidelines include the following:

> "Area Extension Directors, in cooperation with County oversight Committees, will review the roles and responsibilities of educators [for many years known as extension agents] and program coordinators across institutes to work closely with county fairs, whether the county fair is an official county event, or sponsored by a private organization."

> "Adequate clerical staff ought to be employed by county fair organizations specifically to assist with fair responsibilities, so that support for ongoing extension programs can be maintained without disruption. We expect county extension educators

and program coordinators to focus on educational roles at county fairs."

"The following roles should not be performed by Cooperative Extension Staff:

1. Serving as fair secretary or manager or superintendent.
2. Serving as a voting member of the fair board.
3. Booking, contracting, and/or setting up for carnivals or other non-educational entertainment.
4. Scheduling or supervising the maintenance and upkeep of the fairgrounds and buildings.
5. Handling fair receipts and/or disbursements, or selling tickets at the fair.
6. Employing and/or supervising paid personnel for the fair, including judges and departmental superintendents."

"For many years, county extension agents had performed these roles—and in some instances, because a portion of the agent's salary was provided by the county, they were considered county employees with one or more of these managerial roles expected. But the administration's argument, that these agents were primarily educators, should not be compared with other county employees who do not have educational roles."

understanding to ensure "that the Lincoln County Fair remains a successful event" because "a close collaboration between the two groups is essential to achieving that goal."

In the memorandum, the two parties agree that the Lincoln County 4-H program will remain an emphasis of the fair; that the fair association will handle entries and judging for junior division and open division competitions; that the association will pay premiums for junior and open division "as long as state aid is available to adequately cover these expenses" and will provide space to the 4-H Leaders' Association for fair programs and events free of charge; and that the association is "entirely responsible for the business of operating the fair, which includes negotiating and signing the fairgrounds lease, filing the yearly state report, office operations during fair week, and all fair related preparation pertaining to the event." In addition, the agreement states that "neither UW–Extension Lincoln County, nor any state UW–Cooperative Extension employee will in any way be involved in the non-4-H aspects of the Lincoln County Fair."[11]

## WISCONSIN ASSOCIATION OF FAIRS

Organized in 1923, the Wisconsin Association of Fairs proclaims this as its mission: "Increase Wisconsin fairs' quality by providing education and advice on all aspects of producing a fair in Wisconsin mainly through our annual convention and district meetings."

The association offers three types of membership: fair member, associate member, and WAFE (Wisconsin Association Fair Enthusiast). Its membership includes seventy-five county, district, and state fairs. The group's annual convention offers members educational opportunities through workshops, a "fair trade" table where members can exchange information about their fairs, an opportunity to connect with carnival and stage entertainment providers, and a variety of meals and entertainment.

A highlight of the association's annual convention is the crowning of the Fairest of the Fairs, a competition that began in 1966. The Fairest of the Fairs is selected from county and district fair winners and serves a one-year term, with responsibilities including appearances at fairs and other events throughout the state and in the media to promote Wisconsin fairs and the state's agricultural industries.

———————————

NOTE

Wisconsin Association of Fairs, www.wifairs.com.

# PART II
# WHAT MAKES A FAIR A FAIR?

# 3
# EXHIBITS AND CLUBS

Exhibits have long been the core educational activity at fairs, going back to the first fair in the United States, where Elkanah Watson of Pittsfield, Massachutts, displayed his two Merino sheep in the town square. During the early years of Wisconsin fairs, young people were not allowed to participate as exhibitors. Green County, for example, held its first fair in 1853; boys were first allowed to exhibit in 1867 and girls not until 1885.[1]

As fairs in the United States continued to emphasize education as one of their main purposes, agricultural leaders began to realize that agricultural education should include farm boys and girls and not just their parents. Agricultural leaders recognized that one way to approach farmers with new ideas for farming was through their sons and daughters.

## 4-H

By the early 1900s, the University of Wisconsin College of Agriculture began working with young people to improve Wisconsin crops, especially corn. Ransom Asa Moore deserves credit for designing early out-of-school education work for boys and girls in Wisconsin. In 1895, Moore, a Kewaunee County farm boy, rural schoolteacher, and county superintendent of schools, was hired by the College of Agriculture to teach agronomy. Moore became interested in seed selection as a way of improving crop varieties. In the fall of 1903, Moore persuaded the Richland County Superintendent of Schools to allow boys to grow corn plots. Moore's

Banners like this one hung by the Beaver Four-Leaf Clover 4-H Club of Marinette are a common sight at county fairs.
PHOTO BY FRANCIS J. LEWANDOWSKI

In the early 1900s, corn-growing competitions like this one in Grant County attracted many young people to participate in fairs.
WHI IMAGE ID 66418

plan was to sponsor a corn-growing contest with cash awards. In the spring of 1904, interested boys and young men (under twenty years of age) received seed packets with planting instructions and were encouraged to enter the Great Youth Corn Growing Contest, scheduled to culminate at the Richland County Fairgrounds on September 27–30 of that year. Fifty boys enrolled in the contest, and the exhibit drew a large crowd at the fair. This is likely one of the first times that young people became active participants in a Wisconsin fair.[2]

By 1910, youth corn-growing exhibits appeared at forty-five Wisconsin county fairs. The program became so popular that Ransom Moore was able to hire Thomas L. Bewick, a young agronomy instructor, as his assistant for the youth program—soon to be called 4-H. Bewick became the first college-supported farm youth leader in the state. By this time the group's activities included animal care, food preparation, and sewing in addition to various crop-growing projects.[3]

Boys' and girls' clubs soon spread across the country. Some of the clubs featured gardening, some grew wheat, and some baked, sewed, and canned. In 1911, O. H. Benson, superintendent of schools in Wright County, Iowa, was hired to work on Extension activies in the office of the Farmers' Cooperative

Mary Englehart of Dane County's Silver Badgers 4-H Club shows off her Holstein heifer, 1949.
WHI IMAGE ID 58123

Demonstation Work with the United States Department of Agriculture in Washington, DC. It was at this time that Jessie Field Shambaugh of Iowa, later known as the "mother of 4-H," created the four-leaf clover symbol, with the leaves representing Head, Heart, Hands, and Health. The many boys' and girls' clubs operating across the country together became known as 4-H clubs.[4]

In the early 1900s, as interest in improving the country's agriculture continued to grow, the US Congress considered bills to create a formal funding mechanism for agricultural education at the national level. After considerable discussion in both houses, Congress passed the Smith-Lever Act on May 8, 1914, creating the Cooperative Extension Service and stipulating that land-grant colleges would cooperate with counties and the United States Department of Agriculture (USDA) to provide funding and otherwise support educational programs for the entire farm family. Wisconsin's legislature quickly approved the state's particiation in the Cooperative Extension Service. Bewick continued in the position, now called State 4-H Club Leader. He proceeded to work out cooperative arrangements between the public schools and the country school superintendents. The first statewide contest for 4-H corn-growing clubs was held at the Wisconsin State Fair in 1915, with 20,000 boys and girls enrolled in corn, potato, and alfalfa clubs and nearly 2,500 girls in canning and sewing clubs. Next to come were livestock clubs.[5]

In 1917, Wisconsin had two state 4-H club leaders and 235 volunteer leaders. More than 26,000 4-H members were enrolled in 313 4-H clubs.[6] The county fair became an increasingly popular place for 4-H members to exhibit their projects and compete with one another for ribbons and prize money.

## FUTURE FARMERS OF AMERICA

Cooperative Extension programs, including 4-H clubs, were out-of-school programs designed to provide specific information related to all aspects of farm life, from new research on farm production to enhancing farm life. They also provided an array of social and learning opportunities for young people through 4-H club work.

But agricultural leaders were concerned that the public schools were not doing enough to assist farmers. In 1910, only four Wisconsin high schools—Marshall, Janesville, New Richmond, and Plymouth—offered agriculture courses. In 1911, the Wisconsin legislature passed a bill to provide state aid for high schools teaching "manual training, domestic science, and agriculture."[7]

With the passage of the Smith-Hughes Act (formally the National Vocational Education Act) by Congress in 1917, states were eligible for federal aid to teach agriculture, industrial arts, and home economics in high schools. Wisconsin's legislature accepted the provisions of the act and formed the State Board of Vocational Education. By 1925, sixty-five Wisconsin high schools received funds to support vocational education programs.[8]

Madison East High School student and FFA member Duane Lehr, with the help of teacher Irving Gerhardt, readies an alfalfa project for the Wisconsin State Fair, 1951.

WHI IMAGE ID 26229

Local clubs associated with high school agricultural programs began appearing. In 1927, the first mention of agricultural youth groups appeared in a report to the State Board of Vocational Education. The next year, the organization for high school boys studying agriculture took the name Future Farmers of America, abbreviated FFA. Starting in 1969, girls were accepted into FFA. Today, boys and girls in this program exhibit at county and state fairs along with 4-H club members.

## STUDENT EXHIBITS

Until the 1960s, most Wisconsin farm children attended one-room country schools. Many of those schools put together exhibits of student activities to present at their county fairs in competition with other schools. By the mid-1900s, youth exhibits were a major part of county fairs and the state fair. Today, exhibitors have a broad range of exhibit options. For example, in 2019 the junior show exhibits (for 4-H and FFA members) at the Clark County Fair in Neillsville

Raising small animals is a rewarding way for young people to get started in junior exhibits.
PHOTO BY JERRY APPS

included thirty-four departments, from dairy, beef, swine, sheep, dairy goats, horses, poultry, rabbits, and dogs to cultural arts, photography, computers, foods and nutrition, cake decorating, candy making, food preservation, clothing, knitting and crocheting, and more.[9]

Clark County Fair's open-class exhibitors (adults or youth not affiliated with an organization such as 4-H or FFA) could choose from twenty-eight departments, ranging from dairy, beef, draft horses, to cultural arts, woodworking, foods and nutrition, clothing, knitting and crocheting, and home furnishings. A senior division for people sixty-two and older or those with special needs offered opportunities in eight departments: plant and soil science, flowers and houseplants, cultural arts, photography, woodworking, foods and nutrition,

Reserve champion chicken award at the Waushara County Fair
PHOTO BY JERRY APPS

knitting and crocheting, and home furnishings.[10]

Some fairs have awarded money, called a *premium*, to top finishers. And for many people, showing at a fair and earning money from premiums add to the

# ANOTHER FIRST PLACE

Joan Palmer of Madison relayed the story of a neighbor whose grandmother taught him the secrets to a winning entry at the fair. As Joan explained, in the 1950s young Dan Heindl and his grandmother Anna Heindl both entered open class in the Town of Athens Fair in Marathon County.

The Athens Fair was in late August, so the first thing they did was dig the entire garden—every last potato, carrot, and beet. Of the bounty, they selected two matched sets of each variety—no blemishes, perfect form—all uniform in size. They gently scrubbed each with a toothbrush and polished it with a soft cloth so every fruit or veggie gleamed. Their entries would have easily competed for the covers of any seed catalogs.

They handled field crops (clover, alfalfa, grains) differently. When they entered a sheaf of grain, they hand cut the materials in advance and laid them out to dry on beds in the spare bedrooms. When dry, they gently steam-ironed each sheaf if it was not perfectly straight. They placed the perfect stems on the outside of the sheaf, and the not-quite-perfect they hid in the middle. They precisely cut the ends all the same length. The cord binding the sheaf was perfectly wrapped, with every rotation parallel and the knot perfect from years of practice.

They did not leave jars or bags of grain to chance. They hand matched each grain or kernel and then polished it until it gleamed. There was not a speck of dust or chaff in the container. They selected fruits for canning with equal care—nothing was random. One year they canned the absolutely perfect jar of peaches. As they were getting ready for the fair, they noticed that right in the middle of one side of the jar was a fly—perfectly preserved in the golden syrup like an ancient insect trapped in amber. It was too late to can another, so Anna slapped a piece of adhesive tape right over the fly and wrote PEACHES and the year. Another first place.

NOTE
Personal correspondence from Joan Palmer, August 27, 2019.

farm income. As Joan Palmer pointed out, "Back in the 1930s and '40s, fair premiums were vital to my husband's grandparents, as that was cash money and literally the seed money for the next year. . . A family might get a fair check for one hundred dollars or more. There were some years during the Depression that the fair check was greater than the rest of their annual income."[11]

In 1997, Tim and Cathy Wiesbrook moved from Illinois to Iowa County, Wisconsin. Their youngest daughter, Clare, liked goats, and soon she had her first 4-H goat project. She showed her goat, named Lucy, at the Iowa County Fair, one of only two goat exhibitors. Clare began visiting other 4-H clubs in the county, promoting goats as a 4-H project. Goat projects took off in the county.

In 2002, Cathy Wiesbrook served as goat superintendent at the fair, which by that time had added a goat costume class, a goat agility contest, and a public goat milking. As Cathy reported,

> In 2007, Clare thought she had a good enough goat to show at the Wisconsin State Fair. We had never shown at the State Fair. No one from Iowa County had ever shown goats at the State Fair. We had never even visited the State Fair! So, in our naïve excitement, we ventured off to the Wisconsin State Fair. Clare's goat, Laura, won Best Doe of Show at the Wisconsin Fair! Wow! What a thrilling time that was. Exhibitors from Iowa County also won the champion steer, pig, and sheep [contests].
>
> After graduating from 4-H, Clare joined me as superintendent. She shared her knowledge and enthusiasm for goats and became a mentor for many exhibitors. By 2017, the goat project had grown to fifteen exhibitors. After fifteen years of being superintendent, I retired. . . . I will always hold fond memories of the friends we made and the fun we had in the goat barn at the Iowa County Fair![12]

For many young people, exhibiting at the local fair as a member of a 4-H club or an FFA chapter was a highlight of their growing-up years. They learned responsibility, gained new friends, and learned the standards for excellence, whether they be for a dairy animal or for a neatly sewed apron.

# 4

# JUDGES AND JUDGING

After a year spent raising, creating, cultivating, coddling, training, feeding, or otherwise caring for the subject being entered in the fair, the exhibitor faces the culmination of all that activity: the judging. The exhibitor wants to know, "How does my project stack up against what my neighbor has done?" Exhibiting at a fair allows the expression of the competitive spirit that lives in all of us.

Judges evaluate vegetable entries at the Waushara County Fair.
PHOTO BY JERRY APPS

Aside from determining the ribbon won, a judge is also a teacher, imparting important lessons that help the exhibitors improve their efforts. You cannot help but learn something when a friend's display of vegetables receives first prize and yours does not, especially when the judge explains the decision in person and answers your questions.

After months of preparation, fair participants head to the show ring at the Stoughton Fair.
PHOTO BY STEVE APPS

I served as a fair judge for the better part of ten years. In my early career as a livestock agent working in Brown County for the University of Wisconsin Extension Service, I judged 4-H livestock—beef, sheep, and swine—at county fairs. It was a tough job. As a former 4-H exhibitor myself, I appreciated all the work that had to take place prior to exhibiting. Preparing any animal for the fair begins when the animal is born and requires thousands of hours of difficult, time-consuming work, from daily feeding to teaching the animals how to be led with a halter and rope. All of that work comes to a head at the fair, when the 4-H member leads her calf into the show ring with the other competitors. Questions and doubts run through the young person's mind: Will my animal behave in the show ring? How will it handle seeing a crowd of people? How will it adjust to the sounds at a fair, so different from the sounds at the home farm? Have I prepared my animal and myself enough for the show ring? Is its coat spotlessly clean, and are my clothes clean as well? Will I be able to control my fear and anxiety?

As a boy on the farm, I showed dairy cattle for ten years. The first year, when I was just eleven, was the worst. It got easier, but I always felt the anxiety of showing an animal in front of a judge, usually one with a stern, professional face, staring at me with one eye and at my calf with the other (at least, that's what I thought was happening).

I was reminded of my own experience as an exhibitor when I judged a class of beef steers at the Door County Fair. I knew that I must judge the steers honestly and impartially, even though the exhibitors' parents stood on the sidelines, ready to confront me after the judging was finished if I hadn't given the youngster the prize the parent had expected.

## JUDGE REQUIREMENTS

To become a judge for a Wisconsin fair, an individual must submit an application called Registration as a Judge for Wisconsin County and District Fairs, administered by the Department of Agriculture, Trade, and Consumer Protection. Applicants choose from thirty-five departments, ranging from dairy cattle to educational and school exhibits, checking those they are interested in judging and indicating relevant past experience, including any training they've undergone. Additionally, applicants provide up to two references "who may be contacted that will attest to your qualifications as a fair judge." Judges often are Extension agents or vocational agriculture instructors, but the application process is open to anyone. Judges receive a modest daily fee.

## JUDGING SYSTEMS

Fair judging follows two systems: the American system and the Danish system. In the American system, often used for open-class (not youth) exhibits, the top exhibit receives first place, the next second place, and so on. In addition to the rank-order placing, there may be additional categories such as "Best of Show" or "Top of the Class." In this system of judging, exhibitors are clearly competing with one another. Only the top three (sometimes four) finishers receive a ribbon. (For some fairs facing budget challenges, paper "ribbons" have placed ones made of cloth.)

Top finishers at the Waushara County Fair
PHOTO BY STEVE APPS

The Danish system, used frequently for youth exhibits, is based on the premise that exhibits are measured against standards; there may be several exhibits ranked in first place, several in second place, several in third, and several in fourth. First place receives a blue ribbon, second receives a red ribbon, third place receives a white ribbon, and fourth place receives a pink ribbon. When the Danish system of judging is used, nearly everyone receives a ribbon.

# MEMORIES OF JUDGING DAY

Youth exhibitors have many memories of showing at fairs, most of them good, some of them less so. LaVonne Wier from Jackson County recalled her growing-up years as a farm girl in the 1960s, when she spent a big part of her summer preparing for the Jackson County Fair as a member of the local 4-H club, the Franklin Livewires.

My mother had a green thumb. She raised plants and sold them, and she had a big garden. I learned gardening from her. One time I had a beautiful geranium in a pot at the fair. The judge scoffed at it and said, "Someone just cut off the stem and stuck it in the pot." To prove her point, she grabbed my geranium by the stem and yanked it out of the pot. To her surprise, it came out with the roots! I was horrified! I don't remember what prize I received, but I was upset that she would do that to my plant. I think everyone else was shocked, as well.

My best memories, and the most work, were with cattle. I showed Guernsey cattle from sixth grade through eleventh. My first calf was a lovely girl I named Beauty. She was beautiful. That first summer I worked with her daily. I made sure she had just the right amount of feed and curried her often. My brother, Fred, teased me. He told me I wouldn't get any prize at all with that scrawny calf. I worked even harder with her.

Judging day at the fair that fall was nerve-wracking. I washed Beauty and curried her, and she looked great. Back then, the judges worked outside of the barns in a clearing. There wasn't a building for the judging. Beauty and I were in a class with quite a few other competitors. I had Beauty do whatever the judge asked, and she was great. He lined us up before giving out the ribbons. To my amazement, Beauty and I were at the end of the line! Instead of getting a fourth, we were getting the top first prize! After the judging, I was so happy. Right there, I hugged Beauty around the neck and said, "Oh, I love you, Beauty!" Everyone laughed. Our cattle 4-H leader, Basil Finch, never forgot that moment. He teased me about it for years. I took Beauty to the fair four years. Each time, she got a blue ribbon.

NOTE
Personal correspondence from LaVonne Wier, July 5, 2019.

The Danish system emphasizes learning over competition. As one writer explained, 4-H uses the Danish system of judging to "help youth improve their project skills; help them recognize their own efforts and accomplishments; help them develop standards for future self-evaluation; encourage them to continue in the project; and advise them on what they might learn next."[1]

## FACE-TO-FACE JUDGING

In face-to-face judging, generally used for youth exhibits, the judge meets with the exhibitors while judging, having a conversation with each entrant about his or her project. These conversations require the judge to listen carefully to the youngster as well as displaying a good bit of diplomacy.

Linda Kustka, a longtime Cooperative Extension employee and fair judge, recounted one face-to-face judging experience she had with a young person who had an unusual entry.

A judge advises a young exhibitor at the Grant County Fair.
PHOTO BY SHELLY HOLMES PORTRAITURE

Much of my face-to-face judging has been with exhibits best labeled as "Any Other," which brings a wide range of unexpected things ranging from a cartoon like video showing a Lego man using a forklift to move a load, to a genealogy tree, to a short story. A boy around age ten surprised me as I worked one year at the Dane County Fair as a judge. The young man had a gray-haired animal pelt. Our conversation went something like this:

"What did you bring?"

"A possum hide."

"Did you fix it for the fair?"

"Yup."

"It really looks nice. The hide is quite soft. How did you do this?"

"I tanned him by scraping off the meat, cutting out the eyes, rubbing oil into the skin, and letting it dry."

"Was it hard to do? Who showed you how to do this?"

"It wasn't hard. I have a friend who showed me."

"Where did you get this animal?"

"I found it dead on the road." (At this point, his mother in the background looked unsettled and I stifled a physical reaction.)

Speechless about the animal's origin, I said, "Well, you've done a great job and really understand how to tan an animal's hide. You deserve a blue!"

The volunteer superintendent observed this interaction and had the job of tying the blue ribbon on the pelt through the open eye socket before displaying it. After the proud exhibitor left, the superintendent said she knew the boy's family; they were "survivalists" and lived off the land as much as possible.[2]

Face-to-face judging encourages the youth exhibitor to be present at the judging. Parents are welcome as well, although having the parent there can sometimes create problems for the judge. One challenge youth judges face is to determine how much of the work the young exhibitor did and how much the parent did. Fair judge Ila Sanders of Iola explained, "Deciding the degree of parental involvement in a project can be difficult for a judge. Some parents will attempt to speak for the exhibitor—and an overly involved adult is a red flag. Other parents will attempt to invade the judging space, either to hear comments or to offer support. One 4-H'er looked me straight in the eye while simultaneously motioning her mother away with a hand behind her back. Her signal said, 'Mom, I can do this myself.' "[3]

Nancy Franz, who worked as a county 4-H agent and judged county fairs from 1981 to 1999, said that the hardest part of judging was dealing with the parents of 4-H exhibitors: "They could be excessively overbearing and protective of their child and their exhibits," she explained. "Some parents were even bold enough to answer the questions I'd ask of their 4-H'er. I sometimes had to put my open hand in front of the parent's mouth so their child could answer. Some parents were more focused on winning than on their child's education. For example, in judging cultural arts I found a painting with the parent's signature on it. The child affirmed that the parent had created the painting. When I disqualified the exhibit, the parent was mad at me for preventing her from winning money! The fair superintendents kept a close eye on that parent for years to come."[4]

A girl clutches flowers that won the champion ribbon in the "Gladiolus Spike" category and first premium ribbon for "Horticulture Plants and Flowers" at the Wisconsin State Fair in 1955.
WHI IMAGE ID 26217

Pat Ritchie, a volunteer 4-H leader for fifty years in Waupaca County and a judge of crops, vegetables, house plants, and flowers for twenty-five years, described a memorable moment as a judge at the Waupaca County Fair. "A young exhibitor brought in cooked sweet corn. I was trying to figure out where the smell was coming from at first. It had been brought in on Wednesday to be judged on Thursday, and I could see fruit flies flying around the cooked corn. We found out later that Grandmother had helped the youngster because of a family emergency and she didn't know what was required."[5]

# DEPARTMENT SUPERINTENDENTS

Fair organizers designate a superintendent, usually a volunteer, to supervise each of the exhibit departments. A large department—dairy cattle, for example—might also have one or several assistant superintendents. Superintendents are responsible for checking in the exhibits when the exhibitor arrives at the fairground and making sure that the exhibit is placed in the correct category. With the help of assistants, superintendents organize the exhibits to make them easily accessible for judging as well as attractively displayed for the public to see. This work is often done on the first day of the fair, commonly known as entry day. In some exhibit departments, such as dairy cattle, superintendents also review the animals' health records. For some superintendents, entry day is a long one, lasting from morning to late at night.

Judges check in clothing entries at the Dane County Junior Fair, 1959.
WHI IMAGE ID 102637

On judging day, the superintendent serves as the judges' assistant, keeping records of placings, tying ribbons on the entries, and helping organize the displays once the judging is completed.

Dale Simonson, a superintendent at the Waushara County Fair, described his duties as supervisor for plants and crops exhibits: "When people bring their entries in, we make sure they have the tags on. Then we put the exhibits on the tables and make sure they are in the right area and dress up the area a little. On judging day I work with the judge; I tell the judge what class we are judging and how many are in the class."[6]

## LESSONS FROM THE SHOW RING

Both judging and being judged at the fair have created indelible memories for many Wisconsinites. Ronna Ballmer recalled a story from her days as a 4-H member in the 1970s in Rock County, when she showed cattle and participated in the 4-H clothing style revue. One year at the Rock County Fair, both dairy judging and the style revue were taking place on Wednesday. The events were on opposite ends of the fairgrounds, and there were no cell phones, two-way radios, or other means of getting word from one end of the fairgrounds to the other. Furthermore, the style revue classes were large, placing was done with the Danish system, and the judge often gave comments following the classes. Ronna remembered, "I showed two Holstein heifers that year and one outfit in style revue and, of course, my class fell right between the two! There's nothing quite like sporting the smell of bovine as you try to dazzle the judge in a tailored white dress!"[7]

Kassie Schepp of Wausau remembered the long days and nights at fair time preparing to be judged. She wrote, "You start your day around 5 a.m. to make sure you're one of the first ones at the wash rack. You go home around midnight

Youth exhibitors show their cattle at the Jefferson County Fair.
PHOTO BY STEVE APPS

A goat is prepared for its moment in the state fair spotlight.
PHOTO BY STEVE APPS

when they kick you out of the barns. Then you just wake up and do it all over again the next day, prepare for a different animal to show, and maybe grab a cat nap next to your show heifer while in your show whites waiting for your turn." Kassie started showing animals in third grade and showed swine and dairy every year after that, leading to her favorite story from the show ring, when she won intermediate showmanship:

> It was a hot July day. Swine were always shown on Thursday, which was the second day of our fair. My hog and I had been in the ring for what seemed like hours. It was over ninety degrees and my hog decided that he had had enough. I'm not sure how he managed, but he found the one small hole in the fence and decided it would be a great chance to escape the show ring. Being in eighth grade, I thought I could stop his escape. I jumped on top of this squealing, kicking hog. I hung on for dear life and made sure that he wasn't going anywhere. It didn't take long before I had stopped the escape. I had people grabbing me to make sure I was okay. I told them I was fine. The judge said he had never seen someone my age so persistent in trying to keep their pig in a round of showmanship.[8]

In almost every competitive endeavor, someone will try to bend the rules—and in some instances break them. Jim Massey, who worked thirty-four years for *The Country Today* newspaper, remembered a story he covered after blood tests on Wisconsin State Fair steers revealed performance-enhancing drugs. He recalled, "I wrote strong editorials in the *Country Today* criticizing the win-at-all-cost mentality of some of those on the high end of the show circuit." He continued,

> Kids were (and in some cases still are) spending large sums of money to buy an animal in the spring that they thought might perform well in the show-ring in late summer. After several statewide public meetings to tackle this issue, state fair officials put a cap on how much money winners could take home from the sale of their state fair champion show animals, returning some of the money to other exhibitors and providing money for scholarships. The plan has been somewhat successful in "spreading the wealth," so to speak, and has somewhat stifled the big-money atmosphere. It still exists; the competition is still stiff, and some kids still spend too much money on animals that don't end up winning anything—but it's better than it was.
>
> While many young people buy their meat animals in the spring, it has always been rewarding to see the pride in the young people who show livestock that are bred on their farms. When they see their own animals do well against all comers. They may not be the best animals that money can buy; they are the best animals that can be raised on their farms.[9]

Judges and judging are essential to the educational role of fairs. Trained and respected in their fields, judges help participants see how their exhibit stacks up with their competitors'. Judging is an especially valuable learning experience for young people, as they not only can see how their hard work compares with others but also how to apply what they've learned to improve their project for next time.

Clarence Olson, the author's brother-in-law, judged at Wisconsin fairs for fifty years.

PHOTO BY FRANCIS J. LEWANDOWSKI

# 5

# FAVORITE FAIR FOOD

One of my most vivid fair memories is walking down the midway and becoming engulfed by the many smells of food being prepared. As a young 4-H member, I never had much money to try the various foods that smelled so enticing, but I did, on occasion, buy a hamburger piled high with fried onions. Neither of my parents liked fried onions, but I found the taste to be outstanding. As I recall, the cost of a delicious hamburger smothered in onions in those days was twenty-five cents.

It's no surprise that cheese appears in many forms at the Wisconsin State Fair.
PHOTO BY STEVE APPS

# FAMILY FOOD AFFAIRS

The family-run food stand has a long history at fairs. Some stands have been in the same family for several generations. Often the food stand features a special recipe or food that the family is known for.

Fairgoers in southwestern Wisconsin who have attended the Vernon County Fair or the Iowa County Fair fondly remember Hub's Fries. The

business began when Lowell Hubbard, of Viroqua, was working at a food booth at the Vernon County Fair in 1974. Hubbard noticed that many of the stand's customers were buying french fries from a Mr. Clinsman, who sold only french fries at his booth. Folks bought Clinsman's fries before sitting down to eat soup and sandwiches at the stand where Hubbard worked. He quickly surmised that there was something special about those fries. After Clinsman retired a year later, Hubbard bought the business—including Clinsman's secret french fry recipe.[1]

Other members of the Hubbard family became involved in the french fry business. With his brother-in-law Paul Fanta, Lowell built the original Hub's Fries stand in 1975. As daughter Cyndy said, "There was a lot of trial and error at first as we all learned how to make the best fries we could and how to set up the stand so it was the most efficient. I remember the first fair I worked at was the 1976 Iowa County Fair in Mineral Point and held over the Labor Day Weekend—the longest weekend in our lives."[2] Hub's uses Idaho Russet potatoes, cut just before they are fried and served with the customer's choice of apple cider vinegar, balsamic vinegar, red wine vinegar, or raspberry vinegar. As Cyndy Hubbard wrote, "What else we do to the fries to make them special is a family secret, so I'm afraid I can't tell you."[3]

Grandpa Chuck's Kettle Corn, seen here at the Oneida County Fair, is one of many family food stands known for its unique recipes and support of local community organizations.
PHOTO BY STEVE APPS

Young fans of Hub's Fries load up their orders with ketchup.
PHOTO BY DOROTHY ROBSON, *WESTBY TIMES*

Hub's Fries has always been a family affair, starting with the immediate family in 1976 and adding cousins, nieces, nephews, and in-laws over the years. Lowell and his wife, Carol, worked in the stand from 1975 to 2007, and their kids Cyndy, Candace, and David assisted. Now the third generation works in the stand, greeted by their third generation of customers. The serving size has always remained the same, though in 1976 it cost fifty cents and today goes for around four dollars. The most fries they ever sold was on a busy Saturday at the Vernon County Fair, when they sold 1,100 pounds of fries—that's more than a half ton.[4]

In his book *Good Seeds: A Menominee Food Memoir,* author Tom Weso recalled the concession stand run by his grandparents, Jennie and Moon Weso, at the annual Menominee fair in Keshena. It was, he explained, "one of their seasonal occupations." His grandmother's cooking was a major draw for fairgoers:

My grandmother was famous for her meat pies, baked beans, and chili. The meat pies were not a fast-selling item, but not because they weren't popular. My grandmother would not tell everyone she had meat pies, but some people she would let know, and they would get a big chunk of it with homegrown green beans, bread, and butter. . . . Grandma's baked beans were a customer favorite. For the fair, she had a huge roaster filled with beans, slow cooked with real ham, not pork hocks. She did not bake the beans, but rather depended on slow cooking to soften the beans and meld the flavors. The beans were dark and rich, with molasses, tomato sauce, and well-cured ham. These are mythic in my memory. . . . At the fair, other organizations like the Veterans of Foreign Wars had concession stands, as did a few other families. Most stands sold beer and burgers or brats. One served fried chicken and egg salad. Grandma served hot dogs but not brats, since these were available at other stands. Her mainstay was full meals. People would stay at the fair all day and into the night, and they got tired of hamburgers and soda. Friday night would go by, then Saturday was when people would bring the kids early for the cheaper prices on rides. They needed a hot meal by the end of the day.[5]

## NONPROFIT FOOD VENDORS

Some of the most enticing food and drink to be found at the fair is available at the nonprofit food stands: those sponsored by the local Farm Bureau organization, county 4-H club, American Legion post, churches, and school sports teams. At these stands, fairgoers can eat a delicious meal or snack while also supporting community organizations.

The Marquette County Farm Bureau food stands offers a number of fair favorites.
PHOTO BY STEVE APPS

At the Shawano County Fair, St. James Lutheran Church long operated a food stand remembered by some to be "the place" to eat at the fair. Staffed by members of the Ladies Aid, the stand kept fair visitors full from morning to night, offering bacon and eggs for breakfast and chicken dinners and barbecue along with pie and ice cream the rest of the day. They served all the meals on real plates, not paper plates, and visitors would always see several of the church women busy washing dishes in a shady area behind the stand.[6]

Planning for the St. James food stand started about two weeks before the fair. Food stand organizers would go door-to-door visiting church members to ask what they could donate. Some pledged a pie; others offered some garden vegetables. Because almost everything was donated, from the food to the labor to run the stand, the concession was a major income source for the church. The stand ceased operations in the 1960s, when many of the women who donated their time now had jobs and had difficulty taking time off to work at the fair.[7]

Tim Casucci, a former 4-H member, recalled these food memories from attending the Rock County Fair as a youngster:

> To this day, there is one thing that comes to mind that I liked the most. I can still smell the glorious aromas that wafted from the grills of the Grange and church food tents. They were the best. There is nothing like the smell of cheeseburgers on the flat top grill, with onions and all of the other goodness that combined to make my mouth water in approval. The food tents were variations of each other with similar offerings and some unique to that particular location. All were manned by an army of volunteers of all ages. It was fair food, but it was somehow perfect to a kid let loose to make his own choices of what to eat because it was Fair Week![8]

## THE BEER TENT

Whether it is a county fair or the state fair, almost every fair has a beer tent. In Wisconsin, with its large German and Polish population and their brewing traditions, it seemed only natural for fair organizers to provide a place where a thirsty fairgoer could get out of the sun and heat and enjoy a cold one. In addition, beer tents provide an excellent source of income for the sponsoring organization or the fair itself. Some beer tents have long been operated by local veterans' groups, such as the American Legion. At Dodge County Fair in Beaver Dam, for example, visitors enjoy the iconic Legion Beer Pavilion on Wisconsin Street. Sometimes beer tents are the site for special events, such as music or bingo games. At the Sauk County Fair in Baraboo, a DJ provides entertainment in the beer tent.

Many beer tent sponsors have attempted to replicate the feeling of the beer gardens that were associated with Milwaukee's early breweries. I remember as

Visitors to the Wisconsin State Fair in the 1930s could enjoy a glass of locally made Gettelman's brew for five cents.
WHI IMAGE ID 26193

a 4-H member attending the state fair in 1948 and walking past the enormous beer tents operated by Milwaukee's leading breweries, Miller, Pabst, Blatz, and Schlitz. Several had polka bands, the music drifting across the fairgrounds reminding me of my German heritage.

# ICONIC FAIR FARE

It may be a stretch to call cotton candy a food, but it has been a fair favorite since the early 1900s. In 1897, dentist William Morrison teamed up with candy maker John C. Wharton to create an electric cotton candy machine. The machine heated sugar to a liquid state and pushed the liquid through a screen to create strands of sugar. The resulting product, then called *fairy floss*, was introduced at the St. Louis World's Fair in 1904 and became an instant favorite, earning

With a sugary aroma and meltingly sweet texture, cotton candy is the quintessential fair food.
PHOTO COURTESY OF TRAVEL WISCONSIN

thousands of dollars for the inventors. In 1920, after the Morrison and Wharton patent expired, another dentist, Josef Lascaux, created a similar machine, calling his product *cotton candy*.[9]

For many years, cotton candy was either pink or blue. Today the confection comes in every color of the rainbow and a variety of flavors, from dark purple to dill-pickle green. Now more nearly 125 years old, cotton candy remains a favorite for many fairgoers.[10]

Say "Wisconsin State Fair food," and many people immediately think of the famous cream puff consumed by thousands of state fair visitors every year. Cream puffs have been sold at the Wisconsin State Fair since 1924. These days, the fair hires some 220 employees to make them and sells on average around 400,000 of the confections during the fair's eleven-day run. (That requires more than 350 pounds of unsalted butter, 200,000 grade-A large eggs, and 14,000 gallons of fresh whipping cream.) For those counting calories, each cream puff contains 550 calories and about 45 grams of fat.[11]

Generally found only at fairs and carnivals, funnel cakes are believed to have been created by the Pennsylvania Dutch in the mid-1800s. The name *funnel cake* refers to the method used to make this crispy fried confection. Historically, a special batter was squeezed through a funnel to create a circular pattern; the batter was immersed into hot oil, creating a "dizzying pattern of crispy fried dough."[12]

Because they are easily made with readily available ingredients, funnel cakes became a natural addition to fair and carnival food offerings. Traditional recipes for a fairly standard batter include flour, eggs, sugar, milk, and baking powder, plus oil for deep frying and powdered sugar to sprinkle on top just before serving.

Cream puffs are the most popular
food sold at the Wisconsin State Fair.
PHOTO COURTESY OF TRAVEL WISCONSIN

Recipes for "Wisconsin State Fair
Cream Puffs" proliferate online, but
diehard fairgoers say the dairy-filled
pastries just don't taste the same
unless they are made and consumed
at the fair.
PHOTO COURTESY OF TRAVEL WISCONSIN

# HAMBURGER CHARLIE

Some fair food venders become local or even state icons—arguably none more famous than Hamburger Charlie, considered by some to be the inventor of the hamburger. As the story goes, Hortonville, Wisconsin, native Charlie Nagreen was just fifteen when he loaded an oxcart full of meatballs and traveled to the Seymour County Fair (now the Outagamie County Fair) in 1885. Finding the meatball business at the fair to be slow, Charlie struck on the idea that visitors wanted a portable meal so they could continue strolling while eating it. He smashed two meatballs between two pieces of bread, added some onions, and came up with a hit. Charlie named his concoction a *hamburger* after the Hamburg steak popular among German immigrants.

Charlie Nagreen sold burgers at the Seymour County Fair every year for the next sixty-five years. He made a few improvements over time, adding a pickle and switching to a bun, but for the most part he stuck to what worked. His invention became known across the country, at every restaurant, drive-in, and bar—and at every county and state fair. Two blocks from the original site of the Seymour County Fair stands a twelve-foot statue of Hamburger Charlie, Seymour's tribute to the man who invented one of our nation's iconic foods.

---

NOTE

"Hamburger Charlie—Early Days of the Hamburger," www.homeofthehamburger.org/hamburger-charlie.

For those fairgoers too busy to stop to eat, almost every fair offers an assortment of "walk-around meals" commonly known as "food on a stick." The corn dog may always be the king of the food-on-a-stick realm, but here are a few of the more recent innovations:

**Bacon Brat on a Stick:** a handmade brat sausage made with a blend of pork, beef, bacon bits, and special seasoning in a natural casing, broiled and served on a stick with a choice of sauces.

**Blazin' Jalapeño Deep-Fried Olives:** queen green olives stuffed with fresh jalapeños and cream cheese, nestled in a crunchy batter, served with ranch for dipping.

**Breakfast on a Stick:** a battered and deep-fried sausage, wrapped in a pancake, served with a cup of syrup.

**Brownie Waffle on a Stick:** Belgian waffle baked around a double-chocolate brownie with white chocolate chips, served dusted with powdered sugar and drizzled with chocolate syrup.

The corn dog's portability makes it a popular choice for young fairgoers who don't want to miss a minute of state fair fun.
PHOTO COURTESY OF TRAVEL WISCONSIN

**Chicken in a Waffle on a Stick:** chicken dipped in waffle batter and cooked in a waffle iron.

**Deep-Fried Bacon & Cream Cheese on a Stick:** corndog-style breading around a lump of cream cheese, studded with bacon bits and deep fried.

**Frosted Flakes Chicken on a Stick:** chicken tenders dipped in batter and rolled in sweet flakey cereal, then fried.

**Lug Nuts on a Stick:** bacon-wrapped tater tots, deep fried.

**Sangria on a Stick:** a frozen sangria popsicle.

**Deep-Fried Snickers on a Stick:** just like it sounds: a candy bar dipped in batter and deep fried.[13]

# NEWFANGLED FOODS

The Wisconsin State Fair prides itself on offering new and innovative food concoctions. Over the past decade, the fair has offered between sixty and one hundred new foods every year. Here are a few recent examples to illustrate the variety and ingenuity:

**Bud Spuds:** crispy, deep-fried potato boats stuffed with pulled pork and topped with beer cheese sauce, chipotle ranch dressing, and hickory-smoked bacon crumbles

**Bug Tacos:** tacos made with real crickets and worms

**Deep-Fried Milk with Cookie Dip:** deep-fried cubes of milk pudding with Oreo dip on the side

**Elvis Chicken and Waffle Sandwich:** buttermilk-fried chicken sandwiched between peanut-butter-banana-and-bacon waffles served with Sriracha maple syrup

**Snake Soup:** flavorful vegetables, rattlesnake meat

**Spaghetti and Meatballs Mozzarella Sticks:** spaghetti and meatballs wrapped in a wonton with mozzarella cheese, fried to golden goodness

**Ultimate Deep-Fried Cookie Dough Sundae:** vanilla ice cream, chocolate chip cookie dough, hot fudge, and hot caramel fudge, topped with deep-fried chocolate chip cookie dough

The Wisconsin State Fair's "deep-fried brandy old fashioned" is actually a fried piece of orange-flavored pound cake filled with brandy cream cheese and, in some cases, topped with bitters-infused whipped cream. PHOTO COURTESY OF TRAVEL WISCONSIN

---

NOTE

Personal correspondence from Kristin L. Chuckel, Director of Public Affairs, Wisconsin State Fair Park, February 5, 2020; Wisconsin State Fair, "New Foods & Beverages, Wisconsin State Fair," https://wistatefair.com/fair/fair-fare.

⛺

# 6

# THE CARNIVAL
# AND THE MIDWAY

The earliest fairs didn't have carnivals—those traveling collections of rides, games of chance, sideshows, and food stands that are essential elements of most fairs today. The idea of a midway, or central thoroughfare with carnival attractions lining each side, traces back to 1893 and the Chicago World's Columbian Exposition. The 1893 World's Fair, organized to celebrate the four-hundredth anniversary of Columbus's arrival in the New World, covered more than six hundred acres and went on for six months. More than 27 million people attended.[1]

For the first time at a world's fair, an area separate from the exhibition halls was devoted to "amusements," and the word *midway* was used to denote it. This first midway was a mile and a half long and a block wide. Fairgoers could ride the Ferris wheel or merry-go-round, talk with fortune-tellers, play games of chance, and see a sideshow.[2]

Fairgoers stroll along the Waushara County Fair midway, 2014.
PHOTO BY STEVE APPS

Noting the popularity of the World's Fair carnival, county and state fairs soon offered carnivals as well. In 1902, seventeen carnival companies toured the United States. By 1905, the number had climbed to forty-six, and by 1937 more than three hundred carnivals toured the country.[3] Amy Olson, manager of the Grant County Fair, explained that

PHOTOGRAPHED AND PUBLISHED BY H. H. BENNETT, Kilbourn City, Wisconsin.

WANDERINGS AMONG THE WONDERS AND BEAUTIES OF Western Scenery.

CHICAGO AND VICINITY.
312. East on Midway from the Ferris Wheel.

A stereograph view of the 1893 Chicago World's Fair midway taken by Wisconsin photographer Henry Hamilton Bennett.
WHI IMAGE ID 68573

the carnival is a big draw. "If you don't have a carnival, you don't have a fair," she declared.[4]

The life of a carnival worker is hard: four days in one place, pack up and move, four days in another town, pack up and move, and so on. Put the rides together, take them apart, put them together again, take them apart. Load them. Unload them. Work in the rain, work during the hottest days of summer, deal with huge crowds waiting in line for the rides, or have slim crowds because of a cold, drizzly rain that too often visits northern states such as Wisconsin.

Vince Heiman, owner of Badgerland Midways, one of nine carnival companies now located in Wisconsin, described carnival life: "It's hard, physical work that requires a unique set of skills. It is challenging to find employees. And there are long hours spent on the road between fairs and festivals." Running carnival equipment can be demanding—even dangerous—work that requires a unique set of skills. Before he owned Badgerland Midways, Heiman traveled with other carnivals, learning skills in mechanics and hydraulics, useful for his wintertime work when he does routine maintenance on his rides.[5]

Carnival work can also be rewarding, with ever-changing scenery and variety. And some carnival workers are not who they seem to be. Julie Belschner, editor of *Agri-View*, said that as a writer she discovered the "stories behind the

A costumed performer surveys the Wisconsin State Fair midway, 1936.

WHI IMAGE ID 41740

fair." She told one such story: "There was the couple who shared their talents as part of the traveling carnie company. She offered temporary tattoos while he showed his parrots. The two owned a large island off Florida's coast; they had more money than they knew what to do with. As an adventure each year, they signed on with a carnie company."[6]

"Then there was the older man," she continued, "who sold elephant ears—a traditional fair food with no redeeming nutritional value except that it would melt in the mouths of fairgoers. He was at one time a stockbroker from New York. He grew tired of the 'rat race.'"[7]

## CARNIVAL RIDES

Starting with the first carnivals, rides were popular attractions, especially for young people. The Ferris wheel may be the most iconic, but from merry-go-rounds to bumper cars, pony rides to the Wisconsin State Fair SkyGlider, there's a ride for every taste and every age at the fair.

Just as a fair would not be a fair without a carnival, a carnival would not be a carnival if it did not include a Ferris wheel. The enormous wheel towers over other attractions and is one of the first structures a visitor sees when entering

View of the Columbian
Exposition seen from
the original Ferris
wheel, 1893
WHI IMAGE ID 7386

the fairgrounds. The colorful wheel got its start in late 1890, when Daniel Burnham, the architect responsible for laying out a design for the upcoming 1893 Columbian Exposition in Chicago, set out to design a dazzling showpiece. "Make no little plans," Burnham instructed builders. Of course he knew about France's Eiffel Tower, which had opened in 1889, and he wanted to create something even more spectacular. As plans for the Columbian Exposition evolved, Burnham was disappointed. They included nothing that came close to what France had created.[8]

Finally, a thirty-three-year-old steel company engineer from Pittsburgh had a brainstorm for a huge, revolving steel wheel designed to carry people.

Kids hold on tight in the teacup ride at SpinCity, the state fair's amusement park.

"Too fragile," his critics said. But the young engineer persisted. His name was George Washington Gale Ferris Jr., and he was convinced his idea would work. He spent his own money, recruited investors, and hired additional engineers to help him build an answer to the Eiffel Tower. When it was completed, it measured 250 feet in diameter and included 36 cars, each carrying up to 60 people, for a total capacity of 2,160.[9]

The first Ferris wheel began operation on June 21, 1893. Over nineteen weeks of the World's Fair, more than 1.4 million people paid fifty cents each to ride it.[10] Not long after the 1893 Columbian Exposition closed, imitators were building Ferris wheels. They appeared as permanent structures in amusement parks and became a feature of the traveling carnivals that were becoming popular at fairs and community events across the country.

The merry-go-round, sometimes called a *carousel*, dates back to the Crusades in the 1100s, when Turkish and Arabian horsemen competed in a game on horseback later called "little war," or *carosella* in Italian. The Crusaders brought the idea of the carousel back to Europe.[11]

By the 1700s, carousels included carved horses and other animals, plus live bands that provided music; they were powered by draft horses. During the 1800s, when large numbers of Europeans were making their way to the United States, they brought their love for and knowledge about carousels with them, and by the late 1800s a steam engine replaced animal power. With the coming of electricity at the end of the 1800s, electric motors powered many carousels. As carnivals began appearing at fairs and festivals, they soon adopted the carousel.[12]

Another fairgoer favorite, the Tilt-A-Whirl, was invented by Herbert W. Sellner of Fairbault, Minnesota, in 1926. The ride usually consists of seven cars that tip and spin randomly as the ride turns. In his patent papers, Sellner described the objective of the ride this way: "to provide amusement apparatus wherein riders will be moved generally through an orbit, and will unexpectedly swing, snap from side to side or rotate without in any way being able to figure what movements may next take place in the car." Sellner opened the Sellner Manufacturing Company factory in Fairbault in 1927 and debuted his Tilt-A-Whirl at the Minnesota State Fair.[13]

A merry-go-round waits for riders at the Waushara County Fair.
PHOTO BY JERRY APPS

Standing near a Tilt-A-Whirl and listening to the screams and laughter of its occupants confirms that the ride is doing what Sellner intended it to do. The fact that the riders never quite know what will happen next, as compared to the predictability of Ferris wheel or merry-go-round, is one of the ride's great attractions.

In addition to these iconic rides, county fairs offer an assortment of others, some especially for young fairgoers. A popular one that many kids never forget is a pony ride, with real Shetland ponies that walk in a circle, carrying their young riders. A kiddie train also attracts the young crowd, and bumper cars remain popular with teenagers. State fair goers have a vast assortment of rides to consider, including the SkyGlider, which offers a bird's-eye view of the state fairgrounds. Another long-time popular state fair ride is the Giant Slide: hop on a burlap sack and ride down a long incline. What could be simpler or more fun—for all ages?

The Tilt-A-Whirl's cars spin based in part on the weight and position of each rider—meaning no two rides are the same. WHI IMAGE ID 131487

# SIDESHOWS, GAMES, AND ENTERTAINMENT

Along with rides, the carnival midway offers games, demonstrations, and entertainment of every variety. The offerings have changed over the years, but the sights, sounds, and excitement always intrigue passersby—especially children.

Tim Casucci recalls attending the Rock County Fair as a 4-H member during the 1970s:

A family tries out their ring-tossing skills at the state fair.
PHOTO COURTESY OF TRAVEL WISCONSIN

> My favorite ride was the bumper cars, still is. I was a pretty good marksman and fell prey to the crooked gun sights in the shooting games every year as I tried to shoot the red star completely out of the target. All the games looked easy. I won a few trinkets, which were never close in value to what I paid out in hard-earned allowance and other cash I had managed to save. I brought home a few goldfish that I won. I remember looking around on the ground near the change booth in the game arcade. Sometimes I found a quarter, which was enough for me to play a game where I shot torpedoes at passing ships. I got really good at that game.
>
> I sat on the new tractors displayed with other farm implements, pretending I knew what it felt like to drive them. In a little tent on the midway, I watched a duckling climb some steps, reach for some food, and slide down into the tank of water.[14]

At earlier fairs, sideshows featured unusual acts and "oddities" the likes of which are seldom seen today, including two-headed calves, large and small people, challenge events, daredevil escapades, and hoaxes. Sideshows also appeared at circuses; according to the International Independent Showmen's Museum, the date of the first sideshow in the United States is unrecorded, but circus man P.T. Barnum is known to have featured a traveling sideshow as early as 1835.[15]

THE MAN W
BABY THELMA
619 POUNDS OF FEMININE BEAUTY
MIDGET CITY
WORLD'S TINIEST ENTERTAINERS
ELIZ
CULPTOR
EST. PRICE 27¢
FED.TAX 03¢
TOTAL 30¢
COMBINED
SIDE
SHOWS

A barker encourages kids to check out the state fair's side shows. Today's sideshows are more likely to feature daring feats than physical differences.
WHI IMAGE ID 1877

## THE HODAG GOES TO THE FAIR

In Wisconsin, the mythical Hodag made the rounds of the fairs in the late 1800s. The creation of timber cruiser Eugene Simeon Shepard, the Hodag was reported to roam the Northwoods near the lumber camps, but no one had actually seen the creature until Shepard came face to face with one while hiking in 1893 near Rhinelander. He reported that the lizardlike beast weighed about 185 pounds and was about seven feet long, with fangs and green eyes and sporting large horns. Rhinelander's newspaper, *The Near North*, published sketches of the beast that Shepard provided.

Three years later, Shepard, along with several lumberjacks, successfully captured the beast and transported it to the Rhinelander fairgrounds before the opening of what would be Oneida County's first fair. The Hodag became the fair's main attraction. People paid ten cents to enter a dimly lit tent, where they saw the creature move and heard it growl. The event created an audience of believers. Soon Shepard and his Hodag appeared at several county fairs and even at the state fair in Madison.

Eventually the hoax was revealed. Shepard had made the creature from a white pine stump covered with an ox hide, adding horns and spikes from cattle. Its movement was controlled with wires, and its growl was provided by Shepard's son.

———————————

NOTE

"The Living Legend of Rhinelander's Hodag," www.hodagress.com/about.htm.

My father told me a story of an unusual sideshow at the Waushara County Fair in the 1920s. Pa never forgot the year that a tent appeared on the midway with a big sign out front reading: SEE THE HORSE WITH ITS HEAD WHERE ITS TAIL OUGHT TO BE. People lined up to pay twenty-five cents to see the strange creature, something no one had ever seen before. Once inside the tent, visitors saw a big Belgian draft horse backed into its stall, with its tail hanging in the hay manager. The horse's tail was indeed where its head ought to be. Disgusted by being taken in by the hoax, no one who had paid to see the horse said a word to the long line of people waiting for their turn.

Audience participation played an important role in sideshow events at fairs. A popular event at fairs for many years, strong man competitions were an invitation for farm boys to take on the fair's resident strong man. One popular example in the Midwest was Jimmy Demetral's Wrestling Show. The sign on the tent read in large print: JIMMY DEMETRAL'S WRESTLING AREA: WE MEET ALL COMERS. Inside was a raised wrestling ring with spectator seats all around. Any farm boy

A crowd gathers outside Jemmy Demtral's Wrestling Arena at the 1954 state fair.
WHI IMAGE ID 25597

who wanted to challenge professional wrestler Demetral was invited into the ring. The boy usually lost the match, even though he might be stronger than Demetral. The professional wrestler knew the wrestling moves and holds that the farm boy didn't.

Audience participation is the appeal for the many games available on the midway. One old-time favorite is the "guess your weight and age" variety, in which the pitch went like this: "I'll guess your weight within three pounds and your age within two years." The pitch person looked the participant over and then wrote the information on a piece of paper. Often the guesser was wrong, guessing—usually on purpose—that the person was younger or lighter than he or she actually was. If the guesser guessed inaccurately, the person received a prize, usually a stuffed animal. More to the point, the person walked away feeling happy, and the guesser had the money—which was usually more than the cost of the prize.

LaVonne Wier of Jackson County shared this about her experience with the weight-and-age guesser. "I was pretty proud of myself the year I turned fourteen. I looked older than my age. They had three booths where the person would guess your age or your weight within a certain range. I went to each booth and had them guess my age. I think all of them guessed me to be twenty-one or twenty, so I won a prize. . . . Nowadays it isn't as much fun to have someone guess me 10 or more years older than I am."[16]

In another popular game at many county fairs, a volunteer, usually someone well known in the community—the county judge or a local banker, for example—sits fully clothed on a little collapsing platform above a tank of water about five feet deep. A metal arm holding a target is fastened to the platform. The customer buys three chances to dunk the volunteer by throwing a baseball at the target. If the customer hits the target, the volunteer splashes into the tank, and the customer receives a prize while the spectators clap and cheer.

"Step right up and show your girlfriend how strong you are," the pitchman cries as a young couple walk along the midway at the county fair. The couple approached the Ring-the-Dinger, another iconic fair game. The young man grabs the huge wooden mallet, winds up, and takes a mighty swing. When the mallet strikes the pad, it launches a wooden missile up a tall calibrated wooden board with a bell at the top. The wooden missile hits the bell. "Dong!" The young man smiles, his girlfriend kisses him on the cheek, and they walk away clutching a stuffed teddy bear worth less than the cost of swinging the mallet.

Not too many years ago, some of the games offered at fairs were nearly impossible to win—because they were rigged. For example, the popular Milk Bottle Pyramid game seemed easy enough to master. A person tossed a ball at metal milk bottles stacked in pyramid fashion; if the bottles toppled over, the person won a prize. Why did the bottles so rarely fall, even when hit? The bottom bottles in the pyramid were filled with lead, sometimes as much as ten pounds of it. To add to the challenge, the balls were sometimes filled with cork to make them lighter than regulation softballs. Finally, the bottles were often stacked against a backdrop curtain that prevented them from falling.[17]

The Basketball Shoot was another game that seemed easy to win, especially for people who remembered their basketball skills from high school days. It looked so easy: you merely had to toss a basketball through a hoop only a few feet away, closer than shooting a free throw on a basketball court. But alas, the basketball seldom if ever went through the hoop. Why? Because the hoop was

Colorful prizes entice passersby at the Dane County Fair.
PHOTO BY STEVE APPS

often smaller than regulation and oval shaped, not round. Unless the ball was tossed abnormally high, it bounced away with no score.[18]

Then there was the Ring Toss game. In one version, glass bottles were lined up side by side; to win, a person simply had to toss a plastic ring over the mouth and neck of one of the bottles. It was nearly impossible to do because of how close the bottles were to one another. The tossed ring usually bounced off a nearby bottle, and the colorful stuffed animal prizes remained unclaimed.[19]

# ENTERTAINMENT

Almost from the first days of fairs, entertainment has been a feature of the fair experience. Generally, entertainment was available free on the midway; grandstand shows were often considered the elite entertainment, sometimes requiring a separate ticket.

Entertainment has changed with the times. At the 1872 fair in Winnebago County, one of the grandstand events was watching a man walk fast. As the event was described shortly afterward,

> The champion walkist, Mr. James Smith, created considerable interest at the fair on Wednesday afternoon by attempting his feat of walking six miles inside of an hour, one mile backwards. About three o'clock Smith toed the mark and at a given signal started on his tramp. Smith was dressed in a white shirt and pants fitting tight to the skin and walked bareheaded.
>
> He walked half way around the racetrack and back again making twelve times back and forth in front of the stand. Smith seemed to walk with every muscle of his body and walked as hard with his open hands as with his feet. He struck out with his open hands as though cutting the air in front of him and he walked perfectly erect without any bending of the body. But everybody was doubly anxious to see him walk backwards. He took the fifth mile for this heat probably as it would give him a change of motion and consequently rest him a little and thus be able to make time on the last heat. His backward motion was about as fast as ordinary men walk when in a hurry. He however accomplished the feat and came up to the stand making the journey in 54 minutes and 53 seconds.[20]

In the late 1800s, fair entertainment included horse races, both saddle and harness racing. Horse-pulling contests, in which neighbors competed over who had the best pulling team, soon became a feature of nearly every fair. And when tractors became widely available after World War II, tractor-pulling contests became popular. Contests featuring both tractors and automobiles remain big draws today, as Amy Olson, manager of the Grant County Fair, confirmed: "We pack the grandstand with tractor pulls and demolition derbies."[21]

Horse-pulling contests traditionally included a variety of weight classes.
WHI IMAGE ID 78558

Music has always been an essential part of fair entertainment, ranging from the local school band to professional musicians who work the fair circuit, moving from one county or state fair to the next throughout the summer fair season. At both county and state fairs, musical performances by well-known radio and TV stars have been major draws. For many years, especially during the Great Depression and World War II, stars from the popular WLS *Barn Dance* radio show, such as Lulu Belle and Scotty, Red Foley, and others, made the rounds of county fairs in the upper Midwest. In 1942, the entire WLS *Barn Dance* cast performed at the Wisconsin State Fair. Today, local and national musicians and bands continue to attract big audiences at Wisconsin's fairs.

Musical performances in the "Temple of Music" draw crowds at an early Wisconsin fair.
WHI IMAGE ID 8136

A 4-H band entertains visitors to the Wisconsin State Fair.
WHI IMAGE ID 33198

## THE REFLECTIONS

In the 1980s, three young married women in Waushara County formed a band. They started the group, called The Reflections, as an alternative to their days spent, as they described it, "in the company of puppies, children, and jobs." At the start, Dawn DeBraal, Gena Pontow, and Julie Eger faced challenges, including "seven children under the age of eight, lack of musical ability, insufficient time to practice, and tired fingers that refused to consistently hit the right chords." But they kept trying. Gena learned bass guitar, Julie learned to play rhythm guitar, and later Pam Gedmin Schmude joined the band as drummer.

Soon they were entertaining at Lion's, Jaycees, Kiwanis, and Rotary Club events—and fast becoming local celebrities. As they said about their little band, "What we couldn't achieve instrumentally we made up for in enthusiasm." Julie made sparkly outfits for the group, and—armed with an ample supply of smiles, bad jokes, and enough microphone cables to ensure their voices were heard—they continued to fill the county's need for entertainment.

In 1989, the all-girl band was invited to perform as a main attraction at the Waushara County Fair in Wautoma. In their words, "The Reflections had finally hit the big time."

---

NOTE

Personal correspondence from Dawn DeBraal, Julie Jannette Eger, Genna Pontow, and Pam Gedmin Schmude, June 4, 2019, and July 16, 2020.

MOORE 10
CIGAR
E.E.WILLIAMS
INSURANCE.
101 FRONT ST.
HAWLEY & VORECK
CIGARS
BILLIARDS AND POOL.
WE SERVE
POST CARDS
FAIR TICKETS

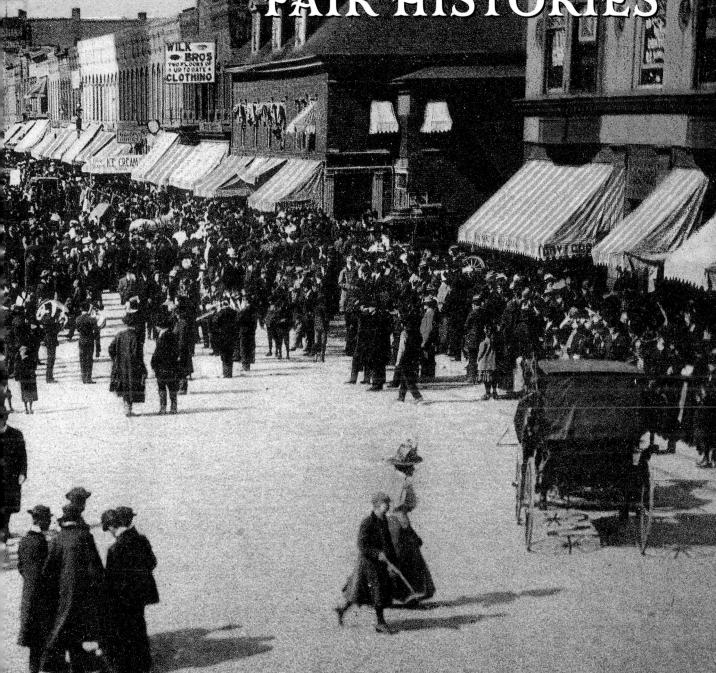

# PART III

# COUNTY AND STATE FAIR HISTORIES

Stoughton Fair

# 7

# SOUTHERN WISCONSIN FAIRS

## COLUMBIA COUNTY

At a meeting of the Columbia County Board in 1851, Jesse Van Ness of Westport suggested that farmers in the county form an agricultural society. Soon some fifty of the county's leading farmers had each paid twenty-five cents to join the newly organized Columbia County Agricultural Society. In 1852, the society sponsored the county's first fair. Secretary of the society John A. Byrne noted this in his report:

> The first fair and cattle show of the Columbia County Agricultural Society was held in the village of Wyocena in November last. But this being our first, it was, as to be expected, somewhat meager. However as a starting point and a beginning it was one of which we may justly feel proud. . . . The notice of our fair had been issued only a few days prior to the time of holding it. Consequently the attendance was thin, and yet large enough to show that, with proper organization and a due share of exertion on the part of each member and officer, Columbia will yet take a proud position among her sister counties in this state, in the cause of agriculture.[1]

A. J. Townsend, a Wyocena pioneer, said this about that first fair, "There was a fine exhibition of grains, vegetables and stock. Jacob Townsend and sons of Lowville had a herd of fine Devon Cattle, on which they took all the first premiums. There were a few fine horses exhibited." The following year, 1853, the society's fair was also held in Wyocena. Nineteen entries of horses, twelve entries of cattle, one for poultry, and two for farm implements made up the exhibits. Over the years, the Columbia County fair has been held, in addition to Wyocena, in Portage, Cambria, and Lodi. In recent years, the fair has been held at the fairgrounds near Portage.[2]

# DANE COUNTY

The Dane County Agricultural Society was founded in 1851. In October of that year, Dane County held its first fair, on a site near the Yahara River in Madison. The fair was held on Wisconsin Avenue from 1856 to 1860, at which time it moved to what is now Camp Randall. No county fair was held during the years 1861 to 1870, when Camp Randall was used as a Civil War training site.

In 1871, the Dane County Fair once more was held at Camp Randall. The years after 1871 were lean ones, and for several of those years the fair operated in the red. The agricultural society began looking for a permanent site for the fair and in 1896 purchased 250 acres that was considered worthless swamp land. The site, formerly Lakeside Park Farm, remains the fair's location today (and is also the site of the Alliant Energy Center).

Tough times continued for the fair, and it was not held every year. To stay solvent, the agricultural society sold some parcels from the 250-acre site but retained ownership of most of the land. The Dane County Agricultural Society sponsored its last fair in 1935. In 1940, the Dane County Fair Association replaced the agricultural society and moved the fair to Stoughton, where it was held for ten years until 1951, when the fair returned to the former park site in Madison. It continues there every July.

As the years passed, the Dane County Fair Association made many improvements to the property. The Veterans Memorial Coliseum was built in 1967, becoming an important building for the fair and hosting other events such as World Dairy Expo, circuses, horse shows, and entertainers such as Frank Sinatra, Bob Hope, Tony Bennett, and Duke Ellington. In 1995, the 255,000-square-foot Exhibition Hall opened, bringing regional, national, and international conferences and trade shows to Madison. In 2014, nine former agricultural buildings were replaced with two new multiuse pavilions totaling 290,000 square feet. Along with the Dane County Fair, the Dane County Junior Fair is held there each year in mid-July.[3]

Grand-prize-winning Brown Swiss bull at the Dane County Fair, 1931

Dane County Junior
Fair poster, 1973
WHI IMAGE ID 58461

# DODGE COUNTY

In 1853, the Dodge County Agricultural Society organized the first Dodge County Fair, held in Juneau that fall and again in 1854. After a lapse of several years, in December 1866 a group of citizens organized the Beaver Dam Agricultural, Mechanical, and Stock Association. For the sum of $1,700, they purchased twenty-one acres of land for a fairgrounds, now the site of Wayland Academy in Beaver Dam.

The Beaver Dam group, not above a little exaggeration, held its first fair in October of 1867 and called it "The World's Best County Fair." The event included horse racing and an assortment of exhibits in a large tent. Twenty years later, on October 5–7, 1887, the Dodge County Agricultural Society and the Beaver Dam Driving Park Association sponsored the fair. The following spring saw the emergence of the Dodge County Fair Association, which became the fair's sponsor after purchasing the property, building, leases, contracts, rights, and privileges plus a debt from the Driving Park Association. At the time there was just one thirty-by-sixty-foot building that housed all the fair exhibits.

As the years passed, the association added more buildings, including a grandstand that held 4,800 people; the group replaced it with a new grandstand in 1921. A 1958 fire destroyed that grandstand and several other buildings; as a result, the 1958 fair was held under large tents. In 1959, the fair board agreed to sell the fairgrounds to Wayland Academy and to purchase property along Highway 33 east of Beaver Dam.

The fair board held the Dodge County Fair at the new site beginning in 1961, with a precast concrete grandstand, five cattle barns, racetrack, and racehorse barn. At the new fairgrounds, encompassing some sixty acres, the board continued to add new buildings. Some of the fair's featured events over the years, in addition to the ever-popular harness racing, included balloon ascensions, parachute jumps, and airplane rides. More recent popular events have included truck and tractor pulls; horse-pulling contests; chainsaw artist demonstrations; demolition derbies; pig, duck, and goat races; and nationally known grandstand shows.[4]

# GREEN COUNTY

On a July day in 1853, a group of people interested in organizing a Green County Agricultural Society met at the courthouse in Monroe. One of the major projects on the new group's agenda was a fair, and they held their first in November of 1853. John A. Bingham, Green County's first attorney after Wisconsin became a state in 1848, deserves major credit for organizing the county's first fair, which included farm produce exhibits and premiums totaling a hundred dollars.

In 1854, the agricultural society purchased seven acres of land for four hundred dollars for a fairgrounds north of Monroe. To acquire funds to fence the fairgounds and build buildings, the association offered "life member certificates" at ten dollars each. The 1854 fair was held on these new grounds, and two hundred dollars were paid in premiums.

In July 1857, the Green County Agricultural Society and Mechanics Institute—the agricultural society's new name—met for the first time. During the late 1850s and early 1860s, the group's fairs were held in the autumn and emphasized handicrafts, especially those associated with Monroe's tin shops, blacksmith, and shoemaker shops. By 1865, the assocation had outgrown its fairgrounds and began looking for new acreage. The association sold its fairgrounds for $105 an acre and, in 1866, purchased two adjacent parcels of land on the east side of town amounting to 13.75 acres for $1,150. The local Jockey Club built a half-mile racetrack on the new property in 1866.

Entertainment in the early days of the Green County Fair took various forms, including, in 1874, hosting Harry Leslie, "Hero of Niagara Falls," who on June 15, 1865, had walked across Niagara Falls on a tightrope. Most entertainment at the fair, though, generally consisted of baseball games and local bands.

The 1909 fair was the first with a carnival and with nighttime offerings. The carnival, traveling with its own train of twelve cars, was the largest show that had appeared in Monroe up to that time. Since those early years, horse racing has remained a tradition at the Green County Fair, which is held in late July each year.[5]

# IOWA COUNTY

Iowa County held its first fair in 1851 in Dodgeville. In 1856, the fair moved to Mineral Point, where it continues to this day. The Iowa County Fair promotes agricultural and industrial education and, like many other Wisconsin fairs, supports and encourages 4-H and Future Farmers of America (FFA) exhibits. In recent years, about five hundred young people have participated in the fair annually; the livestock auction is a major feature supporting local youth and their livestock projects.

Thirty-four exhibit categories are available for 4-H and FFA exhibitors, ranging from long-standing departments such as dairy cattle, beef cattle, sheep, swine, clothing, and foods to newer project departments such as goats, dogs, cats, and computers. The fair also welcomes open-class exhibitors.

Fund-raising opportunities for Boy Scouts, service organizations, local sports teams, and other groups benefit volunteer groups who assist with fair operations, including working the gate, serving ice cream or the free spaghetti supper, parking cars, maintaining the grounds, and operating food and beverage stands. In recent years, the fair draws some twelve thousand people for its five-day run, usually in late August.[6]

# JEFFERSON COUNTY

In 1853, a group of pioneer farmers in Jefferson County formed the Jefferson County Agricultural Society to encourage the improvement of farming and animal husbandry in the county. In September 1853, the group held its first fair in downtown Fort Atkinson near the Green Mountain House Hotel, owned by society president Milo Jones. The location for the fair rotated among the villages of Jefferson, Lake Mills, and Watertown in later years; the fair has been held in Jefferson since 1867.

Today, Jefferson County owns the fair park and states its mission as follows: "The Jefferson County Fair Park provides a county owned facility for all citizens where young and old can gather to display their talents, accomplishments and celebrate their cultures, thereby promoting education, entertainment and economic growth in the country."[7] In the 1990s, the county purchased an additional twenty acres and began extensive remodeling of the park, including building a new dairy barn with milking parlor, a new horse barn, and a new food building. Additional buildings were added in the early 2000s.

Besides being home to the county fair each July, the fair park hosts a horse show every weekend from May through October, spring and fall car shows, a dog show, and many other events.[8]

Jefferson County Fair
PHOTO BY STEVE APPS

# LAFAYETTE COUNTY

In 1857, a group of Lafayette County citizens met to discuss how to improve their county's agriculture, horticulture, household arts, and local industry. They organized the Lafayette County Agricultural Society and began holding fairs. The first was likely held in 1864 at a place called Center Hill. Little is known about these early fairs beyond the fact that they primarily involved livestock exhibits.

On November 28, 1893, the Lafayette County Agricultural Society voted to sell the old fairgrounds and buy land known as the Ellison Meadow. About five hundred agricultural society members contributed to the transaction, and by 1894, the new fairgrounds were ready. Workers built a racetrack, fenced the grounds, and built horse and cattle stables, an amphitheater, a judge's stand, hog and sheep pens, chicken pens, a bandstand, and a grand floral hall. In the center of the floral hall, workers built an aquarium that held one hundred barrels of water and became home to several species of fish from the nearby Pecatonica River.

Fairs at this new site drew hundreds of people, most traveling by horse-drawn vehicles but some also by excursion trains from Monroe, Mineral Point, and Blanchardville. By 1897, baseball games were a popular draw at the fair, and in 1899, workers constructed five new livestock buildings, plus a new entrance and ticket office. In that year, all the fair buildings were painted white, and the fair was unofficially named "The Big White Fair."

By 1900, the crowds coming to the fair were so large that they filled all the nearby hotels, and many found lodging in private homes. Grandstand entertainment included circus acts, dancers, comedians, musicians, and horse acts. Horse racing was the main entertainment draw. In 1925, the fair added fireworks, and in 1926, a dance pavilion was built where couples who wished to dance bought a ticket for ten cents.

Starting in 1927, youth exhibits became an important part of the fair. From 1930 to the 1950s, the WLS radio program *Barn Dance* was a popular attraction at the fair. Horse racing remained popular, too, but eventually a disagreement between the junior fair and the horse racing proponents caused the fair to split into two for several years. Both fairs suffered, and they reunited in 1944.

In 1956, the agricultural society sold the fairgrounds to the county for a dollar, and considerable improvements were made. Throughout the 1950s, popular attractions included circus acts, rodeos, country-western music, and the ever-popular horse races and stock car races. A special attraction in 1955 featured local business and professional people riding ostriches and camels in a race.

In recent years, the fairgrounds has been challenged by the expansion of Highway 81 to the north and the flooding of the Pecatonica River to the south. Today, officials are contemplating conducting a feasibility study to consider moving the fairgrounds to a new location.

Fair manager Kari Ruf notes that the Lafayette County Fair provides "five days to show off the talents of the county." She continues, "You'll see exhibitors sharing their stories in the floral hall or letting visitors ask questions and pet their animals in the barns. The fair is a tool to educate fairgoers about agriculture and its value to the county, as it is one of the most attended events in the area. It provides a perfect opportunity to share the agriculture story of Lafayette County."[9]

# LODI AGRICULTURAL FAIR (COLUMBIA COUNTY)

J. O. Eaton is credited with starting the Lodi Union Agricultural Society in 1863. He had seen the success of the Columbia County Agricultural Society's annual fair and believed the town of Lodi could do something similar. Organizers named their fair the Lodi Union Fair and held the first one October 2–4, 1866. The first competitive classes offered at the fair were "Blooded Horses, Matched Horses, Horses for Work, Mules and Jacks [male donkeys]." Other animal classes included Durham cattle, swine, Merino sheep, and poultry. The fair also accepted exhibits of fine art, fruits, flowers, vegetables, grain, dairy, and a "Ladies Equestrian Display."

In 1875, the fair relocated to a twenty-acre site on Fair Street that included a half-mile horse racing track. The Lodi Union Agricultural Society leased the grounds for fifty dollars each year until 1898, when they secured a ten-year contract for a hundred dollars a year. In the early years, fair admission was fifty cents for a season ticket or twenty-five cents for a single day. Children under twelve were charged ten cents, a team of horses fifty cents, and a single horse twenty-five cents. The fall dates for the fair interfered with the school schedules, so the fair was moved to July, just before of the Columbia County Fair.

Lodi Agricultural Fair
PHOTO BY STEVE APPS

In 1944 and 1945, German prisoners of war were housed at the Lodi Fairgrounds, where they helped with improvements, including laying concrete flooring under the grandstand and making repairs to several buildings. Even though the POWs were housed on the fairgrounds, the fair was still held.

Today the fair charges no fees for exhibiting or attending and attracts some 450 exhibitors each year to its four-day event. Some ten thousand visitors view exhibits of 4-H and FFA members, plus open-class exhibits in a variety of departments. For entertainment, the fair features horse-pulling contests, demolition derbies, tractor-pulling contests, and live music.[10]

# ROCK COUNTY

In the history of Wisconsin fairs, Janesville (Rock County) is notable for hosting the first state fair in 1851. It was almost fifty years later that Rock County held its first county fair. In 1899, business owners and farmers purchased shares in a newly organized Evansville Rock County Agricultural Association. These funds provided for the rental of fairgrounds and tents as well as premiums for the fair's prizewinners. The fair was planned to run for five days beginning September 5, 1899, at the McEwen Driving Park in Evansville. Unfortunately, the night before the fair opened, a huge storm blew down the tents. Fair organizers quickly found two new tents and had them in place when the fair opened.

The county's first fair sparked high interest. As early as five in the morning on opening day, people began arriving. Wisconsin governor Edward Scofield arrived by train; a local band and Evansville dignitaries greeted the governor and other fairgoers. A Methodist women's group rented one of the tents for a restaurant. Exhibits including flowers, baked goods, fancy work, and vegetables were set up in the second tent, and the College of Agriculture at the University of Wisconsin provided judges. Receipts from this first fair were $3,403.36, enough to encourage organizers to plan a second one. With considerable advertising and promotion, plus bringing in a Wild West show for entertainment, the 1900 fair was even more successful, selling 3,500 single admission tickets on one day. In addition to agricultural exhibits, the fair featured displays from local business, including Baker Manufacturing demonstrating its latest windmills, pumps, and feed grinders and wagonmaker Joel W. Morgan showing off his newest wagons and buggies. Two automobiles raced to demonstrate their speed. But harness racing remained the most popular attraction.

Each year the fair grew and became more popular, and the association bought the land that had been the McEwen's Driving Park plus four more acres. They added a grandstand, two sheep sheds, and a floral building. In 1912, twenty-five automobiles traveled throughout the county promoting the fair. A year later, 160 racehorses, some from as far away as Alabama and Montana, came to the fair in Evansville.

Rock County had hired its first county agricultural agent in 1917, and in 1919, with the help of the county YMCA and the Rock County Farm Bureau, four

Prize-winning steer at the Rock County Fair

COURTESY OF MARY CHECK, ROCK COUNTY 4-H FAIR

countywide 4-H clubs were organized: beef, dairy calf, sheep, and corn. A youth fair was held in Janesville a week after the Rock County Fair in Evansville.

Despite its popularity, by 1916 the Rock County Fair was facing financial trouble. In 1923, the fair's events included horse racing, vaudeville acts, fireworks, and the usual exhibits, and the 1924 fair netted the largest receipts to date. Yet financial problems persisted, and in June 1928 the fairgrounds were sold at a sheriff's auction. It was the end of the Rock County Fair at Evansville.

By 1930, in the depths of the Great Depression, the Rock County Fair at Janesville was in considerable economic trouble. Recognizing these financial challenges, on April 16, 1930, a group of 4-H leaders, fair board members, interested citizens, and the agricultural committee of the county board decided to incorporate the county 4-H clubs, creating the 4-H Fair and Livestock Association. This association would sponsor the 4-H Fair, considered to be the first of its kind in the United States. With a grant from the Rock County Board, this first 4-H Fair was held August 20–22, 1930. Exhibits included calves, pigs, sheep, chickens, canned goods, baked goods, sewing projects, and other farm products.

One year later, the fair's financial situation became dire, and by fall 1931, the fairgrounds were in foreclosure. Another sheriff's sale was held to recoup the thirty-five thousand dollars owed. J. A. Craig, a local businessperson and longtime supporter of the fair, sent a representative to the sale to offer what turned out to be the winning bid. Craig rented thirty-nine of the fairgrounds' forty-seven acres to the Rock County 4-H clubs for a nominal yearly fee, and the fair continued.

From 1932 to 1937, annual fairs continued under the name Rock County 4-H Junior Fair and Livestock Exposition. However, the now quite successful fair faced a serious problem in 1938, when young boys playing under the grandstand set it on fire. There was no money to build a new grandstand, but J. A. Craig once more came to the rescue. Craig offered to sell an 18.45-acre site to Rock County for the fairgrounds, so that funds from the Works Progress Administration (WPA, one of the federal government's Depression-era programs) could be used to rebuild the grandstand. In August 1939, the Rock County 4-H Fair opened at its new site, and the new fairgrounds were dedicated in J. A. Craig's honor. In 1952, the fair changed its legal name to Rock County 4-H Fair, Inc. A youth livestock auction was added in 1955. The fair continues to flourish to this day.[11]

## SAUK COUNTY

In 1855, farmers in Sauk County organized an agricultural society. One of its objectives was "the promotion and improvement of the condition of agriculture, horticulture, mechanical manufacturing and household arts." The society sponsored a fair on October 15, 1855, on the courthouse square in Baraboo, just east of the present-day Al. Ringling Theater. The fair continued at that site for ten years, each year doing well and eventually outgrowing the location. In the

Sauk County Fair midway, 1906

WHI IMAGE ID 64166

spring of 1870, the agricultural society purchased forty acres of land east of Baraboo, still the location of the fair today. The land cost $1,540; a few years later, the society sold twenty of those acres for $600. The society went on to build several fair buildings and by 1890 boasted about having one of the best fairgrounds in the state.

By the 1920s, 4-H and FFA youth exhibits had become popular at the fair, along with open-class exhibits entered by adults. In the fair's early days, livestock and horses made up the majority of the exhibits. New buildings for cattle and swine were built in the 1950s, and in 1970 a new commercial building was erected where the fair office is now located. A horse arena and Progress Hall were built in the 1970s, and a new horse barn was erected in 1913.

Exhibits at the Sauk County Fair today include poultry, sheep, rabbits, swine, goats, exotics (llamas, for example), plus dogs and cats. Youth can enter photography, plant and soil science projects, knitting, crocheting, sewing, canning, baking, archery, rock climbing, and woodworking projects.

The fair's attractions include a carnival; popular events have included horse racing, car racing, bicycle racing, horse-pulling contests, tractor-pulling contests, and various types of demolition derbies. Big-name entertainers at the fair have included the Mandrell Sisters, Charlie Daniels, and more. The Sauk County Fair is held in July each year.[12]

## STOUGHTON FAIR (DANE COUNTY)

The earliest Stoughton Fair operated for just two years in the late 1800s. In 1925, the Stoughton Fair opened again, and from 1940 to 1950, the Stoughton Fair was the Dane County Fair.

The Stoughton Fair is a free fair, with no admission charged, and an open fair, allowing exhibitors from anywhere to bring exhibits. In 2018, young people from six counties exhibited. The region around Stoughton was once a major tobacco producer, and the fair still has tobacco exhibits. As Stoughton Fair Board member Rob White said, "We are as close to what an old time fair was as I believe you can find, still concentrating on agriculture with entertainment mixed in. We have no paid employees—all volunteers."[13]

# WALWORTH COUNTY

One of the oldest county fairs in Wisconsin, the Walworth County Fair opened in 1849 in East Troy, sponsored by the East Troy Agricultural Society. At the time, the society boasted that it had 130 members, each having paid fifty cents to join.

At the October 1850 fair in East Troy, Franklin Kelsey Phoenix of Delavan exhibited twenty-five apple varieties, and Josiah F. Brooks sold two bulls, one for $250 and one for $150. The next spring, local farmers gathered in Elkhorn and changed their organization's name from East Troy Agricultural Society to Walworth County Agricultural Society; they also decided to move the fair to Elkhorn on a site along Church Street, south of the courthouse square.

County fairs brought business to their communities, and competition over where to hold the Walworth fair continued. In 1853, Delavan donated a hundred dollars to the agricultural society to hold a fair in its community; that fair was held on September 22 and 23. The following year, Edward Elderkin offered the society six acres of land on the east side of Elkhorn for a permanent fairgrounds at a cost of one hundred dollars an acre. The city of Elkhorn donated three hundred dollars to fence the land, construct pens and a shed, and dig wells. Three thousand people attended the 1855 fair on this site, which remains the location of the Walworth County Fair today. The Elkhorn Hook and Ladder Company appeared in their colorful uniforms, and the Delavan Brass Band played.

In 1862, the agricultural society decided to select fair judges from "the best men in the county." The judges were sworn "to discharge their duties faithfully and impartially and to the best of their judgment and ability." For two days' work, the judges received twelve dollars. The society also decided that any exhibitor who tried to influence a judge would be "worthy of public censure." The society voted in 1864 to build an agricultural hall and in 1868 to construct a building for the fair secretary and treasurer.

In 1888, the fair's premium list included eight classes of cattle, three of horses, sheep, wool, swine, and poultry, two classes of cereals and vegetables, three classes of machinery, household manufacturers, pantry stores, fruit, youth department, fine arts, two classes of plants and flowers, two classes of dairy, and miscellaneous. In 1889, the Agricultural Society passed a motion to contact the railroad and inquire about constructing a sidetrack to the fair-

Walworth County Fair, 1913

grounds, and soon many visitors were coming to the fair by train. At one time as many as nineteen trains arrived at the fairgrounds in the morning and left in the evening after the horse races. Passengers came from northern Illinois as well as from Walworth, Beloit, Madison, Janesville, Milwaukee, and Waukesha.

In 1912, the agricultural society invited farmers from the counties of Waukesha, Racine, and Kenosha to exhibit; each county was also invited to have a representative on the society's executive committee.

Walworth County boys who were members of corn clubs and between the ages of twelve and fifteen were invited to participate in a corn contest at the fair in 1913. In 1918, the executive committee donated one hundred dollars to the county's Boys and Girls Club (the precursor to 4-H clubs). In 1919, L. L. Oldham, the Walworth County agricultural agent, met with the executive committee to request that a boys' calf contest be held at the fair.

The fair continued through World War II, and in 1943 men and women in uniform were admitted free to the fairgrounds. In 1944, the executive committee approved a US Army request to use the fairgrounds' administrative building for housing German prisoners of war. Today, the agricultural society owns about ninety-nine acres of fairgrounds, with land and buildings valued at over one million dollars. The Walworth County Fair is held each year in late August.[14]

Sheboygan County Fair midway

# 8

# SOUTHEASTERN WISCONSIN FAIRS

## KENOSHA COUNTY

A Kenosha County agricultural fair began in 1850. However, it wasn't until 1919 that a fair resembling those of today opened on the grounds of the Wilmot Union Free High School. In addition to exhibits, the 1919 fair included a rooster chase, a greased pig chase, and a pole-climbing contest. On October 15, 1920, the second West Kenosha County fair featured a parade and, according to a poster for the event, "Fine Exhibits of fancy work, cooking, sewing, flowers, vegetable, curios, fruit, grain, poultry, purebred livestock, boys and girls club work and fine school exhibits. Band concerts were offered in the afternoon and evening. Stunts and sports in the afternoon. An evening program of live talks and agricultural discussions, closing with an old folks' dance."[1]

The 1920 fair was a financial success, with over two hundred dollars turned over to the school board. In 1921, the community formed a new fair organization with twelve directors (each representing a Kenosha County township), articles of incorporation, and elected officers. In 1922, the fair proclaimed its exhibits to be as large as those at many of the larger fairs in the state. A University of Wisconsin fair judge said that the Shorthorn exhibit was superior to any that he had seen, with the exception of the state fair. The last West Kenosha Fair was held September 25–27, 1924, and according to one source "from an educational standpoint was far superior to any fair held previously." No fair was held in 1925.

In April 1926, several of the fair directors and other individuals contributed twenty dollars each to start up the fair once more; the 1927 fair featured airplane rides as a major entertainment feature. Unfortunately, the plane crashed, but there were no injuries.

The 1930 fair moved to a dead-end street in Kenosha, with stands and games on the sidewalk and some of the exhibits in vacant stores. The city closed the street for the merry-go-round, Ferris wheel, and other rides. The fair moved locations over the next several years and then went on hiatus during World War II. On April 8, 1947, the fair was incorporated as a nonstock, nonprofit organization and became known as the Kenosha County Fair Association Cooperative, with a fifteen-member board of directors. The association purchased a farm for the fair's use, removed the barn and farmhouse, and in 1950 added a racetrack. In 1954, a Dairy Queen contest was organized to help promote dairy products all summer as well as at the fair. Through the 1960s, the fair continued to prosper, with new buildings built nearly every year. In 1972, a new racetrack was built.

In 1989, the fair constructed a new exhibit building and for the first time in its history did not use the high school as an exhibit site. The fair continues to prosper today.[2]

# OZAUKEE COUNTY

The Ozaukee County Agricultural Society organized the county's first fair in 1859 on leased land in Cedarburg. The fair soon moved to Saukville, where it remained until 1890. In that year, it moved back to Cedarburg, where the society had built a half-mile racetrack for horse racing. The fair was held every year except 1933, when the Great Depression was raging. In 1934, acknowledging the economic climate, organizers reduced the cost of admission from fifty cents to twenty-five. The fair waived admission fees entirely in 1942 following President Roosevelt's admonition that sports and amusements were essential to the wartime morale of the American people and the welfare of communities. In exchange for free admission, the fair encouraged those attending the fair to buy tickets for the "value-priced grandstand shows."

Admission to the Ozaukee County fair has remained free since then thanks to the many volunteers who organize, promote, and operate the fair.

The fair charges for events at the grandstand, which include concerts, truck and tractor pulls, and demolition derbies. The fair also earns rental money from vendors and a percentage of money earned from the various midway rides. In recent years, annual attendance at the Ozaukee County Fair has been between thirty thousand and forty thousand visitors.[3]

## RACINE COUNTY

Under the auspices of the Racine County Agricultural Society, Racine County held its first fair in the fall of 1850 in the Town of York; it there continued until the early 1860s, when it moved to Union Grove. The Union Grove site proved unsatisfactory; according to a local news story in December 1863, "We have had enough of the Union Grove accommodations—if that is the word—which are too well known to need enumeration. Fair-goers—exhibitors and spectators—have fully made up their mind that the location of the Fair must be changed—either to Burlington or to Racine."

After Pliny M. Perkins, a Burlington businessman, offered the society ten acres of land near downtown Burlington, the site selection committee of the Racine County Agricultural Society accepted a motion from J. I. Case (of the J. I. Case Corporation) to move the fair to Burlington for three years. In June 1864, volunteers moved the boards, posts, and other equipment from Union Grove to the new fairgrounds, and that summer volunteers constructed a new racetrack. On a September Saturday, teams of horses pulling all sorts of buggies, carriages, and even lumber wagons packed down the newly created track. For fun, at the end of the day they held a couple of horse races with a five-dollar purse raised among the spectators.

To promote the fair at this new site, the agricultural society convinced the Racine and Mississippi Railroad to carry passengers and exhibits to the fair at half rates. The *Burlington Standard* reported that the fair was a "decided success," with attendance numbering in the thousands.

The fair continued to prosper at the Burlington site. The society added a new floral hall, plus a thousand-seat grandstand, stables, and other buildings. Then in September 1885, the Wisconsin Central Railroad took possession of the fairgrounds and laid its tracks through Burlington, building a depot the next year. The agricultural society, in need of a new location, turned down an offer to rent a suitable grounds for the fair near Burlington.

Meanwhile, the Racine Industrial Association had organized a fair in Racine; it was first held in 1884 and continued until about 1893. Financial failure led to the fair's demise, and for thirty years, until 1923, Racine County had no county fair. The Racine School of Agriculture began holding school fairs for its students' projects starting in 1919, and in 1922 faculty member Earl A. Polley called a meeting for those interested in once more holding a county fair. The Racine County Fair Association was formed, and in January 1923 the group picked Burlington as the host for its first "modern day" fair, held that fall in Schwaller's Grove (now Riverside Park). The fair reported a profit of $2,200. But Union Grove was persistent in expressing its interest in hosting the fair, and the association voted to move the fair to Union Grove. They chose the Old Settlers grounds as the site for the fair, and it has been there ever since.[4]

## SHEBOYGAN COUNTY

The Sheboygan County Agricultural Society was organized July 4, 1851, and sponsored Sheboygan County's first fair, held on October 1, 1851, in Sheboygan Falls. It held its second fair in 1852 in Plymouth; there Henry Eidman of Sheboygan Falls exhibited two Merino rams, the first fine-wool sheep in the county. In 1853, Sheboygan hosted the event, and, beginning in 1854, Sheboygan Falls was once more home to the fair.

In 1888, Sheboygan organized its first Sheboygan Driving Park and Exposition, which led to a competition between Sheboygan Falls and Sheboygan as fair host. Duplicate fairs were held until 1891, and from 1891 until 1895 the fair was held in Sheboygan. A rift developed between the Sheboygan Driving Park and the county agricultural society, and no fair was held in 1896. That year, residents of the Plymouth area reorganized the Sheboygan County Agricultural Association and took charge of the agricltural activities in the county.

The next year, the first fair under this new organization was held in Plymouth, at the present-day fairgrounds east of Plymouth. With its new central location, the fair boomed. A half-mile racetrack was completed in July 1897. Motorcycle racing competed with horse racing in 1909, and spectators began to attend the fair in horseless carriages. In 1910, a special gate was opened just for automobiles in order to prevent spooking the horses carrying riders to the fair.

Ostrich racing at the Sheboygan County Fair, circa 1955

IMAGE PRESERVED BY SHEBOYGAN COUNTY HISTORICAL RESEARCH CENTER

A parade of autos was held one year, with a top prize of eleven dollars to be shared by the top five cars. Only four winners claimed a prize; the fifth became bogged down in mud and didn't finish the race.

The early 1900s Sheboygan County Fair featured a number of modern innovations. Electricity was the big attraction at the 1912 fair, featuring a country home lighted by electricity. In 1914, fairgoers learned how electricity could keep butter and cheese fresher. And in 1919 an airship visited the fair and wowed the crowds. Airplane stunts were a feature of the late 1920s, and stunt fliers entertained fairgoers at the 1927 fair. That year the fair had a negative note as well, as local Ku Klux Klan members burned a cross on the fair's last day. By the late 1940s, stock car racing replaced horse races. The five-day Sheboygan County Fair continues each year at the Plymouth fairgrounds.[5]

# WASHINGTON COUNTY

A group gathered in Hartford in 1855 to organize an agricultural society, and a year later the newly organized society adopted a constitution and bylaws. The Washington County Agricultural and Industrial Society stated its mission: "To promote and improve the condition of agriculture, horticulture, mechanical manufacturing and household arts within Washington County." In 1858, the society held the first Washington County Fair at the courthouse square in West Bend.

The fair was suspended during the Civil War years, but it resumed in Hartford in 1865. The fair ran for three days in September each year, with admission set at twenty-five cents for adults and ten cents for children. Horse racing attracted many fairgoers during the late 1800s.

By the late 1920s, the fair was losing money, and in 1937 the agricultural society, working with Washington County, agreed that the county would take over the fair's operation. After that year's fair, the buildings and fairgrounds were sold. In 1938, the agricultural society dissolved and turned its assets over to the county. A fair committee under direction of the Washington County Board took over fair operations. This first fair under new management was held at the County Highway Grounds in Slinger August 9 and10, 1938. It was called the Washington County 4-H Fair, as youth exhibits had become an important feature. Attendance each year for a decade ranged between forty thousand and sixty thousand.

In 1943, in the midst of World War II, the fair was called the Washington County Victory Fair. By this time officials saw the fair outgrowing its Slinger site, with parking becoming a major problem. Space for exhibits had also become inadequate. In 1945, the fair changed its dates to the last week in July and continued on that schedule, adding a livestock auction in 1970. The first year, twelve beef cattle, seven lambs, and nineteen hogs were sold.

In 1978, the fair management considered moving the fairgrounds to farmland south of Slinger, but a tight budget prevented the move. In the early 1990s, the state health department mandated upgrading or moving the fair, perhaps because of overcrowding. In 1993, the Washington County Development Committee began developing plans for a future site for the fairgrounds. After considerable discussion, the Washington County Board decided to purchase a West Bend site. The first fair held at the newly built Washington County Fair Park took place on July 23–27, 1999, and the fair continues to be held there today.[6]

## WAUKESHA COUNTY

Waukesha County Fair officials say this about their fair: "We are not only the oldest county fair in Wisconsin—we're also the largest event in Waukesha County. The Waukesha County Fair celebrates our rural heritage with barnyard animals, crafts, foods, farm displays—and, of course, the midway!" The fair is a nonprofit volunteer organization "dedicated to supporting 4-H activities and education, and providing a fun time for children and adults of all ages."

The first Waukesha County Fair was held on July 4, 1842, in Poplar Grove on Carroll Street in Prairieville (now Waukesha). The day's activities included a plowing match, with forty dollars in premiums awarded to the winner. In another contest, the farmer with the best yield for an acre of corn received a premium of three dollars.

At the time of that first fair, Waukesha was still part of Milwaukee County; Waukesha County was created in 1846.[7] In 1853, the agricultural societies of Milwaukee and Waukesha Counties consolidated to organize a fair. Tickets were ten cents, and the fair drew up to four thousand people. It featured floral displays, a band, and a women's equestrian display. In 1858, the fair acquired a site at the old state industrial school, but then it moved among several other locations for the next near-century. It wasn't until 1966 that the fair moved to its

Waukesha County Fair, 1987

WHI IMAGE ID 23173

present location at the Waukesha Exposition Center, where, over the next several years, organizers added a youth building, a dairy barn, and a beef barn to the site. The Waukesha Horse Association constructed an outdoor horse show ring at the center, and during the early 1980s the fair association financed construction of a regulation truck/tractor pull track. Fair management began bringing well-known entertainment to the fair; the 1984 lineup, for example, included national acts Loretta Lynn, Mickey Gilley, and the Nitty Gritty Dirt Band. Each year, the Waukesha County Fair leases the exposition grounds for the week of the fair, which is held in mid-July.[8]

The fairgrounds of the Pepin County Agricultural Society in Durand, 1918

# 9

# SOUTHWESTERN WISCONSIN FAIRS

## BUFFALO/PEPIN COUNTIES

Buffalo County held its first fair in 1872 under the auspices of the Buffalo County Agricultural Society, which proclaimed its mission to include "improvement of agriculture and the study of the kindred arts and sciences."[1] This first fair was held in the little community of Cream in the southern part of the county. People arrived in lumber wagons and saw sculptures made of butter, cattle exhibits, and horse races and had an opportunity to hear the first organ in the community. The fair was held for three years at that site, with average attendance about 1,500 each year, before the society moved the fair to the more centrally located Alma in hopes of attracting more visitors. The new location along the Mississippi River was prone to flooding, so in some years the fair had few exhibits and featured logrolling and other water activities as attractions.

In 1884, the railroad took over the location near Alma, and the fair moved to Mondovi, where it continues to be held today. By the early 1900s, the fair was looking for unusual entertainment to help attract attendance. In 1903, a French flier wearing a parachute jumped from a hot-air balloon above the fair. In 1912, Oscar Brindley brought his biplane to the fair; the record does not indicate whether he offered rides. During those years, the association offered unusual entertainment that included seals and bears, bands from across the country, and trick acrobatics, but these acts became too expensive and were discontinued.

In 1919, youth were encouraged to exhibit at the fair for the first time. A few years later, the fair went electric, fully ten years before electricity was available to the public. Crowds continued to grow each year as further improvements were made, include blacktopping the midway and constructing an addition to the commercial building.

The Pepin County Fair celebrated 140 years of operation in 2017. It had become small by that time, and the same year, organizers made a bittersweet decision to close the fair and combine operations with the Buffalo County Fair, in part to provide a better experience for Pepin County 4-H members. Marie Ritscher, Pepin County youth development educator, explained, "Increasing the competition will make students improve their skills to compete, and the end goal will be for youth to learn even more from their fair experience." Today the fair is operated by the Buffalo County Agricultural Fair Association working closely with the UW–Madison Buffalo County Extension office.[2]

## CRAWFORD COUNTY

The Crawford County Agricultural Society was organized on September 10, 1871, with $250 and the stated purpose of promoting "the Agricultural, Horticultural, Mechanical, and Household Arts." Annual dues were one dollar.

A ticket to the nineteenth annual Crawford County Fair, 1890

WHI IMAGE ID 149495

Later that same fall, the society held its first fair in the village of Seneca, near Kane's Hotel. In 1872, the society purchased about ten acres of nearby land from Samuel P. Langdon and held succeeding fairs at that site.

The society set several rules for exhibits, including the following: "Canned fruit, etc. except wine, must be put up this present season. Farm products must have been raised the present year by the exhibitor. Competition is only open to manufacturers of Crawford County, except for farm machinery and arts. Entry fee for exhibitors is twenty-percent of premium. All teams of horses, herds of cattle, sheep or swine, or collection of canned fruit or any other article must be owned by the person who enters it."

Today, the Crawford County Fair Board, a committee of the Crawford County Board, supervises the fair, held at the fairgrounds at Gays Mills in late August each year. Both open-class and youth entries are welcome.[3]

# GRANT COUNTY

On November 6, 1855, a small group of farmers met at a rural church in Beetown and organized the Grant County Agricultural Society. Each member paid a dollar to join. The organization sponsored its first fair in 1856 at Lancaster and paid sixty-nine dollars in premiums. The association bought ten acres of land from J. C. Holloway a mile east of Lancaster in 1859 and immediately built a grandstand that seated up to a thousand people. Later that year they bought an additional five acres from Holloway.

In 1893, the fair featured horse and bicycle racing, and the association constructed its first dining hall. In 1899, the group boasted that it had twenty-five acres with a three-story grandstand, an art hall, floral hall, agricultural hall, and amphitheater. The 1913 Crawford County Fair was electrified and could

An official checks on a driver in the Grant County Fair's "Night of Destruction."
PHOTO BY SHELLY HOLMES PORTRAITURE

now hold evening events; in 1919, the fair raised ten thousand dollars to build the first sales pavilion.

In the midst of World War II, Lancaster businessmen bought out the Grant County Agricultural Society in 1944. This new Grant County Agriculture Extension Committee appointed a fair secretary and soon tore down the old buildings and built new ones, along with a racetrack for harness racing, all with the hope of making the refurbished fair a money-making venture. But the fair lost money eleven out of the next fourteen years, and by 1958 the group was seeking for a buyer for the fairgrounds.

In 1959, the group sold the fairgrounds to Grant County. Under supervision of the county board's Agriculture/Fair Committee, the fair flourished. Management built several several new buildings, including the Youth and Ag Center in 1963. In 1966, the fair held its first meat animal auction, which included forty-nine steers. The fair added a new grandstand in 1967, followed over the next four decades by a pole barn for swine, crops and livestock buildings, a poultry and rabbit building, a new show barn, and a new exhibit hall. Today, the fair attracts about twenty-five thousand visitors each year and offers a variety of entertainment and exhibits, including the popular demolition derby and "Night of Destruction," a race that involves a variety of vehicles—and a lot of crashes.[4]

## JACKSON COUNTY FAIR

The Jackson County Agricultural Society organized in 1854 and sponsored the county's first fair that same year in Black River Falls. Little is known about the county's early fairs, other than that most were held in Black River Falls, with at least one held in the nearby village of Merrillan. With the outbreak of the Civil War in 1860, the agricultural society disbanded and there were no county fairs for several years.

On July 24, 1867, representatives from several Jackson County townships met at the courthouse in Black River Falls and organized a new Jackson County Agricultural Society, which also served as the "fair board." The society negotiated a lease for forty acres of land in Black River Falls for the fair. At the 1869 fair, popular events included a horse-pulling contest and bicycle races. Exhibitors displayed their projects in a log building. In 1877, the three-day fair was held September 20–22 and boasted 1,200 exhibit entries and six thousand attendees. Families arrived on wagons pulled by oxen and in horse-drawn buggies, and some brought tents and stayed for the full three days of the fair. The best plowman over the age of twenty-one received a purebred Berkshire pig, while the best needlework by a young woman under seventeen won five dollars in gold, and seven dollars went to the "best looking lady in the county under the age of 20."

The society built a new grandstand in 1911; it included a kitchen where church members sold food during the fair. Visitors that year could pay twenty-five cents to have their picture taken with an early automobile, a one-cylinder Northern painted bright red. Early rides at the fair included a merry-go-round and a Ferris wheel, both operated by steam engines. The 1913 fair featured Japanese acrobats, bucking mules, and trained dogs, all performing in front of the grandstand. By the 1930s, many young people were exhibiting at the fair; for a time they were excused from school for that purpose, but eventually the fair was moved to dates earlier in the summer to avoid disrupting classes.

With the outbreak of World War I, the fairgrounds became a training site for men from throughout Jackson County. They used the fair buildings as barracks. And in 1942, three Civilian Conservation Camp buildings at Irving and City Point were moved to the fairgrounds and served as exhibit and dormitory buildings for fair exhibitors.

One of the popular features of the late 1950s and early 1960s fairs was a horticultural display organized by 4-H Extension agent Darrel Apps. Tractor pulls also became popular in the 1960s. In 1972, the Jackson County Fair held its first meat animal sale. Special features at the 1977 fair included helicopter rides,

A 1950s ad for the Jackson County Fair's "3 Star Jamboree," which featured popular entertainers of the day

WHI IMAGE ID 149496

performances by the popular group Kids from Wisconsin, hot air balloons rides, and bingo. That year the fair also held its first demolition derby, which has remained popular ever since.

In 2008, most of the fair's aging buildings were sold and moved, replaced a year later by new ones, including a new dairy barn, livestock barn, horse barn, small animal barn, and grandstand. The fair continues to be considered "the biggest yearly event for families and friends in Jackson County."[5]

# LA CROSSE INTERSTATE FAIR

La Crosse County held it first fair in 1858, on the present site of the University of Wisconsin–La Crosse campus. In 1890, local citizens organized the Interstate Fair Association with the purpose of inviting exhibitors and fairgoers from both inside and outside the state to participate.

In 1957, the fairgrounds moved to its present location at West Salem. In 1986, the fair association proposed canceling the fair, possibly because of financial reasons, but county residents and fairgoers rallied to save it. The La Crosse County Agricultural Society, reorganized and incorporated, negotiated with the La Crosse Interstate Fair Association, which agreed to lease the fairgrounds for one dollar, plus the cost of insurance and utilities, for the three- to four-day fair. The new leadership held several successful fund-raising events and offered free admission, except for grandstand events, and free parking.

In 1989, the La Crosse County Agricultural Society assumed complete control of the La Crosse Interstate Fairgrounds at West Salem. The transaction included assuming an outstanding mortgage of $174,000, which was cosigned by several area businesses and local citizens. Fund-raising continued as citizens were committed to keeping the fair, and they paid off the mortgage in 1994. Credit for the fair's continued success, according to the La Crosse County Agricultural Society, goes to the dedicated La Crosse County Agricultural Society Members, 4-H leaders and 4-H members, dairy breed associations, La Crosse County pork producers, many local community organizations, and a huge cadre of volunteers. The La Crosse Interstate Fair is held each year in July and usually includes exhibits from Iowa and Minnesota along with Wisconsin.[6]

# MONROE COUNTY FAIR

The Monroe County Agricultural Society organized the first Monroe County Fair, held in Sparta in 1858. The Sparta Driving and Agricultural Association and, later, the Sparta Fair Association sponsored the fair. Interest dwindled, and the fair died and was reborn several times over its long history. The last of the Sparta fairs was held in the 1930s.

In Tomah, a group called the Eastern Monroe County Agricultural Society, established in 1869, held its first fair in Tomah in 1873, with annual fairs to follow. In 1895, the Eastern Monroe County Fair was held September 22–24. The Tomah *Monitor-Herald* reported: "Rough weather, high winds, and a cold wave reduced attendance on the final day of the fair, Thursday. There was a good field of horses for trotting and running events making the events very interesting. . . . a bicycle craze was sweeping the nation and five riders entered the fair competition."[7]

The fair association pulled out all the stops for the 1907 fair. They boasted having the largest midway in the history of the fair, including a sideshow with a young woman who reportedly weighed 721 pounds, a vaudeville show, Monarch Electric Show, "Madam Smith, a Palmist," and a horse race with the "best 20 gallopers in the Northwest."

In 1921, the fair became known as the Monroe County Fair. The 1925 event featured a pageant and the crowning of a harvest queen, Ruth Gerke, who won in a field of nineteen contestants and received a diamond ring as her prize. Exhibits included gigantic corn stalks and other grains plus vegetables of every type.

Even with the country in the grips of the Great Depression, the 1932 fair, held in August, experienced exceptionally good weather and anticipated a good crowd. However, the carnival that had been booked for the fair had gone bankrupt, and the 1932 fair lacked its main attraction. The record does not indicate how the fair survived, but survive it did. The fair continued through World War II; the 1945 event was judged one of the most successful up to that date, with an attendance of eleven thousand. Harness racing and horse-pulling contests were major draws.

A new attraction was offered at the August 1957 fair: both men's and women's wrestling. Also that year, 1,100 persons entered 4,500 exhibits, from handicrafts to livestock, and sixteen thousand people attended. Special features at the 1972 fair included horse pulling on Friday night, an all-female daredevils show on Saturday night, and tractor pulling on Sunday afternoon.

In the 2000s, the fair continued to try new events to attract visitors. In 2019, the Monroe County Agricultural Society organized free "Learn-N-Earn Activities," a treasure hunt of sorts in which the fair provided questions and participants searched the fairgrounds for answers. According to Monroe County Fair management, "The program teaches both adults and children educational facts and makes it fun to seek them out like a scavenger hunt. We feel it is vital to educate the public on the facts of where their food comes from and how it is grown through interactive experiences."[8]

To support its annual fair, the Monroe County Agricultural Society has sponsored since 1976 the Budweiser Dairyland Super National Truck and Tractor Pull. According to society member Shae Fox, the event, held the weekend before the fair, "has continued to support the community and draws fans and competitors from all over the world. The 'Tomah Pulls' help to support our county fair today."[9]

# RICHLAND COUNTY

Agricultural leaders organized the Richland County Agricultural Society on May 15, 1857. They declared that the major objective of the organization was to improve "the character and operation of agricultural, mechanical and household arts." To meet that objective, in October 1857 the society organized a cattle show and fair at Thompson's Hall on Main Street in Richland Center. The event proved successful, and from 1858 to 1860 the fair was held on the courthouse square in Richland Center. The fair was paused during the Civil War but resumed in 1866.

By 1868, the society purchased a fairgrounds on Haseltine Street for four hundred dollars. The fair remained popular, and in 1873, the society sold the Haseltine Street property and purchased a larger site of twenty acres, the fairgrounds' current site. Admission to the fair in 1873 was twenty-five cents per person, twenty-five cents for a single riding horse or one horse and carriage, and thirty-five cents for two horses and a carriage. The fair continued to grow, and the society purchased an additional eleven acres.

In 1880, J. W. Smith sought permission to build an amphitheater on the fairgrounds designed for watching races. The society agreed, reserving the right to purchase the amphitheater. Admission to the amphitheater was not to exceed ten cents per person. One of the popular races held there in 1895 was a one-mile bicycle race. The winner of the best of two of three races received a purse of twenty-five dollars.

Nine acres were added to the fairgrounds in 1904. One of the 1905 fair's attractions was a football game between the Richland Center team and a Madison team. Growing ever larger, in 1919–1922 the fair added more land, a three-thousand-seat grandstand, and a new racetrack.

By the 1930s, 4-H exhibits were a popular feature of the Richland County Fair, and they remain so today. The fair is held each year in early September.[10]

## TREMPEALEAU COUNTY

Trempealeau County held its first fair October 21 and 22, 1859, in Galesville. Several people exhibited examples of their handiwork; H. Armstrong showed his handmade plows and ox yokes; and spectators watched a horse race on a makeshift track cut out of the brush. After the 1895 event, participants decided to hold another fair, and all the exhibitors agreed to leave their premium money with the society.

A disagreement developed about where to hold the 1860 fair, with some people wanting to move it to Caledonia. But after some protest, the fair was again held in Galesville, in front of the courthouse. The controversy continued, and the fair was moved for two years to the village of Trempealeau, but it returned to Galesville in 1862 on the site where it would remain for the next thirty years.

During that time, the fairgrounds had only enough room for a one-third-mile racetrack, but by 1892, with horse racing growing in popularity, a larger track was deemed necessary. The fair moved to a piece of land large enough to accommodate a half-mile track. Some of fair buildings were moved to the new site, including a small open grandstand and a racehorse judging stand. A new grandstand was built in 1893 and new cattle barns in 1896. Other improvements followed, until the society realized it had accumulated considerable debt and might not be able to continue the fair.

Enter the Galesville Park, Fair and Promotion Company, formed for the single purpose of helping the Trempealeau County Fair meet its financial obligations. The company sold shares in the fair to locals but also to people from La Crosse and Winona, Minnesota. The sale was a success, and the fair continued.

An outbreak of the dreaded communicable disease polio, which afflicted and killed many children in the first half of the 1900s, caused the 1916 Trempealeau County Fair to be a "fair without children," and fair attendance fell by half. And in 1925, when polio once more surfaced in Galesville, the assistant state health officer asked the fair to change its August 25 and 26 dates to a time when cooler weather prevailed. The 1925 fair was moved to October 13–16, but unfortunately the 2,500 attendees on opening day saw bone-chilling, rainy weather.

The Great Depression hit everyone hard, including fairs, and attendance plummeted. In 1933, Trempealeau County Fair management cut admission to 25 cents, and once again there was concern that the fair would have to close its doors. One way to keep the fair going was to encourage young people to participate. Trempealeau County saw the formation of its first 4-H clubs in 1923, and 4-H members were encouraged to exhibit at the fair, but during the Depression years many believed that financially challenged farmers might see such youth activities as frivolous and unnecessary. The opposite proved true. The fair gave farmers the opportunity to prove to others that their work was important and that their children's accomplishments on the farm were worthy of note. Members of 4-H clubs exhibited their projects, and attendance at the fair once more increased. Soon 4-H exhibits exceeded all exhibits at the fair. In December 1936, the Galesville Park, Fair and Promotion Company sold the fairgrounds to the Trempealeau County Agricultural Society for one dollar.

The Trempealeau Fair continued to prosper, and in 1954 the fair recorded 103 junior exhibitors with 3,783 exhibits, plus 797 adult exhibits. The fair held its first County Queen contest in 1964 and its inaugural livestock auction in 1972. Today, the mission of the Trempealeau County Fair is to "create educational, social, and economic opportunities that promote the citizens and businesses of our county and communities; in an atmosphere of education, competition and entertainment." The fair is held in mid-July at the Galesville Fairgrounds.[11]

# VERNON COUNTY

In 1856, the Vernon County Fair began as a humble event on Viroqua's Main Street on a vacant lot next to the courthouse. A group of Vernon County pioneers wanted to promote the agricultural opportunities the county offered and to encourage business and commerce to come to the area. Exhibits at the first fair included two stallions, three bulls, two cows, three woven rugs, some patchwork quilts, and a few jars of home-churned butter, sorghum, and maple syrup.

The following year saw the organization of the Vernon County Agricultural Society. In 1858, the society purchased ten acres for its fairgrounds at a spot near present-day Eckhart Park. The land was surrounded by a ten-foot-high fence and featured a half-mile racetrack. Horse racing was introduced at the fair that year and continued until 1888, when it was banned. With no horse racing, attendance at the fair plummeted. In 1891, a new president of the agriculture society, a Mr. Minshall, reinstated horse races, and they have continued every year since.

In 1891, the Vernon County Fair moved to its present location, a site encompassing twenty-two and a half acres purchased for one hundred dollars per acre. A grandstand, art hall, and cattle barns were the first buildings erected at the new site. Fair admission was ten cents. In 1897, the fair was extended to four days. Featured events during those years included bicycle races, footraces, farmer wrestling matches, and such unusual offerings as performances by Japanese acrobats, elephant rides, and circus acts. Baseball games, which had become popular throughout the country, became part of the fair's activities. Speeches, too, were popular, with the fair awarding a prize to the best orator.

In 1903, the Open Class Exhibition Hall was erected; it also housed the fair office. In 1906, the fair ran for five days, commemorating a half century of the fair's existence. The 1911 fair offered a special attraction: an airplane flight. Hundreds of people came to see the plane, many of them seeing one for the first time. On the pilot's second attempt to fly the machine, it rose to about twenty-five feet and began falling. Its wing caught on a cart, and the plane flipped over. It remained a stationary nose-to-the-ground attraction for the remainder of the fair. To compensate for this failed attraction, fair officials quickly organized an additional baseball game. That year, fairgoers also had the opportunity to enjoy a giant barbecue. A 1,250-pound ox provided about a thousand pieces of well-seasoned meat for sandwiches offered at nominal change.

In 1915, nighttime activities were offered for the first time. Up until the 1920s, adults provided all of the fair's exhibit entries. It wasn't until 1921 that a 4-H livestock show was initiated. That first year, the youth exhibit consisted of three calves. Soon, youth exhibits by both 4-H and Future Farmers of America

Harness racing at the Vernon County Fair, 1963

WHI IMAGE ID 142667

(FFA) members became a major part of the fair. In 1950, the junior barn was enlarged by sixty feet, and in 1952 a new hog barn was constructed.

In 1956, the Vernon County Fair celebrated its one-hundredth anniversary, and ten thousand people attended. As a special attraction, women's groups from eleven communities constructed replicas of homes and shops that had existed in Vernon County in 1856.

More buildings were built over the years, including a new cattle barn in 1962 and a building dedicated to youth activities in 1983. Some thirty thousand people attended the 1989 fair. In 1991, fairgoers paid a dollar to view the largest living steer; he weighed four thousand pounds and stood six feet tall.

As the years passed, the Vernon County Fair continued to grow. A thirteen-thousand-square-foot commercial building was completed in 2009, and a new building for seniors in 2011. As is true of all county fairs, much of the fair's success is due to the contributions of many volunteers. The Vernon County Fair is held in mid-September, making it the latest county fair in Wisconsin.[12]

Marquette County Fair's round barn

PHOTO BY STEVE APPS

# 10

# CENTRAL WISCONSIN FAIRS

## ADAMS COUNTY

The first documented county fair in Adams County was held at the present fairgrounds in Friendship in 1859. Horse racing was featured, in addition to agricultural exhibits.

The 1893 Adams County Fair ran September 20–22 with admission fees of twenty-five cents for adults and fifteen cents for kids under twelve. Special events included a "children's day" with free admittance for children under fourteen and "free open air tight rope and wire performances every day." A "fine American watch" was awarded to the person with the largest number of exhibit entries. Two dollars and fifty cents went to the tallest girl under ten years of age.

In the 1920s, 4-H and school exhibits became popular attractions; since then baseball tournaments, musical performances, commercial displays, political events, airplane rides, stock car races, tractor pulls, and demolition derbies have also been popular at the Adams County Fair.

Today the fair is held in early August with free admission, but with a charge for certain grandstand events, and a full schedule of attractions, including horse, dog, rabbit, poultry, and swine shows. A tractor-pulling contest, the ever-popular demolition derby, a lawn mower race, a dairy milking contest, and a youth livestock auction draw crowds as well.

Another favorite at the fair is the Old Farmers Antique Club, a ten-thousand-square-foot museum located on the west end of the fairgrounds where an assortment of agricultural implements and tools from an earlier day are displayed.[1]

# CENTRAL WISCONSIN STATE FAIR (WOOD COUNTY)

Lovers of horses and horse racing organized the Marshfield Driving Park Association in 1890, a predecessor of the Central Wisconsin State Fair Association. The Driving Park Association purchased land for a fairgrounds and constructed a racetrack and grandstand with seating capacity of five thousand, as well as building horse stables and offices. Their first event featured harness racing and bicycle racing. The city of Marshfield granted the Driving Park Association a fifteen-year, rent-free lease. Sale of memberships to prominent Marshfield-area residents financed the purchase.

As early as 1887, Marshfield residents expressed an interest in organizing an agricultural fair. Local business owners and professionals contributed $1,500 each toward that end, but a huge fire in Marshfield put the plans on hold. Interest in horse racing had begun to wane by the late 1890s, and the Driving Park Association fairgrounds faced foreclosure.

In January 22, 1903, the Central Wisconsin State Fair Association was organized and sold five hundred life memberships at ten dollars each; the association used the money to convert the former horse racing park to a site appropriate for an annual agricultural exposition. The group obtained a fifty-year lease for the fairgrounds from the city and held the first Central Wisconsin State Fair in 1893.

Meanwhile, several Wood County farmers who had become interested in raising purebred cattle formed the Central Wisconsin Holstein Breeders Association in 1912. In 1915–1916, the fair association constructed Wood County's iconic round barn on the fairgrounds. In 1949 and again in 1952, the association added land to the fairgrounds, bringing the total to sixty-six acres.

Starting in 1983, many improvements have been made to the fairgrounds through a partnership of the Central Wisconsin Fair Association, Wood County, and the city of Marshfield. Today there are more than two dozen structures on the grounds, where the fair happens every summer in late August.

Tickets to the 1982 Central Wisconsin State Fair

WHI IMAGE ID 149494

The 150-foot-diameter round barn on the grounds of the Central Wisconsin State Fair, 1936

WHI IMAGE ID 129851

In a welcome letter to the 117th Central Wisconsin State Fair in 2019, Executive Director Dale Christiansen wrote:

In the beginning, most of us either lived on a farm or worked in an industry that supported agriculture. Today most of us are several generations removed from the farm and we are finding ourselves in a position where we have to educate consumers and find out what it takes to produce that cheese and ice cream you are enjoying. Ask how much time and effort it took to raise that steer or that prize-winning head of cabbage as you are visiting with our producers. Take time to thank them for their efforts to keep our store shelves stocked and our bellies full. These are challenging times for American Agriculture, but with creativity and willpower, they will endure. One hundred seventeen years ago, they were the foundation for our fair and they remain our background today.[2]

# GREEN LAKE COUNTY

The Green Lake County Board of Supervisors on May 4, 1939, passed the following resolution: "BE IT RESOLVED that the County Agriculture Committee of Green Lake County is authorized and empowered to conduct a Junior County Fair in Green Lake County and that such a fair be designated as the official Green Lake County Fair to share in the distribution of State Aid by the Department of Agriculture and markets."

The committee held its first fair in 1939, under the direction of A. D. Carew, county agricultural agent, and Annette McDonald, home agent. The fair opened on the courthouse lawn in downtown Green Lake, where booths and exhibits were arranged. City Hall housed the 4-H and Homemaker Club exhibits, and the livestock exhibits occupied the Rowley Tool and Die Company building. In 1940, the fair moved to the county highway grounds.

The war years 1941–1945 curtailed the fair's development, but growth continued in the decades following, with new buildings erected and eleven acres of land added. In 1963, the fair moved to a four-day format.

In October 2009, the fair adopted the following mission statement: "The mission of the Green Lake County Fair is to provide positive youth development and leadership skills, along with promoting agriculture, family and community involvement through education and tradition."[3]

Today the Green Lake County Fair is county supported and held annually the first weekend in August. Its youth and adult exhibitors come from throughout Green Lake County, entering exhibits in categories from pie baking, flower growing, and animal showing to woodworking and photography. Entertainment includes music, educational programs, truck and tractor pulls, and a demolition derby. Of course, there is a carnival, with rides and midway shows and events, and food vendors with their assortment of county fair treats. The Green Lake County Fair is a free fair, with no gate admission or parking fees charged.[4]

# JUNEAU COUNTY

In 1866, a group of farmers and others interested in agriculture met to organize an agricultural society in Juneau County. They wrote:

> The purpose of the Juneau County Agriculture Society shall be the promotion of agriculture, stock raising, dairying, manufacturing, education, and every other activity that can be performed to develop the resources and promote the prosperity of Juneau County. This objective may be obtained by holding a county fair and the sponsorship of other activities that may be deemed appropriate or necessary to promote the above purposes of the corporation. . . . Membership in the Society is open to any person who wants to support the fair. Membership is obtained by paying a ten-year membership fee of $10.00.[5]

The society held its first fair in Mauston in 1866. For the fair's first three decades, it operated only during daylight hours, as electricity was not available. Horses, especially harness racing, were always a major attraction in Juneau County. In 1903, the fair listed 117 classes of premiums for horses. Sixty-nine entries for homemade bread were on display that year. Horse-pulling contests also drew big crowds. When a flying machine was booked for the 1913 event, the fair broke all attendance records to date; tragically, on the third day of the fair, the plane crashed, killing the pilot.

The theme for Juneau County's 150th-anniversary fair, held August 16–23, 2015, was "Down on the Farm." Events included a tractor pull, draft horse–pulling contest, auto/truck demolition derby, junior and open-class dog show, junior pleasure horse show, junior dog agility show, junior and open sheep and goat shows, and the Juneau County meat animal sale. The annual Fairest of the Fair, Junior Fairest of the Fair, and Junior Fairest Attendant appeared throughout the fair.

Just two and a half weeks before the 2019 fair was to open, the carnival cancelled its appearance. Instead, fair organizers offered an assortment of amusements, including paintball competitions, climbing walls, obstacle courses, jousting, bouncy houses, and a bungee trampoline. The fair board also invited several new food vendors to the fair to "satisfy many hungry fairgoers."[6]

## MARQUETTE COUNTY

Local farmers and others interested in the improvement of agriculture organized the Marquette County Agricultural Society in 1863. They sponsored Marquette County's first agricultural fair in 1868, in Montello. The fair continued in Montello thorough 1870 and, like so many of Wisconsin's county fairs, moved to several locations over the years, in this case including Oxford, 1871 and 1875; Montello, 1873, 1874, and 1876–1880; Packwaukee, 1881 and 1882; and Westfield, 1872, 1883–1884, and 1886 to today.

In the early years of the fairs, each township was represented at the fair. Entries topped five hundred in 1889. In 1891, more than four hundred tickets

Marquette County Fair
PHOTO BY STEVE APPS

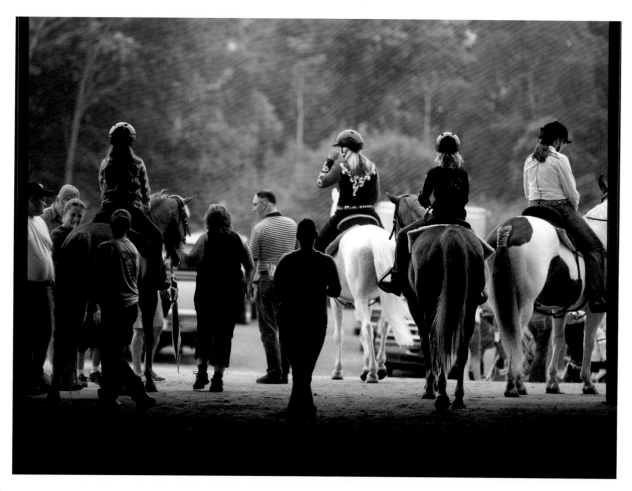

were sold, and the fair sponsored a ball game between Westfield and Montello (Montello was the winner) and a children's day featuring a mule race. In 1892, horse racing drew large crowds, with horses from Chicago, Berlin, Portage, and Marquette County.

The 1894 fair offered premiums including a two-dollar pair of shoes for the most entries, a two-dollar hat for the heaviest man, and a "puff box and puff" for the prettiest baby. Additional prizes included a flowered dress for the person with the best cut flowers, a copy of Whittier's poems for the best loaf of brown bread, buckskin mittens for the best Poland China hogs, and sacks of flour for the best hop-rising bread and the best milk-rising bread.

The 1917 fair's premium list included cakes, bread, cookies, and other baked items made with substitutes to emphasize wartime food-saving efforts. The fair grew, adding a round barn in 1921. In 1926, admission to the fair was one dollar, and anyone caught sneaking into the fair without paying was fined fifty dollars. Gambling, games of chance, and alcohol were prohibited on the fairgrounds. Exhibits in the food division that year included green apple pie, salt-rising bread, canned currants, ground cherries, quince, jams, jellies, pickles, and many types of vegetables.

By 1950, youth exhibits had become a major part of the fair, with 4-H leaders and members contributing to the fair's operations. Dawn Polcyn of Montello, a member of the Mecan Badgers 4-H Club who showed dairy cattle at the 1951 fair, walked away with the grand-champion ribbon for the all-breed dairy cattle contest (she also exhibited the grand-champion bull). The August 9, 1951, issue of the *Marquette County Tribune* reported Dawn's success, along with the winners of the amateur night contest: first place to baton twirler Sandra Trimble; second to the Note-Ables of Montello; third to Donna Wing of Endeavor; fourth to Jack Whirry and his harmonica, from Montello; and fifth to the Elm Grove square dancers. The five winners were asked to perform again on Sunday night before the grandstand crowd.

In 1966, the fair constructed a large animal building where meat animal auctions are still held. Youth and open-class exhibits continue to be major components of the Marquette County Fair, which today runs in early to mid-July. In 2019, the fair added another building to better accommodate poultry and rabbit entries as well as to open the fairgrounds to other activities during the year.[7]

## NEW LONDON FAIR (WAUPACA COUNTY)

The New London Fair operated from 1891 to 1912. During the fair's twenty-two years, the fairgrounds were privately owned by James Henry Cannon, the

leading organizer of the fair and its greatest promoter. The fair was well attended and featured exhibits of livestock, vegetables, flowers, and needlework. Entertainment included trained dogs and a steam-operated "whirly-go-round" that attracted children of all ages. Harness racing became an annual attraction, with horses coming from throughout the Midwest and cash prizes ranging from $75 to $450.

A notable event occurred at the fair in 1897, when three thousand farmers stood in the rain to hear Wisconsin politician "Fighting Bob" La Follette speak. In 1910, fairgoers watched two men with parachutes jump from a hot-air balloon, and in 1912, a crowd observed a biplane circling the fairgrounds. In 1912, the death of fair promoter James Cannon signaled the end of the New London Fair. Wisconsin Historical Marker 559 marks the location where thousands of people once attended this popular central Wisconsin fair.[8]

Fighting Bob La Follette gives a fiery speech at the New London Fair.
PHOTO COURTESY OF RICHARD LUEDKE

## PORTAGE COUNTY

The Portage County Fair Association was organized in 1869 and sponsored the first Portage County Fair in Amherst that year. The fair was held in Amherst until 1917, when the officers of the association voted to sponsor, instead of a fair, a homecoming event for boys returning from World War I service. In 1918, because state aid had been discontinued, the Portage County Fair closed down. A group of citizens organized the Portage County Advancement Association and for several years sponsored cattle sales at the fairgrounds. During the Depression years of the 1930s, these, too, were discontinued.

In 1949, with leadership from the Amherst Lion's Club and a group of citizens, a Portage County Fair Association was organized, with a fair resuming

Calf judging at the
Portage County Fair
WHI IMAGE ID 42443

operation in 1950. The group planned to sponsor a fair every July at Amherst, with emphasis given to providing opportunities for 4-H and Future Farmers of America (FFA) members to exhibit. This fair continues to this day.

The second Portage County fair, commonly known as the Rosholt Fair, resulted from the action of the Rosholt Advancement Association, organized in 1921. The group held a picnic that year in cooperation with the Portage County Guernsey Breeders Association; the gathering was so successful that they decided to make it an annual event. In 1922, the sponsoring committee named the event the Rosholt Community Free Fair. The Rosholt Fair Association is the governing body for the fair, which is held each year over Labor Day weekend and welcomes substantial participation from area 4-H and FFA members.[9]

# WAUPACA COUNTY

Waupaca County held its first fair in the city of Waupaca in the summer of 1873. Declaring it a success, organizers planned a second fair for the summer of 1874. This one was less successful, and planners decided to move the fair. Farmers and other public-minded citizens met to discuss a county fair at a new site and to organize an agricultural society. Township chairmen attending the meeting passed a resolution to organize an agricultural society in the county of Waupaca, "having as its aim the promotion of agriculture, horticulture, domestic manufactures, and mechanical arts."

The newly organized Waupaca County Agricultural Society held its first meeting on October 3, 1874, "for the purpose of completing the organization and making arrangements for holding the first annual fair." Members attending the meeting voted to organize a fair to be held in Weyauwega October 15 and 16, 1874. The exhibit list included horses, cattle, sheep, poultry, farm and garden, dairy and household, fruit, fancy work and fine arts, and mechanical items. Admission to the fair was forty cents for a season ticket and twenty-five cents for a one-day visit.

The fair at Weyauwega was a success, and directors of the agricultural society agreed to continue. They planned an 1875 fair for October 7–9 and, after some deliberation, agreed to pay two hundred dollars for twelve and a half acres near Weyauwega as a more permanent setting for the fair. The 1875 fair also proved very successful, and then next year the directors agreed to build an exhibition building.

After 1900, the fair was held in the September, and a one-half-mile racetrack was built for racehorses. A grandstand was added in 1902. In 1912, the fair directors voted to give all schoolchildren in Waupaca County a free ticket to the fair.

For the 1915 fair, an airplane was contracted to give flights each of the fair's four days. The society bought fourteen additional acres for the fairgrounds and added a racetrack. In 1917, a new grandstand was constructed using lumber from the old one; a cow stable was built at a cost of $455, and the fair added a merry-go-round. At the 1925 fair, a grandstand show was held in the evening for the first time, featuring several acts, followed by fireworks.

In 1938, the Great Depression led the Waupaca County Agricultural Society to sell the fairgrounds and all the buildings to Waupaca County. After a windstorm blew down the cattle barn in February 1946, the county built a new steel barn, at a cost of ten thousand dollars, in time for the 1946 fair; a new grandstand was erected in 1948. In 1970, organizers moved the fair to August with the hope of boosting attendance and to avoid competing with harvest work on farms in September.

Today, junior entries make up a major part of the fair. At a recent fair, youth exhibits included clothing, knitting/crocheting, home improvement, woodworking, communications, health sciences, family living, home environment, photography, plant and soil science, flowers/house plants and crops, nature-space, electricity, mechanical projects, rabbits, poultry, sheep, beef, swine, market goats, horses, junior dairy calf and heifers, junior dairy cows, and nonmarket goats. Entertainment featured everything from pig and duck races to a magician, rock-and-roll band, tractor and truck pull, and demolition derby.[10]

# WAUSHARA COUNTY

Waushara County farmers organized the Waushara County Agricultural Society in March 1857. The society held its first fair September 22–23, 1858. Fruits, vegetables, and flowers were exhibited at the Wautoma courthouse, and livestock were shown at the north end of St. Marie Street.

In 1861, at the start of the Civil War, both the agricultural society and the county fair were discontinued. In 1866, agricultural leaders attempted but failed to revive both. By 1875, the Waushara County Agricultural Society was active once more, and a county fair was planned. At a meeting held in early April 1875, Phineas Walker of Wautoma offered to donate twenty-five acres of land on the Richford road near Bird Creek. The offer was immediately accepted. However, at a meeting in May 1875, the society decided for reasons unknown not to locate the fairgrounds at the Walker site. The society appointed a three-person committee to negotiate with a Mrs. Johnson for twenty acres or more for a fairgrounds at a price not to exceed eight dollars per acre. The society quickly raised enough money to pay for the Johnson property, which was a quarter mile east of Wautoma and declared "probably the best location that could be had."

A clear title to the Johnson property was not immediately available, so the 1875 fair, held September 30 to October 1 in Wautoma, included temporary cattle sheds erected in a vacant lot near Coon's Hotel. Nearby rooms were obtained to display produce, fine arts, and other exhibits. Because the society had next to no funds, no prize money was offered. As reported, "Although rain threatened the first day, there was a fine showing of cattle and horses, hogs, sheep, and fowl. In the department of farm and garden produce, there were excellent specimens of small grains as well as vegetables. The fair of 1875 also exhibited articles of merchandise and homemaker skills."

The fair continued through both World War I and World War II. In 1994, the county purchased ten additional acres for the fair. In 2019, Waushara County celebrated its 145th county fair. The fair is still located on the land on Fair Street.

While most of the buildings on the fairgrounds have been replaced over the years, the Family Living Building remains. It began as the gymnasium for Wautoma High School and was moved from the corner of Fair and Elm Streets in the late 1920s. The Family Living Building is used to display home arts, clothing, foods, knitting, and crocheting. A photo gallery was added in 2004, and in 2005 the building was re-sided and re-roofed, and new windows were installed. The Family Living Building has withstood the test of time and has become a nostalgic symbol of the Waushara County Fair for many people.

The Exhibition Building was constructed in 1972, a cooperative project of the county, the fair association, and local 4-H clubs. During the fair, this building houses displays of vegetables, flowers, and plants as well as offices for fair staff. In 1990, the Farm Progress Committee (a joint program of several agencies, including Cooperative Extension) donated the Farm Progress Shelter House after a very successful festival. During the fair, the shelter is a popular place to relax with refreshments and friends.

The year 2019 marked the Waushara County Fair's forty-fifth annual Junior Livestock Auction. Auction records exist to 1986, when sixty-three head were sold. In 1995, rabbits and poultry were added to the market sale, with forty-four businesses and individuals supporting the youth selling animals. In 2018, the Waushara County 4-H/FFA Market Animal and Dairy Sponsorship Auction had eighty-eight buyers. Members of thirteen 4-H clubs participated in the market and animal dairy sponsorship projects that year.[11]

Poultry competition at the Waushara County Fair

Victory Garden contest at the Manitowoc County Fair, circa 1942

# 11

# NORTHEASTERN WISCONSIN FAIRS

## ALTO 4-H AND FARM BUREAU FAIR (FOND DU LAC COUNTY)

The Alto 4-H and Farm Bureau Fair began in 1946 as an alternative to the Fond du Lac County Fair. With deep conservative Dutch roots, this unincorporated community wanted to operate a fair without beer sales or Sunday activities. The fair is held in Alto Township, a township of thirty-six square miles and 1,100 residents. The fair is just two days long, held midweek, and bills itself as "The Biggest Little Fair Around."

The Alto fair receives no county or state funds; money earned from food sales covers much of the event's expenses, and local businesses sponsor entertainment. The township's 4-H clubs exhibit their animals, and a livestock auction is held each year. Premiums for a blue ribbon range from two to fourteen dollars.

One of the fair's unique features is a pie-baking contest, with a different kind of pie featured each year. The 2019 competition, featuring cherry pie, awarded one hundred dollars for first prize, fifty dollars for second prize, and twenty-five dollars for third prize. The fair is managed by a board of directors numbering twenty-one, all volunteers. Volunteers also coordinate various fair activities. The fairgrounds is off Wisconsin Highway 49 and County AS in Fond du Lac County, northwest of Waupun. Admission to the fair and parking are free.

Activities in recent years included an antique tractor pull, pedal tractor pull, livestock auction, 4-H archery shoot, fireworks in the evening, and the annual fair parade featuring the University of Wisconsin Marching Band.[1]

# BROWN COUNTY

On June 19, 1856, the Brown County Agricultural Society purchased sixty-five city lots near Astor Park on the south side of Green Bay. On that property, in October 1859, the society sponsored Brown County's first fair. In 1868, the Society mortgaged the sixty-five lots, presumably to finance the construction of fair buildings. Then in 1870, the John Jacob Astor estate sued the society for nonpayment of the mortgage. The fairgrounds near Astor Park faced a sheriff's auction set for August 27, 1870. The fair did continue at this site for two more years, 1870 and 1871, but 1871 saw the last county fair in Brown County until 1879.

In 1871, the Brown County Agricultural Society purchased land from Woodlawn Cemetery, located east of Webster Avenue in Green Bay, but the society never held a fair at that site. In 1877, the society again faced financial problems and a lawsuit from the Woodlawn Cemetery Association for nonpayment of the mortgage on the new fairgrounds. This second fairgrounds was sold at a sheriff's sale on July 6, 1878.

Not giving up, in 1879 the Brown County Fair was once more established, and the fair opened for one year at Cormier Park in Ashwaubenon. In addition, that same year the Brown County Agricultural Society approved a ten-year lease at the Fox River Driving Park in West De Pere. The first Brown County Fair opened at this new site in 1880 and continued through 1886.

In 1887 and 1888, Brown County held two fairs, one in De Pere at the Fox River Driving Park site, and one at the east end of Walnut Street in Green Bay sponsored by the Brown County Horticultural and Agricultural Society. The fair would continue at the latter site until 1905. In October 1894, a fair was held on the Oneida Indian Reservation. For the years 1906–1908, there were no county fairs, only the Oneida Reservation Fair. In October 1906, the Oneida Fair moved to the De Pere fairgrounds site. Two years later, in 1908, the county tried to purchase the Fox River Driving Park land from the city of De Pere, but the city refused to sell. In 1909, the city of De Pere agreed to lease the park to the Brown County Fair Association for twenty years for purposes of holding an annual county fair. Meanwhile, in 1919, Brown County organized 4-H clubs, and youth were allowed to exhibit at the fair.

In 1920, wanting to include more exhibitors and increase attendance, the Brown County Fair changed its name to the Northeastern Wisconsin Fair and began welcoming exhibitors from outside Brown County. In 1930, the fair association negotiated with the city of De Pere to extend the lease for ten more years. In 1968, the fair changed its name back to Brown County Fair. To this day, discussions continue between Brown County and the city of De Pere about ownership. The county owns about 35 acres of the fairgrounds, and the city of De Pere owns 18.5.

Just as the fair's names and locations have a rich history, so too do its entertainment options, for example: 1859 to 1968, horse races; 1868, ladies' horse race; 1900, balloon ascension; 1912, motorcycle races; 1913, first merry-go-round; 1914, trained seals; 1915, first Ferris wheel; 1920s, vaudeville acts and night fireworks; 1941, auto racing for several years, which stopped during the war years of 1942–1945; 1946, return of auto racing; 1960s, circuses; 1972, tractor pull. Today the goal of the Brown County Fair "is to teach urban and rural residents of all ages about Brown County history, traditions, and accomplishments through agriculture, family living, and business. We strive to provide a welcoming environment for our guests and promote agriculture through exhibits and demonstrations, and are committed to supporting lifelong learning for our young people and our community."[2]

## CALUMET COUNTY

The Calumet County Agricultural Society was organized in 1856 and operated until 1865. The first Calumet County Fair was held in the fall of 1856 in Stockbridge. The newly formed *Chilton Times* said this in promoting the one-day event: "A giant opportunity to meet people one seldom saw during the year, to exhibit your best wares, and most of all to exchange ideas and learn from others." It clearly was a successful event, as evidenced by the community's search for a permanent fairgrounds.

Calumet County residents were supportive of holding subsequent fairs, but they couldn't agree where the fair should be held. The 1857 fair was held in Stockbridge on October 6 and 7. In 1858, the fair moved to Brothertown and was held there September 29 and 30. New Holstein hosted the 1859 fair, and 1860 it was held at Gravesville, where Leroy Graves offered the agricultural society four acres of land, including his red barn, for twenty-five dollars to become a permanent site for the fair. The fair continued at Gravesville until 1864.

These were two-day events, the first day devoted to judging exhibits and a speech or two on the theme of agricultural improvement. Often two speeches were given, one in English and one in German. The second day of the fair was an open market where people could sell livestock, grain, or farm implements. Farmers exhibited the first horses at the Calumet County Fair in 1863. The best stallion received a premium of four dollars, and the best "blooded bull" won three dollars.

The Gravesville fair suffered from bad weather three out of four years and was moved back to Stockbridge in September 1865. Meanwhile, dissension within the agricultural society boiled over, and the society closed down. No fairs were held for the next five years.

The *Chilton Times*, always a supporter of the county fair, pushed to open one again in 1871. It had been a very dry year, and fires raised havoc in Chicago, Peshtigo, and several communities along Green Bay. Marshes and woodlands east of Chilton burned, and local Calumet County citizens were concerned. Rains came on October 14, and a week later the Calumet County Fair opened at a place called Aesseu Woods (now Brooklyn Heights), south of the Manitowoc River in Chilton.

The railroad arrived in Calumet County in 1872. No longer did county residents have to depend on the stagecoach for transportation. Chilton boomed, and by 1874, a housing development had crowded out the fair. The fair moved again, this time to Hobart's Grove.

Meanwhile, interest in horse racing was growing, and Calumet County leaders began advocating the formation of a Calumet County Trotting and Fair Association. After several failed attempts, the organization was formed in 1878, with membership dues of fifty cents. Only members could exhibit and compete at the fair. The association agreed to temporarily lease land from Harrison Hobart, a Chilton attorney, and fairs continued each year until 1884, when the association, near bankruptcy, dissolved. No fairs were held from 1884 to 1890.

In 1887, Hobart donated land along the Manitowoc River for a fairgrounds, and efforts began in 1889 to reestablish the county fair. A new organization, the Calumet County Agricultural and Driving Park Association, was formed to take charge of the county fair, and in 1891 a fair was held, featuring "trotting races, running races, bicycle races, fat men and boy's racers, a balloon ascent, English and German speakers, fireworks and a grand ball at Turner Hall in the evening. Admission would be twenty-five cents for adult and ten cents for children." Also in that year the association became known as the Calumet County Agricultural Association and remains in charge to this day.

In 1891, the Calumet County Agricultural Association purchased an additional 8.5 acres from Hobart for $651. Soon the fairgrounds included a racetrack and a grandstand.

In 1922, the county hired its first 4-H club agent to work with rural youth enrolled in corn clubs, calf clubs, and sewing clubs. In 1924, the agricultural association purchased additional land that included buildings used by the Schuetzen Verein, a German shooting club.

During the Depression years of the 1930s, while most other activities slowed down, the fair continued. When Prohibition ended in 1933, all stands at the fair offered five-cent beer and five-cent sandwiches. In 1934, the association board and the Calumet County Cheesemakers sponsored a Dairy Queen Contest.

In 1942, there was considerable discussion as to whether a fair should be held during a time of shortages and rationing. The Wisconsin Association of Fairs urged counties to hold fairs but to cut out the frills, such as flower and artwork exhibits. In 1944, with labor in short supply, seventy-five Barbadians traveled to Chilton to work on farms and in canneries. The fairgrounds became headquarters for this war labor camp, as it was called. The 4-H building became the camp's kitchen and mess hall; the secretary's office, the boiler and shower room, and the poultry barn became sleeping quarters. The camp was closed by fall, and the fair went on as usual as a four-day event over the Labor Day weekend.

Management cancelled the fair in 1955 because of a polio epidemic but resumed operations the following year. That year, fair management purchased three additional acres from Joseph Sell for eight hundred dollars. By 1988, the city of Chilton owned about 15.5 acres of the fairgrounds, and the agricultural association owned 16 acres.

The Calumet County Fair, which calls itself "the Biggest Little Fair in Wisconsin," is held Labor Day weekend and features a family-friendly midway and youth and open-class exhibits.[3]

# DOOR COUNTY

Door County, located between the waters of Green Bay and Lake Michigan, has long been known for its apple and cherry orchards. According to Hjalmar Holand's 1917 history of the Door Peninsula, "The earliest farm orchards of which there are records are those of Joseph Zettel and Robert Laurie. Zettel began setting out trees in 1862. Laurie planted trees about that same time. At the first county fair, held in the old courthouse, October 20, 1869, Robert Laurie exhibited thirteen varieties of apples, for which he received much praise."[4]

The Door County Agricultural Society formed in 1858 and began sponsoring annual fairs on a forty-acre plot of land just north of Sturgeon Bay in 1871. The fair moved to a baseball park on Delaware Street and in 1908 began operations at its present location on 14th Avenue. Unfortunately, the depression of the early 1920s forced the fair to close down in 1923.

The first county agricultural agent in Door County, Ben Rosy, arrived in November 1927. That year, Rosy organized a fair for county 4-H club members. It proved so successful that the county fair once more began operations in 1928, this time with considerable volunteer help. Mule and horse races were added as attractions.

The fair continued to operate throughout the Depression of the 1930s, thanks to help from the Works Progress Administration (WPA), one of Franklin D. Roosevelt's Depression-era initiatives. WPA workers built the fairgrounds' grandstand, livestock buildings, roads, and other structures during that time.

As was true of many county fairs, one person emerged as a champion of the fair. In Door County, it was John Miles, a former fruit farmer from Iowa who arrived in Door County in 1928. He took a special interest in the fair and began as fair secretary in 1937. He had a great love of youth exhibits, but he also recognized the importance of entertainment as a way to attract more people to the fair, especially those not from farms. Miles brought in high-wire acts, Wild West rodeos, harness racing, and the latest carnival rides. In 1948, when Wisconsin was celebrating its centennial, Miles organized a three-hundred-member cast production of a show called *Peninsula Cavalcade*, which highlighted both state and county histories.

In 2021, the Door County Fair celebrated its 150th anniversary. Along with 4-H junior, school student, and open-class exhibits, attractions included pig and duck races, a "DockDogs" jumping dog show, stock car and motorcycle races, tractor pulls, the University of Wisconsin Marching Band, and a midway music stage featuring headliners Head East and the BoDeans. Fireworks closed out the sesquicentennial celebration.[5]

## FOND DU LAC COUNTY

The first Fond du Lac County fair was held in Rosendale on September 29, 1852. It ran for two days and featured exhibits of dairy cattle, wood products, tools, locally manufactured items, household arts, and garden vegetables. The best stallion exhibited received a four-dollar premium; the best working oxen and steers received three dollars. The top-rated sample of butter, "not less than 50 pounds," won five dollars, while the best sample of sugar received a four-dollar premium. (At the time Fond du Lac County was becoming a major producer of sugar from sugar beets).

Exhibits continue as a major component of the fair today. According to Fond du Lac County Dairy and Livestock Agent Tina Kohlman, "Exhibits representing the best of Fond du Lac County 4-H, FFA, and junior Holstein project work are put on display to be judged and viewed by the public. The way the exhibits are placed helps producers see and understand the impact of breeding management or new practices. Exhibitors learn how their project management and work 'measures up' compared to others." But as Kohlman explained, exhibiting at the fair is about far more than learning about agriculture: "It's about our youth learning to become more self-sufficient and growing into tomorrow's leaders."[6]

The Fond du Lac County Fairgrounds is located on seventy-five acres in the city of Fond du Lac and features over sixty thousand square feet of exhibit space. Besides the annual fair, the fairgrounds welcomes trade and craft shows, livestock events, and a host of other activities all year long. The annual county fair is held in mid-July each year.[7]

## KEWAUNEE COUNTY

In 1872, Kewaunee County residents interested in agriculture organized the Kewaunee County Agricultural Society. The society sponsored Kewaunee County's first fair in Kewaunee that fall and continued it there every year until 1917, when it moved to Luxemburg, its present site.

Kewaunee County
Fair horse race at
the Luxemburg
fairgrounds, 1918
UW DIGITAL COLLECTIONS /
COFRIN LIBRARY, UWGB

The 1932 Kewaunee County fair featured several special events: a doll parade for the kids and an exhibit offered by the US Department of Agriculture called an "egg factory"—a mechanical hen some six feet tall with a voice to match its size. The artificial hen was constructed of wood, wallboard, feathers, and steel. The hen's voice explained how she produced eggs.

The fair was cancelled in 1942 because of World War II and in the 1950s because of the polio epidemic. Over the years, the fair developed a reputation for outstanding grandstand attractions; in the 1960s, Myron Floren from *The Lawrence Welk Show* played back-to-back years, and major country headliners Minnie Pearl and Mel Tillis also appeared. During the 1990s and early 2000s, performers included REO Speedwagon, Rascal Flatts, and Little Texas. The BoDeans set a grandstand attendance record of 6,556 in 1998. The big grandstand productions ended in the mid-2000s, but the fair continues to bring in national acts.

While some of the buildings at the fairgrounds have been renovated over time, longtime fair board member Al Hoppe noted, "Some of the features, like livestock judging that draws about 20,000 people each year, remain unchanged. Tradition is part of the fair's charm."[8]

These days, the Kewaunee County Fair features live music; carnival rides and games; thousands of livestock, small animal, and 4-H displays; grandstand shows; kids' entertainment; and a wide variety of food and beverage offerings, all included in the admission ticket. The fair is held annually during the second week of July.[9]

## LANGLADE COUNTY

The Langlade County Agricultural Society was organized on August 21, 1886. Charles Gowan, a prominent farmer in the county, and A. B. Millard, a publisher, were elected the society's president and secretary, respectively. The group held its first county fair October 4 and 5, 1886, in Antigo, featuring speaker W. D. Hoard, who later would become governor of Wisconsin and publisher of *Hoard's Dairyman* magazine.

Logging had been the region's major economic activity up to this time, and the 1886 fair helped create interest in the possibilities of agriculture in the county. After the success of the 1886 fair, the agricultural society searched for

Bicycle race at the Langlade County fairgrounds, circa 1895

WHI IMAGE ID 98611

a permanent fairgrounds site, and the Langlade County Board appropriated $1,500 to purchase a forty-acre site in Antigo and an additional $1,000 to build an exhibition building, which was completed by October 1, 1887. As historian Robert M. Dessureau wrote in 1921, "Agriculture exhibitions have been supported since; farmers and citizens generally have taken a keen interest in the annual fair and its success is a source of civic pride."[10]

In 2019, the Langlade County Fair continued at the fairgrounds in Antigo as a family event, with no gate fee for fairgoers entering the grounds on foot. Some five thousand 4-H exhibits and more than thirty carnival rides attracted youth of all ages. Grandstand shows included "loud, action-packed" entertainment. The fair also included musical entertainment on three stages, plus three auctions: market animal, small animal, and a cake auction.[11]

## MANITOWOC COUNTY

The first fair in Manitowoc County was held in 1859 at Washington Park in downtown Manitowoc. It was sponsored by the newly formed Manitowoc County Agricultural Society. The fair soon outgrew the confines of the park and moved to what was known as Northwestern Hill in Manitowoc. It was held there until 1874, when the three-day event moved to Clarks Mills, deemed to be the geographic center of the county. At the time, fair rules mandated no games of chance, no gambling, and no intoxicating beverages. In 1884, the fair moved back to Manitowoc. By 1905, interest in holding an annual fair was declining, and there was talk of closing it down.

William Rahr, a former mayor of Manitowoc and associated with the Rahr Brewing Company, decided the fair should be saved. He bought stock from the Industrial Association, which had run the fair for more than twenty years, paying three times the stock's value. He then spent more than $70,000 on fair improvements, including rebuilding the racetrack and the grandstand. He also allowed the sale of beer at the fair. The 1906 fair was a huge success, with some four thousand people attending on Thursday, the opening day. Friday's attendance was even higher, estimated at twelve thousand. Friday was children's day: schools and many businesses were closed that afternoon, encouraging folks to attend the fair.

Rahr continued supporting and organizing the fair until 1911. No fair was held that year, as no one stepped forward to take charge. But by 1912, a fair was

VIEW OF THE MANITOWOC
COUNTY FAIR GROUNDS,
MANITOWOC, WIS.

Manitowoc County
fairgrounds, 1909
WHI IMAGE ID 138857

once again held, with the support of a citizens' committee. The committee posed a letter in the 1912 fair program that in part read: "An abiding faith that Manitowoc County, as one of the leading Agricultural Counties of the State will support a County Fair, has prompted the committee of ten in charge of the fair to undertake its management and the public is asked to show its loyalty and patriotism."[12]

The Manitowoc County Fair continues, held in late August and recently offering a vast array of entries in both the youth and open-class divisions, plus a horse-pulling contest, a cream-puff-eating contest, a market animal show, and a tractor- and truck-pulling event. In contrast to the early years, when no intoxicating beverages were allowed, recent fairs have included a Blue Ribbon Brew Competition, open to amateur home brewers twenty-one and older.[13]

# MARINETTE COUNTY

The Wisconsin Legislature created Marinette County in 1879. Not long after, agricultural exhibits at public events became popular, including a "dairy day" held at the former Marinette County Farm near Peshtigo. No full-fledged county fair was held until 1928, and that fair was held in Iron Mountain, Michigan, in cooperation with the Dickinson County (Michigan) Fair.

By 1930, Marinette County's agricultural leaders decided it was time to have their own fair. They deemed Wausaukee, in the center of the county, to be a good location and chose Emil Jicha's farm, on the east side of town, as the site. The first fair was held in 1931, with just a few pens and tents. The Wausaukee Recreation Building and bowling lanes were used for exhibit space. The fair was an immediate success. But with the Great Depression stifling almost all economic activity, it wasn't until 1940 that there was enough money for the construction of fair buildings.

The fair ran for three days through 1961. In 1962 a fourth day was added "to allow for a better livestock show." The 1981 event, held August 21–23, marked the fair's fiftieth anniversary. Today, the fair is held at the Wausaukee Fairgrounds at the end of August. The fair features live bands, 4-H horse competitions, livestock and domestic animal displays/awards, food vendors, truck pulls, tractor pulls, demolition derbies, carnival rides, booth displays, photo and food competitions, and paid displays from merchants.[14]

# OCONTO COUNTY

On September 1, 1873, several farmers and businesspeople from Oconto and Shawano Counties met in Gillett to discuss the formation of a Shawano-Oconto County Agricultural Association. The association's purpose was to sponsor fairs in these two counties. The first Oconto Fair was held in Gillett on October 16 and 17, 1873, with exhibits including eighty-five head of cattle, forty-six horses, several hogs, chickens, grains and vegetables, and household products such as breads, jellies, and pickles. Schoolchildren from the country schools exhibited examples of their schoolwork. The first fair was deemed a great success.

The following year, fairs were held in both Oconto and Shawano, and separate fairs continued until 1876. Shawano County had become unhappy with the joint arrangement, arguing that all of the agricultural association's officers were selected from Oconto County. By this time, agriculture in both counties had developed to the point that each county believed it could sponsor its own fair. In 1876, the Oconto County Fair was moved to Gillett and was sponsored by the newly formed Oconto County Agricultural Society. As this was the first fair held with no ties to Shawano County, there was some concern about its success. But entries were strong: sixty-two head of cattle, twenty-one horses, twenty-six sheep, and several hogs, among others.

The 1877 fair moved again to Oconto. Interest in the fair lagged, and no fair was held in 1880. In 1886, the Oconto County Agricultural Society began offering higher premiums for farm and household products and less money for horse racing purses, and the 1886 fair was one of the most successful to date.

However, for several years in the 1890s, no fairs were held, in part because of the 1893 economic depression and the 1898 Spanish-American War. In 1900, local business owners formed a new organization, the Oconto County Fair Association, and held a fair that year. Starting in 1907, the fair association urged every township in the county to exhibit at the fair, and the fair prospered.

In 1910, boys' and girls' corn- and barley-growing contests were added. These contests drew considerable interest and demonstrated a close cooperation between the home farm and the schoolroom. In the years 1911–1917, the fair suffered from bad weather nearly every year, forcing organizers to close it down in 1911 and continue for an extra day in 1912. The fair also suffered financially during these years. No fair was held in 1918 because of World War I.

Today, organizers say the fair's mission is to "annually organize a welcoming family-oriented, safe, affordable, educational and entertaining event that addresses the interests of all ages." They hope to bring together both residents and visitors in celebration of the talents and skills of local citizens and organizations and "focus on the goal of advancing knowledge of Oconto County history, people, culture, and traditions." The fair is held each year in mid-August at the fairgrounds in Gillett.[15]

## OUTAGAMIE COUNTY

The earliest fairs in Outagamie County were held in 1859 in Appleton and Hortonville. Noting the success of those first fairs, Seymour businessmen began investigating the possibility of holding their own fair. A group of businessmen led by W. B. Comee, D. H. Kenyon, and William Cirkel met on August 11, 1884, to organize a "Fair and Driving Park Association."

With support from local banker William Michelsteter, Falck Hotel owner George Falck, and flour mill owner J. A. Stewart, the association purchased land northwest of the railroad tracks in Seymour and made plans to construct a half-mile racetrack. The association also pledged to support the development of agriculture and improvement of livestock husbandry.

The first Seymour fair opened on October 6, 1885, for a three-day run. Horse racing was the major attraction. *The Appleton Post* reported:

> Numerous agricultural products were exhibited—Fancy stocks of vegetables and grain, prize cattle, sheep, and hogs. The Exhibition Hall was the central attraction for all visitors; where household comforts, ornamental work, flowers, fine art, and the products of factory and foundry were arranged side by side to demonstrate the diversified industries of the people. . . . Phillip Muehl's furniture created a desire in spectators to make themselves confortable while they inspected novelties and dry goods. On the grounds outside there was a great variety of labor saving farm machinery. . . . The horse trot is a source of income that agricultural societies all over the country have been compelled to take advantage of, but in no instance represents the best interest of farmers. . . . On the other hand the improvement in the style of travel and speed of the horses is most impressive. . . . Of Seymour and its citizens and leading industries we will have something to say in the future. . . . In the meantime we congratulate the town on the splendid success of the first annual fair. May each succeeding exhibition grow in importance until the expositions there held fully equal if they do not excel any in the country.[16]

The Seymour Fair continued to grow and prosper, and by 1900 it attracted thousands of visitors. In 1920, the Seymour Fair became the official Outagamie County Fair. By the late 1920s, as 4-H clubs were organizing across the state and Future Farmers of America chapters were forming in high schools, youth exhibits became popular at the fair.

Harness racing with sulkies continued as a huge draw for the fair into the 1950s. As horse racing began fading late in that decade, the fair brought in nationally known performers, automobile thrill shows, and stock car racing. Entertainers who performed there included Pee Wee King, Red Foley, Jimmy Dean, Roy Acuff, and the Lennon Sisters from *The Lawrence Welk Show*. People traveled from all over the state to see their favorite TV performers. The fair has continued to present major nationally known entertainers to the present time, with country-and-western singers being most popular.[17]

## SHAWANO COUNTY

The Shawano County Fair began as a joint enterprise between Shawano County and Oconto County, when people from both counties formed the Shawano-Oconto County Agricultural Association in 1873. The first fair was held that year in Oconto County, and, declaring that one a success, the group planned another for the following year in Shawano County. The 1874 fair was held on a fifteen-acre tract just north of Shawano leased from local farmer John A. Winans.

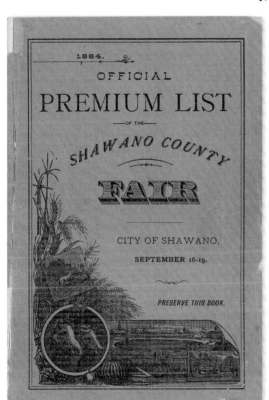

Premium book from the 1884 Shawano County Fair
IMAGE COURTESY OF THE SHAWANO COUNTY FAIR

In 1876, a group of Shawano farmers organized the Shawano County Agricultural Society, leaving behind the relationship with Oconto County. The agricultural society operates the fair to this day. In 1876, the group improved the fairgrounds and decided to hold a fair of their own; records suggest it was well attended. In 1883, the society purchased land from Herman Naber east of the center of town on Green Bay Street to add to the fairgrounds. Fair management built several exhibit buildings, a large racetrack, and a grandstand. All of the buildings have since been replaced, except for the judge's stand, which was moved to the grounds of the Shawano County Historical Society in the 1970s.

For many years, horse racing was popular; eventually it was replaced by stock car racing. The racetrack, now named the Shawano Speedway, is a popular place on Saturday nights in summer. A loud roar can be heard across town as cars zip around the track. The county fair has hosted many other exciting attractions throughout the years, including a reenactment of Custer's Last Stand in 1889, a "flying machine" in 1912, Joe

Greer's Western Rodeo and Society Circus in 1931, and country singer Tracy Byrd in 1998.

While entertainment has changed over the years, the fair has always featured a wide variety of exhibits. In 1923, 4-H exhibits were added, when there was but one countywide 4-H club. Today the county has twenty-one clubs, with more than six hundred members exhibiting at a recent fair.

The citizens of Shawano County always look forward to Labor Day weekend and the fair, which continues to thrive. It is a social event where one can run into old friends, have a beer or two at the VFW stand, and listen to the polka music at Presidents Park.[18]

## WINNEBAGO COUNTY

The Winnebago County Agricultural Society sponsored the county's first fair October 10 and 11, 1855, in Oshkosh and continued sponsoring the fair for several years. These early fairs featured exhibits of fruits, vegetables, grain, and livestock. In 1862, a US Army regiment had its headquarters at the fairgrounds, and the place had a very martial appearance.[19]

On April 6, 1867, the Winnebago County Stock-Growers Association was organized with the following stated objectives: "raising, improving and training horses and other animals and holding public shows, fairs and exhibitions." The organization declared it would further "have the power to establish, procure and prepare grounds and places in the city of Oshkosh, in Winnebago County for the exhibition and for testing the quality and speed of animals and for the exhibition of agricultural and mechanical implements and productions; and it may for such purposes, from time to time hold such fairs, shows and exhibitions as it may deem advisable, and it may establish such rules and regulations therefor, and offer and pay such rewards and purses to the competitors at such fairs, exhibits, & c., as it may seem fit." In 1870, the Northern Wisconsin Agricultural and Mechanical Association took over operations of the Winnebago County Fair. The stated purpose of this association was "promoting agriculture, manufactures, mechanic and household arts by holding fairs."[20]

For its first fair, held in 1870, the association welcomed entries from residents of sixteen counties in addition to Winnebago County. The fair was deemed by the association "a complete success, far in advance of the most sanguine expectations of its friends, the citizens of Oshkosh, with their accustomed liberality and public spirit, giving freely to arrange the grounds and buildings without cost to the Society, and the people of the surrounding country turning out almost en masse, thus giving the Society a good start."[21]

Exhibits at the next year's fair included "horses for all work, carriage horses, trotting horses, matched horses . . . shorthorned cattle, Ayrshire Cattle, Devon or any other cattle, grade and native cattle, Merino sheep, Cotswold and Leicester sheep, medium wool sheep, fine wool sheep, swine, poultry, grain, apples, pears, plums, grapes, wines, preserves, jellies, canned fruit, pickles, flowers, dairy and household products, vegetables, domestic manufacturers, works of art, machinery and implements, leather manufacturers, printing and binding, manufacturers of wood, and miscellaneous items."[22]

In 1879, the fair set an attendance record of twelve thousand for one day and claimed to be the largest fair in the state at the time. In 1910, the fair's sponsoring organization became the Winnebago County Fair Association; the next year's fair was held September 26–29 and was funded with five hundred dollars from the Winnebago County Board for "fair purposes."

The fair grew from four days to six in 1952, resulting in an overall attendance of one hundred thousand people. Joey Chittwood's auto thrill show drew the largest single-day attendance. In 1954, Winnebago County took over ownership of the fairgrounds and leased it to the fair association. Attendance in 1955 suffered from the polio epidemic, as children under sixteen were advised not to attend. Tragedy struck the fairgrounds on September 4, 1965, Labor Day weekend, when fire destroyed the grandstand and the Expo Building.

In 1988, the Winnebago County Board voted to move the fairgrounds to a larger site, which it did in 1990. The Sunnyview Exposition Center, north of the city of Oshkosh, includes seventy-eight acres of grounds, a covered arena, 31,000-square-foot exposition building, five barns, a food court building, an outdoor show arena, and a grandstand that seats 4,600 people. Many activities and events besides the county fair take place at the Exposition Center all year. Today's Winnebago County Fair is held for five days in early August.[23]

Three 4-H members display their cows at the Iron County Fair, 1935.
WHI IMAGE ID 87343

# 12

# NORTHERN WISCONSIN FAIRS

## ASHLAND COUNTY

Tucked up against Lake Superior, Ashland County was organized on March 27, 1860, with a population of 500. By 1870, the population had dipped to 221, but it grew to 24,538 by 1920.[1]

There is some confusion as to when the first Ashland County Fair was held. An 1861 Ashland map shows "County Fair Land" on the east side of Orange Street. In 1883, the *Ashland Press* reported that a fair was held that year at the fairgrounds in Ashland, noting that the fair opened with a double balloon ascension. The 1902 county fair featured horse racing with eight departments for exhibits including everything from livestock to farm produce to flowers, plants, and fine arts.

The Ashland County Fair has operated at the fairgrounds in Marengo since 1963. Today the fair runs from Thursday to Sunday, usually in mid-August. A recent fair featured a truck pull, mixed-doubles horseshoe-pitching tournament, market animal sale, 4-H pie sale, pie-eating contest, pool tournament, bingo, and a "mud run." With paid admission, fairgoers have access to free rides and grandstand events.[2]

## BAYFIELD COUNTY

In 1865, the Wisconsin Legislature created Bayfield County, originally part of La Pointe County. The newly created county became the second largest in Wisconsin. Bayfield County's agriculture includes some dairy farming plus berries and other fruits.

In 1894, the first county fair was held at the Bayfield County Fairgrounds in Iron River. The fair continued to be held at the Iron River site and was sponsored for many years by the Bayfield County Agricultural Society. Sponsorship of the fair changed in 1939, as the county agricultural agent reported: "By direction of the County Board, the Agricultural Committee assumed the management of the County Fair, with the County Agent as Secretary. Considerable repairs and improvement were made to the grounds. This year's premium list was revised and added to in order to more adequately represent the agricultural and home products within the county. While the attendance was less than last year, the exhibits increased by 50 percent."[3]

The fair continues to be held in Iron River in early August each year. A recent fair, with the theme "Fair, Food, and Fun," featured a carnival, pony rides, live music, a petting zoo, plus an antique tractor pull and bull riding in addition to the many exhibits. The admission price to the fair includes carnival rides and grandstand activities. Parking is free.[4]

## CLARK COUNTY

In 1872, farmers in Clark County organized a Clark County Agricultural Society with the purpose of sponsoring a fair. According to John S. Dore, an original organizer, their goal were "to improve and develop the agricultural program and to present a county fair which will be the show window of our county."

The society purchased a forty acre tract of land near Neillsville for a fairgrounds. They paid $1,200 for the property and $2,500 to build bleachers and an exhibit building. During the spring and summer of 1873, the society added a dirt racetrack in the center of the fairgrounds and built a permanent grandstand on the east end of the track. The first fair was held October 14–16, and fairgoers arrived by foot, by wagons drawn by oxen, and by horse-drawn buggies to see exhibits of farm and garden crops, cattle, chickens, and hogs. During this first

Congressman David Obey talks with constituents at the Clark County Fair, 1977.
WHI IMAGE ID 101168

fair, exhibitors staked their cattle and other livestock outdoors; in later years, fair management constructed exhibit buildings. Harness races were the big attraction at the grandstand and continued for many years.

At the 1900 fair, management raised the admission price from twenty-five cents to thirty-five cents. A family ticket was $1.50 and admitted "a lady and a gent, horse or team, and unmarried children under the age of 16."

A special feature at the 1910 fair was an airplane built by Walter Moldenhauer of white oak two-by-fours, bamboo, and airplane cloth. The wingspan was about twenty-five feet, and Moldenhauer had whittled the propeller himself. Unfortunately, he could not get the plane in the air. (Later, after the fair, he did get the plane to fly, but it crashed into a rock pile.)

In 1921, the hog house at the fair was moved near the livestock pavilion and enlarged. Also in that year, organizers added a fifteen-acre tract of land purchased from the farm adjoining the fairgrounds. In 1924, Clark County Agent H. M. Knipfel organized a calf club for the youth of Clark County, and the county board appropriated three thousand dollars to build a barn for the calf club at the fairgrounds. The activities of 4-H members, both boys and girls, at the fair became "the center of interest, and certainly of most importance."

At the 1929 fair, Margaret Newton of Humbird was chosen as the healthiest girl at the Clark County Fair and Tom Fagan of Owen the healthiest boy. The criteria used for these awards were not recorded.

In 1931, Clark County 4-H members saw a new 4-H club dining hall at the fair that accommodated up to three hundred members. In 1943, a horse-pulling contest on the last day of the fair became an added attraction. By the late 1960s, a highlight at the Clark County Fair was the annual contest to select the "Fairest of the Fair" to represent the Clark County Fair at the state fair in Milwaukee.

In fall 2018, the Clark County Fairgrounds (through the Clark County Forestry and Parks Department) started an initiative to raise money for the Clark County Fairgrounds Revitalization Project. Two of the largest planned projects were the construction of a new livestock building and a new multipurpose event center, together estimated to cost about $1.65 million. The Clark County Fair is held at the fairgrounds in Neillsville during the second week of August. Over the many years of its operation, it has been cancelled only twice: in 1949 because of the polio epidemic, and in 2020 because of the COVID-19 pandemic.[5]

## DOUGLAS COUNTY

Douglas County, in the far northwestern corner of Wisconsin, became a county in 1854. Soon farmers began showing and selling their animals and produce at what we would today call farmers' markets. Some years later, exact date unknown, the Douglas County Agricultural Society organized a tri-state fair, welcoming exhibitors from Wisconsin, Minnesota, and Michigan.

When the Douglas County Extension office opened in 1914, county agriculture agent J. M. Walz became the fair secretary and held that role for several years. Sometime between 1880 and 1890, the fairgrounds were donated to Douglas County with the proviso that the land must be used for family education and recreation. The fair continued at this site, adding 4-H and Future Farmers of America (FFA) exhibits by the 1920s, but not without serious challenges between the county, which owned the land, and the fair board, who was responsible for operating the fair.

In 1983, the fair took the name the Head of the Lakes Fair, under the supervision of a fair board. As longtime fair board member and fair department superintendent Pat Luostari said, "The challenge was for the fair board and management to keep [the fairgrounds] up. The county owned the land and all the buildings. If 4-H or FFA and the fair board put up a structure that was attached to the ground in any fashion, the county would own it. The county complained about the conditions of the fairgrounds and the [fair] people complained that they didn't get enough money to maintain the buildings."

The Head of the Lakes Fair is held at the fairgrounds in Superior in mid-July each year. It accepts both open-class and youth exhibits. Open-class exhibitors may reside in Douglas County or in Minnesota or Michigan, but youth exhibitors must reside in Douglas County.

The fair continues to operate, even though there are fewer exhibits and attendance has decreased. Luosatri noted that Family Day, with special activities for kids, is the biggest draw, as families with young children "like to go to the barns and see the animals, the lambs and baby chicks and the other animals. They do not have that opportunity anywhere else."

In addition to the exhibits, the fair features rides, bluegrass music, free grandstand shows, stock car races, commercial exhibits, a demolition derby, and a variety of food.[6]

## FLORENCE COUNTY

Florence County, tucked up against the Upper Peninsula of Michigan, was founded in 1882. The region had been a major logging area beginning in 1865; in 1877, iron ore was discovered in the area, and soon mining was a major economic endeavor in the region. Farming emerged first as a service to the logging companies, providing them food and other agricultural products. By 1935, there were 580 farms in the county.

The first Florence County Fair opened in 1903. Today, the fair continues to operate at the Florence County Fair Park, located in Florence. The fair, held in late August each year, features not only the exhibits and judging, but also a horse-pulling contest, tractor pull, music and science shows, "mud bog," and much more.[7]

## FOREST COUNTY

Forest County was created in 1885 from land formerly designated to Langlade and Oconto Counties. Like its neighboring counties in northern Wisconsin, Forest County is heavily wooded, and logging was one of its early economic activities. Farming followed the loggers, and the first Forest County Fair opened in Crandon in 1894.

The fair continues at Crandon and today features "midway thrills, demonstrations, food and family fun," as well as youth and open-class exhibits.[8]

## IRON COUNTY

The first Iron County Fair was held in 1927 at Saxon, Wisconsin. Exhibits were primarily of an agricultural nature, along with some household items and several displays from the county's schools. Over the succeeding years, fairs continued at the Saxon site. In the early days, some Iron County farmers also exhibited cattle at the nearby Gogebic County Fair in Ironwood, Michigan.

The Iron County Agricultural Society managed the fair until 1944, when Herbert Kinney was hired as county agricultural agent. Kinney and the Extension office took over administration of the fair; Kinney also expanded the county's 4-H program considerably, and 4-H members began exhibiting at the fair. The fair did not have dairy cattle exhibits until the mid-1940s, when they were housed in a tent on the fairgrounds. Eugene Luoma, Iron County Fair Board member from 1996 to 2018, noted, "In the 1950s, Iron County had several small dairy farms with from 12 to 25 cows each. Today there are few dairy farms left."[9]

In the 1950s, Iron County's population was considerably larger than it is now; mining still provided a significant number of jobs in the region. In that decade, the fair added a carnival, and in the 1940s and 1950s a fair dance held in the old school gym on Sunday evening attracted as many as two hundred people. Around 1962, when the Saxon schools consolidated with those of Hurley, the fair association bought the old gym for use for the fair. The association also bought about eight acres of land from a local farmer for the fairgrounds. The fair association owns the fairgrounds, while Iron County carries the fair's insurance and contributes twenty thousand dollars each year to the fair association.

An exhibitor shows her quilt at the Iron County Fair, circa 1935.

WHI IMAGE ID 87350

Horse-pulling contests, which began in the early 1940s, are held on the racetrack in front of the grandstand. Today homemade doodlebugs (four-wheel-drive vehicles) also compete in pulling contests. Demolition derbies and mud runs, in which pickups, jeeps, and other vehicles race on a muddy course, attract many folks to the fair. According to Eugene Luoma, mud run viewers fill the grandstand each year.

A recent addition to the fair's program include a youth market auction for beef, hogs, turkeys, and chickens. The fair continues to have its challenges, including limited attendance numbers due in part to the small population. But the fair perseveres and has replaced a number of older buildings over the years. "Today, I believe we have one of the nicest fairgrounds in northern Wisconsin," Luoma said.[10]

# LINCOLN COUNTY

On October 10, 1885, the Lincoln County Land Commission paid $4,500 for a piece of land it then dedicated for use as a county fair. The land had been used for horse racing, baseball, and other public recreation activities, and on November 11, 1886, the land commission gave the land to the Lincoln County Agricultural, Mechanical, and Driving Association, stipulating that the land remain public and the building and fences be cared for.

In 1887, the Agricultural, Mechanical, and Driving Association quit operations, and Lincoln County citizens formed the Lincoln County Agricultural Society with the purpose of sponsoring a fair, which was planned for 1888. The fair emphasized agriculture, livestock, and homemaking. Entertainment included horse and pony racing, plus local entertainers and a professional group performing "Turkish Dances by Oriental Maidens." The dance show proved to be a crowd pleaser, according to reports of the day.

A dog-sulky race attracted considerable interest, but it had problems. According to a centennial history of the fair, "The dogs did not cooperate in either pulling the sulkies or staying on the racetrack. Two dogs ran away immediately; two others got their reins and sulkies tangled and got into a fight. When the owners got the fight stopped and equipment straightened out, they had to pull the dogs through the finish line."

The fair continued each year, with the fairgrounds used for a variety of events when the fair was not in operation. Horse racing at the fair was suspended for several years but resumed in 1908 under the cosponsorship of the Lincoln County Fair Association and the American Trotting Association.

At the 1916 fair, horse races were once more suspended, but not without considerable rancor between the horse racing fans and the agricultural community. A citizen wrote a letter to the *Merrill Daily Herald* dated August 4, 1917, that stated: "Ours is a fair for the farmer where he can meet with his neighbor and compare grain and stock. It is to stimulate production on the farm and boost our agricultural resources. . . . You can have horseracing without having a fair with it, but you can't have a fair without exhibits and the farmers. The farmer is the man you should want to exhibit."

No county fair was held in 1918 and 1919. However, a small community fair was held in September 1919 for farmer exhibits. In 1920, interest in resuming a county fair emerged, and a group of local businessmen offered their services to the Lincoln County Agricultural Society to once more sponsor a fair. They raised over five thousand dollars, and the Lincoln County Board organized a Lincoln County Fair Board; the exhibit list was expanded, and horse racing was reinstated. To promote fair attendance, the mayor of Merrill issued a proclamation that all businesses, including the banks in Merrill and Tomahawk, be closed for two afternoons of the fair. The 1920 and 1921 fairs were successful. For the 1921 fair, each township was invited to set up a booth. Competition among the townships was fierce.

In 1920, with the assistance of County Agent A. H. Cole, several 4-H clubs were organized in Lincoln County, though they were not yet exhibiting at the Lincoln County Fair. Their first projects were calf raising, poultry, and canning. A Tomahawk Community Fair was held September 14–16, 1920, with junior exhibits from 4-H members and an open-class exhibit for adults. A second fair featuring 4-H exhibits was held in 1921.

By the late 1920s, 4-H club members had become a major part of the Lincoln County Fair. The 1929 fair, held at the Merrill fairgrounds, took place August 26–30 and was once more sponsored by the Lincoln County Agricultural Society. In 1934, the Lincoln County Board, which owned the fairground site and buildings, passed a resolution declaring "that the 4-H clubs of Lincoln County be hereby granted the permission of the board to use and occupy the fairgrounds site and all of the buildings located thereon for the conducting and carrying on of a 4-H Club Fair."

Bob Sumnicht, county agricultural agent starting in 1953, served as president of the Lincoln County 4-H Fair Board and worked with the fair for more than thirty years. In 1977, the rock band Styx brought six thousand people to the fair in one day. That year also saw the largest number of exhibits in the fair's history. Tractor-pulling contests proved popular in later years, with local farmers competing with each other; another popular feature has been the County Fair Bake-off Contest, initiated by the Lincoln County Homemakers Association, under the leadership of Beverly Peterson Topinka. The fair takes place in mid-August and has free admission.[11]

## ONEIDA COUNTY

In 1891, the Oneida County Board appointed a committee to find a fairgrounds site. But it wasn't until 1895 that the board voted to provide five hundred dollars to help the Oneida County Agricultural Society purchase a fairgrounds on Coon Street in Rhinelander, now a part of the Rhinelander Industrial Park. The first Oneida County Airport had once been located at that site. The society erected buildings, including a grandstand and a half-mile racetrack, and held the first Oneida County Fair in 1896. Wisconsin lumberman and humorist Gene Shepard is said to have brought his famed Hodag to the fair that year for all to see. He claimed to have captured the mythical creature—said to be a clawed, horned, seven-foot-long beast—and had some people believing it was worth a dime to see the creature up close.

By 1903, the Oneida County Fairgrounds racetrack was known as one of the best in Wisconsin. In the early 1920s, the fair association spent nine thousand dollars to improve the fairgrounds, including adding a new exhibition building and two racehorse barns and rebuilding the racetrack. In 1924, the original grandstand was replaced at a cost of $9,761.80. The new building could seat 3,200 people. The fairgrounds was also the site for Rhinelander High School football games and other events. In 1960, a huge crowd attended the Lakes States Logging Congress, which met for three days at the fairgrounds.

The fair, originally held in September, was moved to August in the 1930s. For many years, Oneida County potatoes highlighted the premium list. Each town in Oneida County had a booth, with exhibits of vegetables, fruits, flowers, canned goods, and clothing, all from Oneida County farms. Another building housed exhibits from the one-room country schools.

The fair took place at the original site from 1896 to 1968, when the Oneida County Board turned the fairgrounds into the Oneida County Industrial Park. From 1968 to 1992, there was no fair in Oneida County. But the fair did not die. It reopened at the Hodag Country Festival grounds in the town of Pine Lake in 1992. In 2009, after several years of declining attendance, the fair moved to Pioneer Park in the heart of Rhinelander. Each year the park is transformed into an old-fashioned county fair, with 4-H and open-class exhibits, entertainment, good food, contests, games, and carnival rides.[12]

Oneida County Fair

## PRICE COUNTY

Price County's first fair was held in 1885, on the courthouse lawn in Phillips. This fair took place nine years after the Wisconsin Central Railroad had come to Price County in 1876, and the same year that surveyors platted the city of Phillips. Price County bought land for a fairgrounds in 1888 and added more land with another purchase in 1907. The fairgrounds is located on the shore of Lake Duroy, between the Big Elk River and Squaw Creek at the edge of the city of Phillips.

The open-class exhibit building at the fairgrounds is over 107 years old, and the livestock barn was 100 years old in 2020. These buildings were constructed of old-growth pine from the area. In early years, the fair had a racetrack, with saddle and harness horse racing being popular attractions. Other popular entertainment has included demo derbies, rodeos, and baseball games between teams from different towns. Over the years, exhibits have changed, with fewer dairy cattle but more sheep, swine, poultry, and beef exhibits. The fair has about equal numbers of open-class and youth exhibits.

The Price County fairgrounds have been witness to some fascinating history. In 1894, many residents of Phillips took refuge at the fairgrounds as the city burned down on the other side of Lake Duroy. During World War I, troops were trained at the fairgrounds, which was called Camp Moose when it was used for that purpose. And in 1977, a windstorm known as a derecho hit Phillips hard and destroyed several fair buildings. The well-constructed open-class and livestock buildings survived.[13]

## RUSK COUNTY

Rusk County, deep in Wisconsin's Northwoods, became a county in 1901 but at that time was named Gates County after the Gates Land Company. In 1905, the name was changed to Rusk County after Jeremiah Rusk, governor of Wisconsin 1882–1889.[14]

In 1931, University of Wisconsin graduate student Katharine Woodrow Dresden wrote this about early Rusk County fairs:

Another popular Rusk County institution was the fair. Local fairs or harvest festivals were held in most of the communities, but the big event was the county fair held every September. Originally, there had

Rusk County Fair, Ladysmith, Wis.

Early postcard depicting the Rusk County Fair
WHI IMAGE ID 132560

been two of these, one in Bruce and one in Ladysmith . . . but in 1915 Bruce gracefully resigned her position, she [the fair] was sadly in debt, and let Ladysmith have full sway. It, too, had its financial difficulties, despite appropriations from the county board, progressing from [a debt of] $500 in 1915 to $1,500 in 1918, and in 1919 it found itself over $6,000 in debt. The county board decided to take it over and let a committee operate it. Passed one day, the measure was rescinded before the board had finished its session. By 1929 [the fair] was in such a state that it had a debt of $6,500 besides a first and second mortgage. Bravely it asked the board for $5,000 but no action was taken. The fair seems to have served its place in rural development and is about to follow the nickelodeon [in its demise].[15]

That was apparently the end of the county fair in Rusk County. But the fair rose from the ashes and today is known as the Rusk County Junior Fair, held in early August each year at the fairgrounds in Ladysmith. Some of its recent events—in addition to exhibits, judging, and the carnival—include donkey races, livestock auction, truck and tractor pull, pie judging, Fairest of the Fair competition, mud bog, a demolition derby, and the North Country Pro Rodeo.[16]

## SAWYER COUNTY

Sawyer County 4-H Club members show calves at the Sawyer County Fair, circa 1930.

WHI IMAGE ID 87355

Sawyer County was formed in 1883 from land originally designated to Chippewa and Ashland Counties. Like many of the state's northern counties, logging was big business here from the 1870s into the early 1900s. After the loggers left the county, some of the land was sold for farms.[17] The county boasts 691 lakes within its boundaries, making the county a major tourist attraction.[18]

The first Sawyer County Fair was held in 1907 under the leadership of the Sawyer County Agricultural Fair Association and continues so to this day. It takes place in mid-August on the fairgrounds in Hayward. As fair organizers describe their fair, "Families, youth and adults may enjoy different programs and activities that promote positive youth and young adult development. The fair hosts a carnival, demo derby, kids pedal power, cow milking, racing pigs, tractor pull, veggie races and more."[19]

## TAYLOR COUNTY

Logging as a business enterprise began in the late 1850s in what later became Taylor County. The county was established in 1875 from parts of Marathon, Chippewa, and Lincoln Counties, and Medford was named the county seat. After the trees were gone, the lumber companies sold cutover acreages to farm families who tried making a living selling milk, eggs, beef, wool, cucumbers, and peas. Dairy eventually became the predominant form of agriculture in the county and peaked there in the early 1940s.[20]

The first Taylor County Fair was held in 1885. Today, the fair is held in late July each year at the Taylor County Fairgrounds in Medford and features exhibits, judging, children's activities, entertainment, music, a variety of food, commercial vendors, and midway rides.[21]

## VILAS COUNTY

Vilas County was formed on April 12, 1893, having previously been a part of Oneida County. Like several other northern Wisconsin counties, it is a land of lakes and trees. The first Vilas County Fair was held September 7, 1916, under the auspices of the Vilas County Agricultural Society. The fair continues today, opening in the middle of August each year at the Eagle River Fairgrounds. Attractions include judging of junior and open-class exhibits, chainsaw carving, petting zoo, bean bag toss, face painting, and a beer garden. The midway offers rides and games and, of course, all kinds of fair food. Admission to the fair is free.[22]

# WISCONSIN VALLEY FAIR (MARATHON COUNTY)

The Marathon County Agricultural Society sponsored Marathon County's first fair on September 24 and 25, 1868. According to the *Wisconsin River Pilot*, a local newspaper, this fair opened with a parade of some two thousand people. One of the opening event speakers, a Mr. C. Hoeflinger, spoke these words in German: "Nobleness of labor and the trial pursuits of life, giving the farmer the highest rank and praise for his patient toil, and the benefits derived therefrom." Exhibits at this fair included horses, cattle, sheep, swine and poultry, along with displays of flowers and vegetables. A Siberian crab apple was on display and was recommended for planting in Marathon County.

August Kickbush and Bradbury Plummer later gave the agricultural society eighty acres of land, which the society deeded to Marathon County in 1920 for a fairgrounds known as Marathon Park. That same year, the society commissioned Alexander Eschweiler, a Milwaukee architect, to design a new pavilion for stock judging, a grandstand, and cattle barns for the fairgrounds. The tallest building at the fairgrounds is an exhibition building constructed in 1924. The hexagonal-shaped building with cupola has six rectangular wings, with gable roofs that radiate from the building's center.

In addition to the many fair activities and exhibits, fairgoers can visit the Ingwal S. Horgan Agricultural Museum, with various displays depicting Marathon County's agricultural history. In a relocated one-room school at the east end of Marathon Park, visitors can see how rural education was conducted for many years.

The fair is held each year at Marathon Park in early August. Today, the fair sees its purpose as being a "leading venue for agriculture, exhibits, entertainment, and education . . . all which enhance the social and economic benefits to Marathon County and its residents. . . . We are committed to supporting youth, promoting agriculture and enriching our community. Our commitment to excellence and integrity continues to strengthen loyalty among our guests, vendors, sponsors and the public."[23]

# 13
# NORTHWESTERN WISCONSIN FAIRS

## BARRON COUNTY

The Barron County Fair, held annually in Rice Lake, began in 1877. Harness racing was introduced in the late 1800s and continues to draw people to this fair today. Recent fairs have also included chainsaw-carving shows, tractor pulls, and 4-H youth group activities.

The Barron County Fair invites both open and junior class exhibits. Young people can enter projects in the following categories: dairy cattle, beef cattle, swine, goats, horses and ponies, poultry, rabbits, dogs, small animals, llamas, cats, field crops, fruits and vegetables, flowers, house plants, natural resources and environmental education, cultural arts/photography, computers, wood-working, electricity, mechanical arts, food and nutrition, clothing, knitting and

Crowds in and around the grandstands at an early Barron County Fair
WHI IMAGE ID 55194

crocheting, home furnishings, child development, communications, health, social and political sciences, plus school exhibits.

According to fair organizers, the fair's mission "is to provide for people of all ages opportunities to exhibit their talents or products and to enjoy and participate in the entertaining, educational and affordable activities in a safe, wholesome environment."[1]

# BURNETT COUNTY

When Burnett County became a county in 1856, it included land that later split off as Washburn County.[2] Today Burnett County hosts two fairs. The Burnett County Agricultural Society Fair opened in 1877; it continues to this day, held in late August at the fairgrounds in Grantsburg. The fair welcomes exhibits from anyone of school age along with adults, and exhibitors can reside outside Burnett County. Exhibits welcomed at this fair include baking, crafts, photography, animals, gardening, flowers, and more. The fair includes a carnival, with rides and games, and grandstand entertainment such as tractor pulls and demolition derbies. Admission is free.

The Central Burnett County Fair began in 1917. It continues today at the fairgrounds in Webster in mid-September. Besides the exhibits and judging, events include a Sunday car show, children's pedal tractor competition, various musical events, Saturday bingo, and a craft and business expo on both Saturday and Sunday. Grandstand events include a tractor and truck pull, demo derby, and Midwest farmers' horse pull. A carnival with an assortment of rides and games is available each day of the fair.[3]

# DUNN COUNTY

A trapeze act captivates the crowd at the Dunn County Fair, 1910.
WHI IMAGE ID 7950.

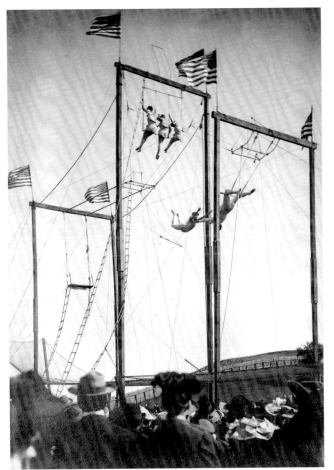

Dunn County farmers organized an agricultural society in 1872 and held a fair that year but suspended the fair for the next several years because of "difficulty of transportation." Thirteen years later, in 1885, a new Dunn County Agricultural Society was organized and requested $3,500 from the Dunn County Board to purchase fifty acres of land for a fairgrounds. The society stated the purpose of their fair as being "not to make a profit but to create an enterprise of the highest service bearing in mind that prudence requires a margin of safety for continuance of the life of the institution and as provision against the rainy day." They held fairs every year except the war years 1916, 1917, and 1918.

In 1956, the agricultural society ceased operations, and a sheriff's sale was scheduled to sell the fairgrounds. The Dunn County Board of Supervisors stepped in, stopping the sale and offering to assume responsibility for operating the fair. The board appointed a three-person fair board and charged them with conducting the annual fair, which included bringing in a carnival and reviving interest in both commercial and junior exhibitors.

In 1970, the Dunn County Board of Supervisors expanded the fair board by two additional members and instructed the board to develop a long-range plan to examine how the fairground facilities might be used year round. The Dunn County fair is held each year in late July at the fairgrounds in Menomonie with a variety of exhibits, events, and entertainment.[4]

## EAU CLAIRE COUNTY

The first Eau Claire County Fair featured exhibits plus a carnival and horse races and was held in Augusta in 1924. In 1930, the fair building burned, and the fair moved to Fall Creek. The city of Eau Claire hosted the fair in 1934 and 1935, followed by a return to Augusta, where it remained until 1939.

Exhibits at the fair reflected the tough times during the Depression years of the 1930s, which included entries for the best patched garment and the best darning on a sock. In 1940 the fair returned to Eau Claire, but in 1941 it moved to Altoona; a dairy barn, exhibit building, and dormitory were built on the Altoona grounds in 1942. During World War II, the fair switched to paper ribbons to conserve fabric, and 4-H clothing project members made use of printed feed and flour sacks for their projects. Near the end of the war, German prisoners of war were housed at the fairgrounds for a short period.

A new hog barn, beef barn, and food stand were built in 1946 and 1947. During the polio scare in the late 1940s, some youth members did not participate in the fair. The fair continued in Altoona until 1996, when it moved to its present site on the south side of Eau Claire. Several new buildings were constructed there, including three barns, a main exhibit building, an arena, an outdoor food stand, and a dog agility ring.

Fair organizers note that the fair is a youth- and family-focused event, with an emphasis on education. The fair does not have a midway or carnival.[5]

## NORTHERN WISCONSIN STATE FAIR (CHIPPEWA FALLS)

The first Wisconsin State Fair opened in Janesville in 1851 and moved around between southern locations for a number of years. Northern Wisconsin residents felt a bit left out, as the trip to southern Wisconsin in the late 1800s was not an easy one. Realizing that what the farmers in the north called the "Southern Wisconsin State Fair" was not likely to move, Chippewa Falls–area citizens drafted a charter to create the Northern Wisconsin State Fair. The state enacted the charter inw1897 with the stated purpose to "improve

Workers assemble tents and rides at the Northern Wisconsin State Fair, 1930.

agriculture, horticulture and mechanical and household arts." The 1897 fair was considered a financial success, with "a small balance . . . left in the treasury." Twenty-seven counties in northern Wisconsin were soon associated with the fair.

Reporter Dan Lyksett discovered that the foundations of the Northern Wisconsin State Fair go back to 1881, when Chippewa County held a fair that included baseball (called "base ball" at the time) and a horse trotting race. An article in the *Chippewa Herald* on September 30, 1887, reported on the variety of exhibits at the 1887 fair, praising the agricultural exhibits with the comment, "It would be a good thing if those who think Chippewa County is solely a lumbering county could have been present."[6]

The Northern Wisconsin State Fair faced tough times during the Great Depression. A November 11, 1931, issue of the *Herald Telegram* carried this headline: "Local Fair Is Facing Bankruptcy."

On September 9 and 10, 1932, a Chippewa County 4-H Club Fair was held under the auspices of the Northern Wisconsin State Fair. In addition to the 4-H exhibits, the fair included a baseball game, performances by "the Stanley band," and a horse-and-buggy race among local farmers. Eventually, a community campaign was conducted through the nonprofit Chippewa Foundation to purchase the Northern Wisconsin State Fairgrounds in 2007.

Today, the Northern Wisconsin State Fair Association, Inc., a 501(c)(3) nonprofit organization, is responsible for the operations and management of the fairgrounds. The fair is held each year in early July at the Northern Wisconsin State Fairgrounds. Youth exhibitors must belong to a Chippewa County youth group, such as 4-H or Future Farmers of America. Open-class exhibitors are welcome from the area as well.[7]

## PIERCE COUNTY

Located along the Mississippi River, Pierce County became a county on March 14, 1853. The county's first fair, sponsored by the Pierce County Agricultural Society, was held in 1859 in Prescott, the county seat at the time. The agricultural society moved the fair to Ellsworth in 1884, and it continues at that site today. In 1942, the county purchased the fairgrounds from the agricultural society; Pierce County has sponsored the fair from that time to the present.

The fair is held in mid-August each year at the Pierce County Fairgrounds in Ellsworth. Featured events, besides the hundreds of exhibits, are truck, tractor, and horse pulls and a demo derby.[8]

# POLK COUNTY

Polk County became a county in 1853, and the Polk County Agricultural Society was organized in 1861. The society sponsored Polk County's first fair on September 17, 1861, at Farmington Center, two miles south of Osceola. Exhibits at this first fair included livestock, crops, vegetables, blacksmithing, wood carpentry, baking, sewing, knitting, handiwork, dairy (five pounds of butter, five pounds of cheese), one-half bushel of carrots, and one bushel of potatoes. Popular events included oxen- and horse-plowing contests and horse racing. The cost of admission was ten cents per person; a food stand permit cost three dollars. Membership in the Polk County Agricultural Society was required of all exhibitors.

Fairs were held at the Farmington site through 1866 but stopped for an unknown reason. Attempts were made to start up the fairs again in the 1870s, but it didn't happen until 1881, when the Polk County Agricultural Society sponsored a fair at the St. Croix Falls fairgrounds. The fairs continued until 1885. Horse races were a popular attraction.

The Polk County Agricultural Society was reactivated in 1886 and sponsored a fair held October 7 and 8, 1886. Admission was twenty-five cents; children not yet in school got in for free. The fair was held near St. Croix Falls every year except 1893 and 1946. Besides the variety of exhibits, these fairs featured prominent speakers, horse races, and band tournaments.

Today, the Polk County Fair is held in late July at the fairgrounds in St. Croix Falls under the auspices of the Polk County Fair Society, a nonprofit organization. Organizers note, "Many learning experiences and lifelong skills are learned through exhibiting at the fair. . . . We pride ourselves in providing an opportunity for town and country to come together to celebrate our county." In addition to the many exhibits at the fair, activities include a demolition derby, tractor pull, carnival rides, and live entertainment.[9]

# STANLEY FAIR (CHIPPEWA AND CLARK COUNTIES)

The Stanley Fair started as a street fair in the city of Stanley in 1903, offering exhibits and entertainment. After local stores closed for first event and decided that the lost sales weren't worth it, no fair was held in 1904. The fair was held in 1905 but then was discontinued again. In 1908, the Stanley Driving and Athletic Association, made up of farmers and business owners in Stanley and surrounding communities, purchased land in Stanley for an athletic and driving park and racetrack. The new fair opened on July 4, 1909, with a parade led by a band, the mayor, and other city officials. Some five thousand people attended to watch harness racing, greased-pig races, a basketball game, fireworks, and "a grand ball at the opera house that kept everyone up until the wee hours of the morning." A series of "small sports" took place as well, including a footrace, a "fat man's race," an egg race for girls (carrying a spoon with an egg balanced on it), a bologna-eating contest, a boy's race, and a pie-eating contest. A featured event was a "money shower," in which two thousand pennies were tossed from the roof of a local hotel. The fair was deemed a success.

The following year, 1910, Governor James Davidson visited the fair, which in that year included more than one thousand exhibits. In 1913, the association built a dairy barn with room for 140 head of cattle. By that time the fairgrounds also included fine arts and horticultural buildings. The 1914 fair, which ran September 15–18, was billed as an "Inter-County Fair, Bigger and Better Than Ever" with this featured attraction: "The World's Greatest Aviator, Ralph E. McMillan, Two Flights Daily From the Fairgrounds, Rain or Shine, in a gentle wind or a tornado." The fair also offered a side show: "Extra, by special arrangement from Riverview Park, Chicago: Dwarf Cannibals from Central Africa."[10]

The *Stanley Republican* in September 1916 proclaimed, "The buildings and grounds of our fair association constituted the best equipment of any fair in northern Wisconsin." For the 1917 fair, the association installed electric lights at the fairgrounds, and more than two thousand exhibits were on display. Seventy horses from all over the northern part of the state entered the horse races. Unfortunately, bad weather that year and the next caused considerable financial loss. The 1919 Stanley Fair would be the last. Even with good weather and large crowds, the fair could not recoup its losses. The great days of the Stanley Fair were no more. The fairgrounds was abandoned and eventually sold.[11]

## ST. CROIX COUNTY

Fairs have been held in St. Croix County for more than 125 years. In 1895, Glenwood City hosted an agricultural fair. In 1910, an inter-county fair (for St. Croix and Dunn Counties) was held at the site of former lumber mills. A county fair was held in New Richmond for several years. Hudson hosted a fair for a few years, and Hammond had a fair from the 1930s to the early 1950s where dairy cattle were exhibited in the county highway shops and exhibits were on display in a nearby school building. A fair was held somewhere in the county every year except during the polio epidemic of the 1940s.

In 1948, the St. Croix County Board of Supervisors designated the Glenwood Inter-County Fair as the St. Croix County Fair. The fair runs for five days in mid-July at the Glenwood City fairgrounds. Fairgoers can see agricultural exhibits, competitions of various types, entertainment, carnival rides, tractor pulls, the ever-popular mud bogs (where off-road vehicles compete by driving through a pit of mud), commercial exhibits, and a variety of food booths. No admission is charged.[12]

## WASHBURN COUNTY

The first Washburn Fair opened in 1912 on fairgrounds located "where the road ended" on the north end of Spooner. The fairgrounds comprised twenty-two buildings and a racetrack. The Washburn County Agricultural Association advertised its first fairs as "Farmers Festival and Agricultural Shows." At the 1912 fair, an exhibitor could win not only cash prizes but also a box of cigars, seventy-five cents toward shoe repair, and even five dollars for dental repairs.

The association cancelled the 1918 fair to focus on war efforts. In 1932, the Washburn County Agricultural Association disbanded, putting the future of the fair in question. The county Extension agent and Washburn County Board's Agricultural Committee decided to sponsor a Junior County Fair in 1933 so that 4-H members could meet the club's requirement to display their projects at a fair. When a polio outbreak threatened in 1946, the fair was postponed until October and ran for just one day, long enough for the 4-H youth to show their projects.

Members of the "Bashaw Famers Club" gather for a community fair in Washburn.
WHI IMAGE ID 42438

After taxes went unpaid, the fairgrounds reverted to county ownership, and today all that remains of the original fairgrounds is the curved tree line crossing the swamp on the west side of Highway 63 as you leave Spooner. Those trees grow where once there was a racetrack considered one of the fastest in Wisconsin.

In 1947, H. B. Rasmusson donated twelve acres on the south side of Spooner as a permanent home for the fair. The original deed stated, "It is the intention of the grantor to give said lands to the grantee provided that they are used always for fairgrounds, educational, or civic recreational purposes." Some of the original buildings were moved from the north end of town to the newly acquired property. Today only two buildings remain from 1947, Plainview Schoolhouse, where open-class exhibits are held, and a log cabin.

Janet McNabb was a longtime president of the Washburn County Fair Board, starting in that role in 1934 and holding it for forty-nine years. After McNabb passed away in 1982, her longtime friend Oscar Johnson bequeathed his estate to the county 4-H program in honor of McNabb's memory. Fair management used that bequest to upgrade and replace buildings on the grounds as well as to provide scholarships for local 4-H youth. In 1995, a dedication was held at the fairgrounds for the newly constructed Janet McNabb Small Animal Building and the Oscar Johnson 4-H Center.

In 2010, the Washburn County Junior Fair Association dropped the word *Junior* from its name to encourage participation from all ages in both the junior and open classes, but the fair remains dedicated to the youth of the community, encouraging 4-H, Boy Scouts, Girl Scouts, and schools to exhibit.[13]

# 14

# WISCONSIN STATE FAIR

In March of 1851, just three years after Wisconsin had achieved statehood, a group of legislators and other citizens met to discuss the organization of a state agricultural society. Several county agricultural societies had already been organized by that time, and agricultural reformers recognized the power of fairs, with their competitive exhibits and demonstrations, to improve the state's agricultural practices. The state society also supported the formation of additional county agricultural societies.[1]

Shortly after the March meeting, the newly formed executive committee of the Wisconsin State Agricultural Society decided to hold the first state fair and cattle show in Janesville on the first and second days of October 1851. "The Society members including farmers, mechanics and citizens formed a procession in Madison at 8 a.m. on September 30th and began their march to Janesville, led by the Madison Brass Band."[2]

Rufus King, then owner and editor of the *Milwaukee Sentinel*, wrote a detailed account of what occurred on each day of the fair. "An area of something over six acres, on the edge of a plateau which looks down upon the rapid and silvery Rock [River], and enclosed by a high board fence, constitutes the fairgrounds. Along two sides of the enclosure are pens for sheep and swine, and stands for cattle. Near the centre is a large and lofty tent for the display of fruits, flowers, fancy articles, paintings, jewelry, etc. In the open space between these centre pieces and the cattle stands on the sides, there is ample room for exhibition and trial of all sorts of agricultural implements, as well as the display of single and matched horses."[3]

Stamp commemorating the 1915 Wisconsin State Fair

WHI IMAGE ID 33247

This first state fair attracted large crowds—thirteen thousand to eighteen thousand people, by most estimates—many eager to exhibit their produce, and even more of them interested in seeing their neighbors and learning something about the farm practices of others. Exhibits included samples of Wisconsin wheat, a two-hundred-pound squash from Dane County, sweet potatoes, broomcorn, and a barrel of "Superfine Family Flour." Livestock exhibits included 52 entries of cattle, 68 horses, 120 sheep, and 20 hogs. On the second day, the fair featured a plowing contest held in a field about a quarter mile from the fairgrounds. Ten farmers competed, eight with horses and two with oxen and each plowing a quarter acre. After the plowing match, everyone hurried back to the fairgrounds to hear an address by University of Wisconsin Chancellor John Hiram Lathrop. The speech was delivered in the floral tent, which was "crowded to suffocation," according to Rufus King. The newsman noted, "If the State Fair produced nothing else than the Chancellor's address, it would have amply repaid the Society and the farmers of Wisconsin for the time, money, and labor expended for [sponsoring the fair]." In summary, King wrote: "There must have been in the afternoon [of the second day] fully eight thousand persons within the enclosure, all orderly, well-behaved, and decently dressed. There was not a single intoxicated man in the crowd, no riotous or disorderly contact; no gambling appliances, no liquor booths, no profanity, nothing in short to offend the eye or mar the general enjoyment." This first state fair was credited with being the largest gathering held in Wisconsin up to that date.[4]

Before moving permanently to its present location in West Allis, the state fair moved around a good deal, landing six times in Janesville (1851, 1857, 1864–1866, and 1877), eighteen in Milwaukee (1852, 1854–1856, 1859, 1870–1876, 1886–1891), eleven in Madison (1858, 1860, 1867–1869, 1878–1880, 1883–1885), twice in Fond du Lac (1881 and 1882), and in Watertown (1853).[5] The state fair was cancelled during the Civil War years 1861 and 1863, in 1893 when the Columbian Exposition was held in Chicago, and once more, in 1945, during World War II.[6]

Abraham Lincoln, then a lawyer from Illinois, spoke at the 1859 Wisconsin State Fair in Milwaukee on September 30. His speaking fee: $150. The man who would one year later be elected president summarized the importance of agricultural fairs this way:

> [T]hey are useful in more ways than one. They bring us together, and
> thereby make us better acquainted, and better friends than we oth-

erwise would be. . . . They make more pleasant and more strong and more durable the bond of social and political union among us. . . . But the chief use of agricultural fairs is to aid in improving the great calling of agriculture, in all its departments and minute divisions—to make mutual exchange of agricultural discovery, information, and knowledge; so that, at the end, all may know everything, which may have been known to but one, to but a few, at the beginning—to bring together especially all which is supposed to not be generally known, because of recent discovery or invention.[7]

An artist's rendering of the Wisconsin State Agricultural Society fair held in Milwaukee in 1859, the year Lincoln spoke there

WHI IMAGE ID 33371

Over the years many other notables would visit the Wisconsin State Fair: President Rutherford B. Hayes (1878), former president General Ulysses S. Grant (1880), President William Howard Taft (1909), Wilbur and Orville Wright (1910), and Henry Ford (1922).[8]

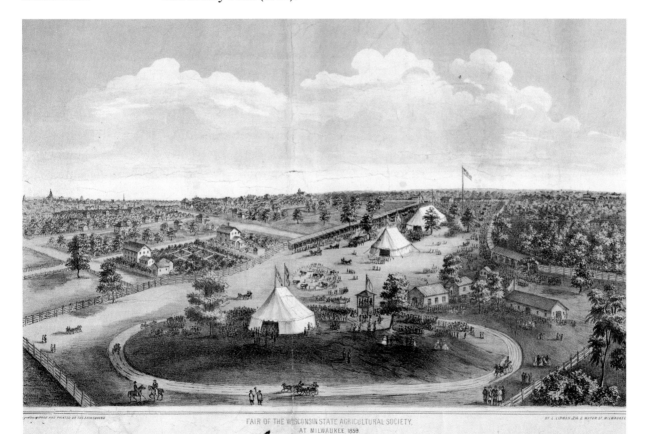

FAIR OF THE WISCONSIN STATE AGRICULTURAL SOCIETY,
AT MILWAUKEE 1859.

The 1860 Wisconsin State Fair was held September 24–28 in Madison at what was known as the Bruen Estate. The fair had more than two thousand exhibit entries and featured scientific lectures held at the state capitol. John Muir, then of Montello, displayed several of his inventions.

In 1864, the fair returned to Janesville, where it remained through 1866. At the 1864 fair, Manufacturers' Hall featured a competition between cooking stove brands, with fairgoers sampling roast beef and bread. Back in Madison in 1867, the featured speaker at Camp Randall was University of Wisconsin President P. A. Chadbourne. This fair was described as "one of the largest and most satisfactory held." The fair continued in Madison each year through 1869; it returned to Milwaukee in 1870 and remained there through 1876.[9]

The 1876 fair ran September 11–20 and celebrated the nation's centennial. Heavy rains lowered both attendance and receipts. Madison's Camp Randall was the site for the state fair once again in 1878 through 1880. The fair moved to Fond du Lac for 1881, but rain dampened attendance, and the fair lost money. The machinery department had more than 280 entries and covered eight acres. In Madison at Camp Randall in 1883, increased attendance brought receipts up to $25,000.[10]

The Madison Brass Band performed at the 1879 state fair at Camp Randall.
WHI IMAGE ID 1866

It wasn't until 1892 that the state fair found its present home in West Allis, where it has been ever since. The year before, the Agricultural Society of Wisconsin purchased land from a dairy farmer, George Stevens, for $136,000. The land included a horse racing track that would later become the legendary auto racing track commonly referred to as the Milwaukee Mile. Auto racing began on the Milwaukee Mile in 1903 and has taken place on the famous racetrack every year since. Some of the big names who've raced there include Barney Oldfield in 1905 and again in 1910 with his famous Blitzen Benz race car, Rex Mays, A. J. Foyt, Al Unser, and Mario Andretti. In the 1930s, a new grandstand overlooking the track was built, replacing one constructed in 1914. The new structure held 14,900 spectators and stood until 2002. State fair management have continued to make improvements over the years to both the track and the viewing area.[11]

Crowds eagerly anticipate the start of a car race at the 1956 state fair.
WHI IMAGE ID 33348

In 1916, the Wisconsin State Fair had its first exhibits of boys' and girls' club work. Projects entered included potatoes, dairy calves, and pig projects. In 1940, when the fair celebrated its ninetieth anniversary, about two thousand young people from seventy-one counties took part in youth programs. Attendance exploded over the first half of the twentieth century, growing from 172,620 in 1916 to 674,683 in 1946.[12]

As the fair grew in popularity, a plethora of dining options was added, and several of Milwaukee's prominent breweries, including Pabst and Schlitz, built beer gardens on the ground. The fair added an amusement park in 1921, with traditional fair rides such as a merry-go-round, a roller coaster, and a Ferris wheel, making the fair an even more appealing attraction for families with kids.

## WISCONSIN STATE FAIR MISSION AND MANAGEMENT

Today the Wisconsin State Fair is overseen by the State Fair Park Board, a state agency. The State Fair Park board of directors comprises seven governor-appointed members, along with four state legislators and the secretaries of the Department of Tourism and the Department of Agriculture, Trade, and Consumer Protection. The board provides financial oversight for State Fair Park; paid staff, led by a CEO/executive director, manage the day-to-day work for the state fair and other events that take place on the grounds.

The Wisconsin State Fair defines its mission as celebrating "agriculture and other industries paramount to Wisconsin's rich history and promising future by producing family-friendly, affordable, safe, and educational event for all ages and ethnicities, creating memories and traditions to be carried on for generations." State Fair Park receives financial support from the Wisconsin State Fair Park Foundation, a non-profit fund-raising organization.

---

NOTE

"About Wisconsin State Fair," wistatefair.com; "Wisconsin State Fair Park Board of Directors 2019," Kristin Chuckel, Director of Public Affairs, Wisconsin State Fair Park, February 5, 2020.

The fair also added extensive exhibits and demonstrations by Wisconsin manufacturers and other businesses during this time.

In 1948, to celebrate the centennial of statehood, the Wisconsin State Fair was titled the Wisconsin Centennial Exposition. It took place August 7–29 and still is considered by some to be the most significant in the history of the fair. In preparation for the event, management completely renovated State Fair Park. Admission that year was fifty cents, and close to 1.8 million people attended. New buildings and exhibit spaces were added to the grounds, including "Wisconsin at Work," a $320,000 industrial building where every type of manufacturing in Wisconsin was demonstrated; a Women's Building, "a tribute to all Wisconsin women who played such an important role in the molding of the Forward state"; an "on the farm exhibit . . . telling the history of Wisconsin from the cradle to the combine"; and a Conservation Exhibit, a "two-acre wonderland where the beauties of Wisconsin's splendor are presented in nature's authentic form." A Wisconsin Youth building was constructed where "Wisconsin youth, yesterday and today, are honored at the giant youth exposition—as they take part in every phase of the Centennial Exposition." An Alice in Dairyland building was also added to the grounds.[13]

Evening fairgoers stroll
the Centennial Expo
midway.
WHI IMAGE ID 87638

Entertainment that centennial year included the world premiere of the play *Paul Bunyan* at the grandstand and Paul Bunyan Sports Show on the midway, which included log rollers, wood choppers, and canoe tipping. An Indy Car race and the fair's first stock car race were held. During the evenings, the coliseum floor was covered with ice for the "Ice Vogues" show. During the day, the ice was covered for livestock judging.

Kids and teens take a break for a cool drink at the state fair.

WHI IMAGE ID 33334

As the unknown author of *The Wisconsin Century Book* wrote, "State Fair Park is the fitting amphitheater for this spectacular production [the history of Wisconsin]. Every structural and natural facility of the two-hundred-and-twenty acre stage has been carefully arranged and designed to add distinction and splendor to this living tribute to our state. . . . Within these buildings are displays which radiate the glory of Wisconsin. Exhibits which portray the achievements, the progress, and the ultimate leadership which Wisconsin has assumed in so many fields."[14]

It would be hard to beat the record attendance of the Wisconsin Centennial Exposition, which ran for twenty-three days (compared to the typical state

Booths lining the midway at the Centennial Exposition advertise a variety of attractions.

fair's nine-day run). The 1967 state fair recorded attendance at 974,757, the fourth straight year that the fair had drawn more than 900,000. In 1968, in an attempt to boost attendance at the State Fair to one million, management decided to offer all the shows in the grandstand without an additional charge beyond the fair's entrance fee. Grandstand performers included Johnny Carson, Doc Severinsen, the American Folk Ballet, Mike Douglas, Don Adams, James Darren, the Statler Brothers, and the Cowsills. Three United States Auto Club auto races were also held. Fair management increased the fair entry fee from $1.00 to $1.50. When officials added up the numbers, 1968's state fair attendance hit 1,032,740.[15]

## ALICE IN DAIRYLAND

The Wisconsin Department of Agriculture (now Department of Agriculture, Trade and Consumer Protection, or DATCP), along with several other dairy industry leaders, created the Alice in Dairyland program in 1948 to promote the state's dairy industry.

Workers erected the Alice in Dairyland building measuring sixty by three hundred feet, later described as a "wonderland unlike anything ever attempted in Wisconsin or any state in America. It is conceived as the fairyland story of our beautiful dairyland . . . the dairyland of all the world." Margaret McGuire was selected as Wisconsin's first Alice in Dairyland. She served as a model for the construction of a ten-foot-tall mechanized "Alice" that served as master of ceremonies for the events taking place in the building. The mechanical Alice was operated by remote control; according to a report from the time, the Dairyland device "sits down, stands up, gestures, has facial expressions and answers queries about the dairy industry and the dairy display. . . . Alice may very well become a legendary figure in Wisconsin, loved and remembered for many years to come."

The Alice in Dairyland program has indeed become an iconic representation of the state's dairy industry. The role continues to this day as a salaried position in DATCP. Alice's duties include traveling the state, appearing at a variety of

The first Alice in Dairyland, Margaret McGuire, rides on a float at the 1948 state fair.
WHI IMAGE ID 121244

events, including speaking at schools and doing media interviews, all in support of promoting Wisconsin's agriculture.

NOTE
*The Wisconsin Century Book* (Milwaukee, WI: Wisconsin Centennial Exposition, 1948), pp. 79–80.

Youngsters enjoy the state fair's kid-sized roller coaster.
WHI IMAGE ID 33152

Free attendance at the grandstand shows continued until 1974. The grandstand went back to all-paying shows in 1975, when grandstand tickets were from one to three dollars and fair admission was two dollars.[16]

In addition to the many educational exhibits, great food, an exciting carnival, and live animals of every description, the Wisconsin State Fair has offered big-name grandstand entertainment for decades. As Blaine Schultz

Hmong dancers take a break from performing during the state fair.

USED WITH PERMISSION BY UW–MADISON DIVISION OF EXTENSION

wrote in a 2019 Milwaukee *Shepherd Express* article, "In recent years, the Fair has presented country western superstars Blake Shelton and Reba McEntire, pop sensations Shawn Mendes and Demi Lovato, Christian bands, Casting Crowns and Hillsong Live, and rock legends John Mellencamp, and Foreigner. Past performers of note included Frank Zappa, Neil Young, Whitney Houston, Alex Chilton and the Box Tops, and the Texas Tornadoes."[17] Also among its broad range of entertainment and education opportunities, the state fair showcases the foods, music, dances, and traditions of dozens of cultural groups.

Wisconsin State Fair attendance reached 1 million again in 2013, and the upward trend continued for seven years in a row. In 2019, attendance was over 1.1 million, the highest attendance other than the centennial celebration in 1948.[18] In 2020, the state fair was cancelled because of the COVID-19 pandemic—the first time in seventy-five years the fair could not be held.

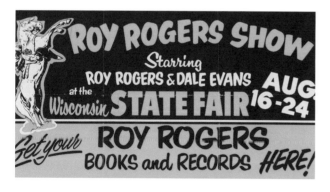

Poster promoting an appearance at the fair by entertainers Roy Rogers and Dale Evans, 1958

WHI IMAGE ID 33629

Menominee Indian High
School students dance
during UW Extension day
at the state fair.
USED WITH PERMISSION BY
UW–MADISON DIVISION OF
EXTENSION

To adapt to changing conditions—and accommodate those who missed state fair food, fair organizers created a drive-through for classic fair foods at State Fair Park in August 2020. Thirteen vendors offered everything from corn on the cob, Cheddar nuggets, and deep fried Oreos to cotton candy and a walking taco. Of course, the world-famous state fair cream puffs were also available, a six-pack selling for twenty-two dollars.[19]

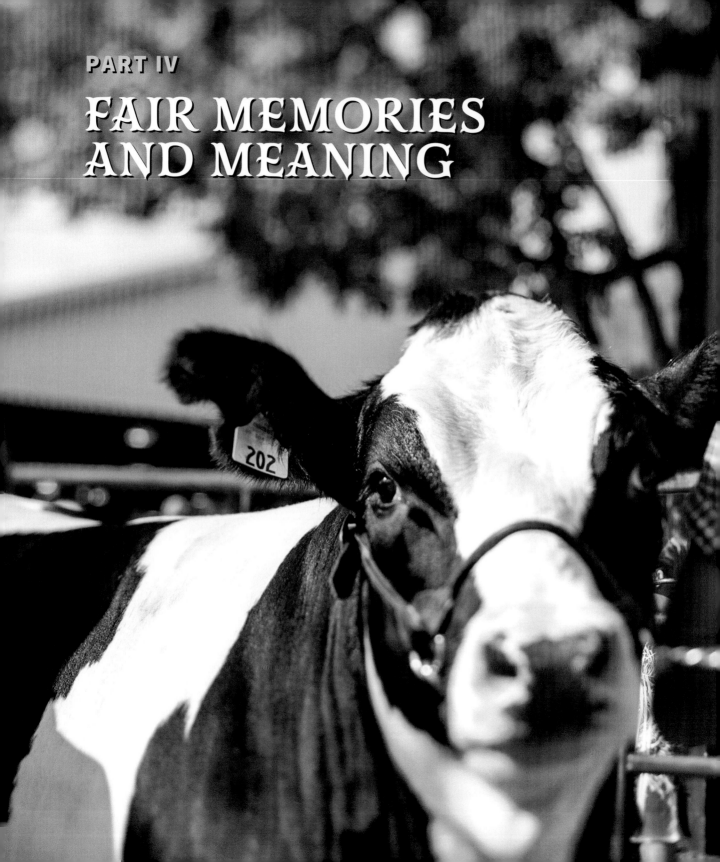

# PART IV

# FAIR MEMORIES AND MEANING

# 15

# STORIES FROM THE FAIR

From the whirling colors of the carnival, to the sights and sounds of the animal barns, to the thrill of winning a ribbon, a trip to the fair creates indelible memories. It seems everyone who's ever attended a county or state fair recalls lessons, stories, and friendships that came from the experience.

Pam Jahnke, today a broadcaster for *The Mid-West Farm Report*, explained, "It's a shared experience. No matter your age, there is a certain camaraderie when you start talking about showing or being at the fair. The wash rack, telling stories in the barn, the knots in your stomach before you go in the ring, the way you hang on every word the judge shares about your project or the crazy rides you went on afterward—heads start to nod when you start sharing those stories."

Working together and helping one another has always been part of the farming life; it's only natural that this sense of community would extend to the local fair. Remembering her time as an exhibitor at the Oconto County Fair, Jahnke continued,

Parents, families, everybody worked together. You helped one another. You saw kids from other school districts that you might only see once a year. You learned patience and commitment. Whether it was taking care of the vegetable garden to make sure you had a selection for fair display, or the countless hours of walking, walking, walking, to get the fair animal ready and at ease for the ring.

You learned to listen to your parents, grandparents, club leader, and FFA advisor. They taught you, showed you, listened to you—all to

Some fair memories are unforgettable.
PHOTO COURTESY OF TRAVEL WISCONSIN

make the fair experience the best! . . . Today—as a farm broadcaster—I see the same stories repeating with exhibitors and families everywhere I cover fairs.[1]

Author Tom Weso, who grew up attending fairs both in Shawano and on the Menominee Reservation, where his family lived, also recalled how fairs created a sense of kinship and belonging. "Fair time was a time for the Menominee community to come together. Late at night, after the rides closed down, the men would get together and talk past midnight," he wrote. At the Shawano fair, the food stands were the place to buy cream puffs, bratwurst, and beer, Weso recalled, but they also functioned as "a meeting place for members of the opposite sex, important to me as a young teenager." (For more about romance at the fair, see page 211.)[2]

Former 4-H member Kassie Shepp of Lincoln County said that "show kids" form strong bonds at the county fair. "The 4-H members you show with and spend that week in the summer together become your family," she wrote. "You may only see them for five days of the year, but you discover your best friends in a hog show ring."[3]

Young people wait to enter the show ring at the Jefferson County Fair.
PHOTO BY STEVE APPS

# MY COUNTY FAIR STORY

I joined 4-H in 1946. In those days, you had to be ten years old to join, and you could belong until you reached age twenty-one. Pa told me that if I signed up for the dairy project, I would be able to stay overnight at the Waushara County Fair in Wautoma, and sign up I did. I also signed up for the forestry project.

Pa helped me pick out a calf from our dairy herd. He suggested a bull calf that he thought had the best potential for winning at the county fair. I named my calf Stormy—and I quickly discovered his rather "stormy" personality. Teaching the little bull calf to lead with a halter and rope proved to be one of the most challenging things I had ever done. I worked at it every day when I had spare time from all the others things that farm kids had to do in those days. Some days I believed I was making progress. Other days the little bull simply shook his head and refused to move a step. Sometimes I led him out of the barn and he took off at a trot, with me holding the rope tied to his halter and stumbling after him to keep up.

Pa constantly coached me. He showed me how to hold one hand on the rope closest to the halter with the rest of the rope coiled in my other hand and how to make sure that Stormy

Author Jerry Apps and Stormy, 1947
PHOTO COURTESY OF JERRY APPS

held his head high. Day after day, Stormy and I practiced with Pa watching, commenting, demonstrating. I was learning. Stormy was learning. Soon the fair was only a month away. Would Stormy be ready? Would I be ready? Pa told me, "Showing a calf is a team effort. You and your calf are one. The calf must trust you. You must trust the calf."

*(continued on next page)*

# MY COUNTY FAIR STORY

*(continued from page 197)*

By late July, Pa was teaching me the fine points of leading a calf in a show ring. "Keep his head up, walk slowly, and keep a little distance from the animal in front of you. Keep one eye on the judge and the other on your calf."

At the same time, I was working on my forestry project, an exhibit of wood samples from different kinds of trees. It took a few hours of work—nothing compared to the process of teaching a calf to lead.

At our July meeting, our 4-H club discussed the county fair. Someone asked where we would sleep while we were there. Someone else said he'd heard that you could buy a used army surplus tent for ten dollars that would hold a dozen people. Our club's treasury at the time had about $1.50 in it. What to do? Our 4-H leader, Clayton Owens, suggested that we sponsor a pie social as a money-making event. Our mothers made the pies, and we bought the ice cream. When it was over and we'd paid the bills, we had nine dollars. Pa tossed in the extra dollar, and soon we had our tent and a place to sleep at the fair.

The first days of August flew by, and then it was mid-August and fair week. We asked Ross Caves, the community's livestock trucker, to haul our 4-H calves to the fairgrounds. He arrived at our farm at noon on opening day of the fair. I led Stormy up into the truck. I could tell that my calf was as nervous as I was. I rode along with Mr. Caves as we picked up calves from other 4-H members—the Yorks, the Kolkas, and the Dudleys.

Arriving at the fairgrounds, Caves backed up his truck to the cattle barn, and I helped him unload and tie the calves in the barn. Stormy was on his best behavior, as were all the other calves, none of which had ridden in a truck before. Pa arrived at the fairgrounds about the same time. He brought along my forestry project, which I took to the exhibit building for forestry projects, woodworking projects, soil conservation exhibits, home furnishing items, tractor maintenance, and other project materials.

Other members of our 4-H club began arriving, and Clayton Owens organized us in an open area on the south end of the fairgrounds near the carnival people's travel trailers. He put us to work, and we soon had our tent assembled, along with our army surplus canvas cots, which we each had purchased for two dollars apiece.

The following morning, I was up at 5:00 a.m., and by 5:30 I was busy feeding and watering Stormy. Next, I brushed him, washed the bushy end of his tail, and combed it out and fluffed it up. I put black shoe polish on his horns, a trick I had learned from Pa.

Shortly after eight o'clock, 4-H members led their calves into the show ring, and the judging began. When the announcer called the junior bull class, I removed Stormy's halter and put on the special halter that Mr. Gorman, the harness maker in Wild Rose, had made for me. I backed Stormy out of his stall and led him toward the show ring. I scratched him on top of his head; he always liked that. He looked at me; I looked

## MY COUNTY FAIR STORY

at him. "This is it," I said. I was scared to death, and I think Stormy was, too.

I tried to remember everything that Pa had taught me. Keep Stormy's head up, walk slowly, stay a few feet in back of the animal in front of you, keep one eye on Stormy and the other on the judge, do what the judge asks you to do, remember to smile. Stormy and I walked around the ring with a dozen or so other bull calves. A couple of them were jumping around, acting up, but not Stormy. He did everything I asked him to do and more. After one trip around the show ring, the judge pointed at me and signaled for me to lead Stormy where he pointed. As I did, I looked over at Pa, who was standing just outside the show ring fence. Pa was smiling. I then knew that I had received first prize, a blue ribbon. All of my hard work with Stormy had paid off.

I have never forgotten the feeling I had that day so many years ago. I showed calves at the Waushara County Fair for nine more years, but none were as memorable as that first experience. I learned so much showing cattle at a fair, including the wonder of developing a relationship with an animal, the importance of patience, the rewards of keeping going even when things do not go well, the fun of sleeping in an old tent, and much more.

## A FAMILY AFFAIR

For many folks, participating in the fair—whether as workers, exhibitors, or visitors—becomes a treasured family activity, often one that brings together multiple generations and forges lasting memories. Julie Belschner, editor of *Agri-View*, noted that her memories of attending a county fair in Iowa are shared by multiple generations of her family. Her son and daughter spent every August of their childhood preparing a booth in the same exhibitor barn where Belschner admired cakes, pies, canned goods, and other exhibits with her dad a generation earlier. "Each year was a celebration," she remembered. "My daughter was born during fair week, as was one of the carnie's daughters. A goat tended to disappear from the petting zoo each year, destined to be grilled over a homemade temporary pit as part of a celebratory birthday party we were blessed to be a part of."[4]

Betty Lassa-Blauvelt shared these memories of assisting her grandchildren with their projects for the Central Wisconsin State Fair in Marshfield:

Siblings ready to show
their cows in Green
County, 1959
WHI IMAGE ID 25063

Summer was off to a good start. Gardens were planted and livestock were let out to pasture, all except the two Black Angus steers that were chosen to become 4-H projects. Jack and Julius had been specially fed all winter, and my thirteen- and fourteen-year-old grandsons were enthusiastic about entering them in the Central Wisconsin State Fair. James and Matthew's ten-year-old sister, Colleen, was also getting started in 4-H with her huge, fluffy Brahma rooster. He had soft feathers from his head down to his toes. She handled him every day.

My son and his wife took a part-time summer job requiring them to be gone several days out of the week. So I had the opportunity and responsibility of babysitting. With all of the outdoor activities, the grandkids and I didn't spend much time indoors. The grandsons led Jack and Julius around each day. [The steers] were bathed, brushed, and made to obey commands as they would when being shown. They had an excellent rate of gain, staying within the middle-weight class of 1,100 pounds. Despite James and Matthew's athletic strength, the steers were becoming quite a handful.

Entry day was busy loading up and getting the animals to the fair. Riley the rooster was assigned a cage in the chicken barn, and Jack and Julius were given stalls between other Black Angus steers. James and Matthew stayed with their animals during the five days of the fair, feeding, watering and providing clean, fresh bedding. Judging day was an exciting but somewhat stressful time as Jack and Julius competed against ten other Black Angus in their weight class—all looking perfect in comparison to one another. With so many in this class, judging took a long time. Both the contestants and the cattle were becoming anxious for it to be over. Jack and Julius ended up 5th and 6th, and the boys were very disappointed.

After two more classes to be judged, it was time for the showmanship classes to begin. I had gone for some sandwiches, and when I got back to the cattle barn, my son met me saying the boys didn't want to go out in the ring anymore. I went over to question them. They responded that they had given up, they were done. I said, "Nonsense, you're going out there. You didn't work hard all summer to quit now. It doesn't matter if you don't win. What's important is that you tried! Now get out there and hold your heads up high." I followed close behind and patted each one on the back as they led their steers into the ring.

The showmanship judging didn't take long. The boys each got a blue ribbon and came out of the ring all smiles and with a bounce in their step. I hugged them both and even hugged Jack and Julius. When all were settled back into the cattle barn, James came up to hug me and said, "Thanks, Granny, for making us go out there." Matthew was right behind, shyly repeating his thank you.

I couldn't have asked for any more thanks than the expressed love and appreciation of my grandchildren. What a wonderful reward knowing that I made a difference in helping to make memories. And the local fair gave our family that opportunity."[5]

Pam Jahnke recalled that her family became a beehive of activity leading up to and during the Oconto County Fair. "Our farm was on the far east side of the county, with the fairgrounds on the far west side. The week leading up to the

A family takes in the midway sights and sounds in Washington County, 1966.
WHI IMAGE ID 25600

fair was crazy with activity. Dad was nailing boards up on the pick-up truck to transport my heifer. I was organizing pails, feed, combs, brushes—everything I'd need to use for that beloved ribbon!"[6] Things were similar in my family during the years that my two brothers and I were 4-H members and exhibiting dairy calves, woodworking projects, garden produce, and forestry projects. Everyone in our family was involved—not only on fair days, but for weeks ahead of time as we taught animals to lead, tended the vegetable garden, and updated record books kept for each project.

Family members often meet up at the fair—sometimes crossing paths in unexpected ways. Phyllis Sonsalla grew up on a Buffalo County farm and recalled this memory from when she was about ten or eleven:

> I was taking a vegetable box to the fair. The box was an old peach box (mom would buy a case of peaches and can them for the winter), which I decorated. . . . [I]n the box we would put six [each] of six different vegetables. Mom would get so upset because sometimes we'd have to dig up six or seven hills of potatoes to get six matching potatoes. The beans, peas, and carrots were also difficult to match. That year Mom planted cabbage and cauliflower. You only had to take one each of those vegetables. I got my box to the fair, checked in and all. I was not there for the judging, but my cousin Ed Pronschinske was a summer youth agent. As the judge was looking at the beautiful vegetable boxes, the judge said, "Well, it's too early to have a cauliflower from a garden, they must have bought it." My cousin piped up and said, "I know my aunt has cauliflower already in her garden." The judge wanted to disqualify my box, but Ed persisted. Finally, the judge gave in and gave me a pink ribbon, fourth place.[7]

## EXPECT THE UNEXPECTED

One common lesson learned at the fair is that anything can happen. It seems combining animals, kids, unpredictable weather conditions, and who knows what else can sometimes lead to chaos—and some of the funniest fair stories.

Cheryl Ehrke, a superintendent for the Jefferson County Fair, shared this story:

Sometimes a little coaxing is necessary to move an uncooperative partner.

WHI IMAGE ID 23169; © JOURNAL SENTINEL INC.

I have been involved with the Jefferson County Fair for nearly fifty years in different capacities. It all began in 1970, when I was a shy ten-year-old 4-H member showing a calf at the fair. My registered Holstein junior calf, named Marcia, was well trained and spoiled. She was fed and groomed to perfection, but when we entered the ring, she began kicking at her belly, acting up, and ultimately got away from me—four times. Friendly spectators caught her and returned her to me as I fought tears and tried to hide my embarrassment at having attention drawn to me. Marcia placed 4th in the class of about twenty-five calves, and I felt a little better when the older boy whose calf won the class told my dad that my calf should have won.

Despite this less than illustrious start, I continued to show registered Holsteins at the county and state fair through all ten years of 4-H and continued to be involved as cousins and neighbors showed our cattle at the fair. I was also the dairy leader for our club and chaperone/leader for the county dairy exhibit at the state fair.[8]

The Wolf family of Memory Lane Farm in Marshfield told a similar story:

In the fall, our daughter, Diane, purchased her first young black feeder steer for purposes of raising him for the Central Wisconsin State Fair 4-H and FFA market animal sale held annually over Labor Day weekend in Marshfield. Over the winter months, the steer, affectionately named Harvey, grew steadily and filled out proportionately as a future market steer. During the summer, Diane worked to build trust with Harvey, halter trained him, and exposed him to the sights and sounds of nature and the farm environment. She taught him to walk and set-up and washed and groomed him so that the 900-pound, muscular steer was ready for show time at the fair.

Fair entry day finally arrived. Harvey appeared peaceful at home, swatting flies off his back with his tail. He tolerated the drive to the fairgrounds in the trailer uneventfully. Diane led him off the trailer to the scale (he met the weight goal!) and then on to the steer barn to be tied in his stall. Diane organized his feed, bedding, and carefully placed the show trunk in its proper location. With her 4-H friends, she decorated the area and placed Harvey's name card above him. Meanwhile, Harvey chewed his cud, suggesting that he was indeed a "happy camper" at the fair. Considering everything and everybody was tucked in satisfactorily, Diane's father left the fairgrounds for much needed evening farm chores.

As other animals arrived at the fairgrounds, Harvey seemed quite peaceful. Diane thought this would be an ideal time to give him his final bath in preparation for show time. She eyed the wash rack and saw two openings, just perfect for Harvey and her brother's steer. With a pail, washrags, towels, and soap in hand, Diane led Harvey to the sturdy wooden plank rack. Her brother tied his steer to an adjacent wooden plank. They both started the washing routine, using a water hose to wet the animals. Nearby, another exhibitor brought his show animal to be washed. This exhibitor, however, had a power washer. As the power washer roared to life, Harvey started to rock back and forth, pulling on the plank with ever widening eyes. And then, a large cracking sound, and Harvey broke loose, running away from the washing station, still tied to the wooden plank. Diane, her brother Dale, and others quickly followed. Harvey was spooked and ran directly toward the midway.

Fairgoers yelled, screamed, and ran to safety as Harvey continued his sprint past the carnival and Ferris wheel. Harvey continued to run, evading people [who were] yelling and screaming, right through the enter-exit fair gate. Diane and others tried to catch up to Harvey, but he was too fast, even while dragging the wooden plank. Heading into the downtown via a main road, he passed a grade school football field. The football players couldn't believe their eyes and ran to the sideline bushes to take cover. By this time, the police joined the pursuit, with the sirens blaring and lights flashing. In an effort to block the steer from running further through town, a police car tried to cut off Harvey only to have its back door smashed by the 900-pound beast. Harvey turned south, heading straight out of town on Maple Avenue. Somewhere along the route, the plank broke free and Harvey bounded forward full speed. Diane and Dale tried to keep up on foot with Harvey, but they were winded and could barely keep him in sight. Somehow, after traveling another three-quarter mile south of town through gardens, roadways and yards, Harvey became wedged between two semi-trailers at a loading dock. Unable to move forward, backward or sideways, he took a break! Diane and Dale finally caught up with him, now exploring their options as to how to get Harvey back to the fairgrounds.

Suddenly, a small cattle truck came towards them and stopped upon seeing the police cars and people surrounding the semi-trailers. The cattle truck was in route to the fairgrounds; the driver, Russ, asked if he could help! Diane and Dale could not believe it as he had an extra lead rope with him. With clear experience, the driver crawled under the semi-trailers to reach Harvey's head, snap the lead rope on his halter and led him into the partially loaded truck. All watched in amazement!

With Russ's vast experience handling cattle, Harvey returned to the fairgrounds via the entry gate for animals! Diane and Dale rode back with Russ in his truck. We led Harvey back to his stall after being weighed. After all of the running, Harvey came in under weight and could not be sold at the market sale.

Diane learned many lessons along the way and chose to focus her future market sale efforts on raising sheep![9]

Lynda Ketelboeter recalled belonging to a 4-H club in White Creek and showing chickens and pigeons at the Adams County Fair in the mid-1960s. "I received several ribbons for the chickens and pigeons, but my best memory was my live demonstration on how to clip chicken wings so they couldn't fly away. The chicken I chose for the demonstration was a particularly ornery Long Island Red that put up quite a fight but I persevered. I received a blue ribbon."[10]

Larry Meiller of Wisconsin Public Radio recalled a time his 4-H club had to improvise: "I remember a float that we made for the Dane County Junior Fair. We had a horse lined up to pull the float. Unfortunately, the horse would not cooperate and it looked like we would not be able to compete. Then our 4-H leader, Hilmer (Red) Gust, took over. He installed himself where the horse should have been and pulled our float! We got first prize. The local newspaper ran a story about it and we were all pretty proud! One of many great memories for a lifetime!"[11]

## EVERYONE HAS A FAIR STORY

It isn't just exhibitors and midway visitors who remember their fair experiences fondly. Fairs have left their mark on the many county agriculture agents, fair board members, volunteer judges, and other folks who share their time and skills to make fairs go off without a hitch (or, often, even with a hitch).

Linda Kustka, retired 4-H youth development specialist, recounted when she was hired in 1973 as the first female 4-H youth agent in Brown County.

It was a large youth fair with around 12,000 exhibits, which meant that the experienced staff stressed the need to be well organized, follow and enforce the rules strictly, and try to keep the fair secretary, fair board, volunteers, members, and public happy.

My tasks (with the other 4-H youth agent and Extension staff) included hiring/supervising high school and college students who recorded the entries from registration forms onto fair tags and judges' sheets for weeks in the Extension office. Several days before fair, the 4-H staff and volunteers (youth and adults) went to the fairgrounds to

Volunteers make fair activities like this hog judging in Waushara County possible.
PHOTO BY STEVE APPS

prepare the non-animal exhibit space where vehicles were stored during winter. This involved washing display cases, painting, sweeping, and constructing a makeshift office. My philosophy was that if I was present where volunteers were doing this physical work, I worked with them. Thus, every year we roller-painted lots of chicken-wire, five- to six-feet-high project security fences with wooden borders and legs. I learned quickly that it was a bad idea for me to be painting with another person doing the same facing each other. I wondered how that teen explained to his parents that the new 4-H agent had painted him.[12]

According to Kustka, volunteers were key to the fair's success. "We probably had fifty people involved as superintendents, judges' helpers (recorded comments and placings), and project protectors (keep exhibits safe from theft or damage)," she recalled, noting that she learned she needed to hire the best qualified judges available.

The arts area was a challenge because people who are experts in one area probably don't know much about another area. Thus, we needed different judges for leather craft, ceramics made from molds, hand built pottery, hand stenciling, painting, etc. Parents will quickly let you know if a judge doesn't have the needed knowledge or supportive personality. After the first fair, I had a list of where we needed "better experts" and recruited that kind of person to become certified judges for the future. Years later, I had a dream or nightmare that I was judging horses and the audience started throwing vegetables at me because I was so bad in the equine area.[13]

Melanie Miller, a longtime Cooperative Extension employee, worked for more than forty years at the Wisconsin State Fair in a variety of roles. Some of her best stories come from the years that she worked as an assistant superintendent for the open-class beef department. One of her jobs was to check the ear

Cattle judging at the Waushara County Fair
PHOTO BY JERRY APPS

tags or tattoos and the registration papers for the beef exhibitors' cattle. This was a relatively easy task—until she faced a huge Chianina bull, six feet tall at the shoulder, whose name was Krypton. Miller and the other judges decided to wait until Krypton was lying down so they could more easily read the tattoo in his ear. But the big bull clearly wanted to stay standing, and every time someone grabbed his rope halter to try to lower his head, he offered a look that said, "Don't mess with me." It took most of a day before they were eventually able to confirm his identification.

On show day, the Angus breed preceded the Chianina breed. After the Angus judging ran late, Krypton's owners were becoming uneasy. They finally confided to the superintendents that in preparing Krypton for his public walk into and around the show ring, the owners' herdsman had used an age-old method for helping the bull to relax:

they had given the big bull just enough beer to mellow him out and make him easier to manage in the show ring. Then, not knowing the herdsman had already given Krypton his dose of beer, the bull's owner gave him a second serving of Wisconsin's finest. A drunken bull was not difficult to handle, but it became hard to keep him on his feet. The herdsman was able to get the bull into the Coliseum, take him around the show ring (where he won his class) and start back to the barn before the inevitable happened. Halfway back to the stalls, Krypton lay down on the blacktop. He lay there snoozing, snoring, belching, and smelling like a brewery. Drunken Krypton provided an unusual point of interest for the fairgoers the rest of that day.[14]

As the thirty-fourth Alice in Dairyland, Debbie Crave of Waterloo had a unique view into many behind-the-scenes fair activities. She recalled that she served as cohost of the 1981 Wisconsin State Fair, which had the theme "Days of Swine and Roses," and stayed overnight on the fairgrounds in the old administration building, where there were rooms upstairs. "The night sounds of fairgoers laughing as they left the grounds, Midway screams, and garbage trucks outside my room were my night sounds for the eleven nights of the state fair. I loved it," she remembered. She continued,

> Every day I had a different schedule; . . . I might give out ribbons in the dairy cattle show ring, mingle with people in the Ag Products building, or serve cream puffs to fairgoers. We always stopped by the radio and television exhibits to make sure to talk to media about the fair events and the importance of Wisconsin agriculture. I traversed the grounds in a golf cart in my dress, and every day I had a new corsage to wear, courtesy of the Wisconsin Florists Association.
>
> I met all the Ag queens of the time—Honey, Maple, Apple, Cranberry, and Holstein. We were lucky to have so much diversity and interest in promotion of Wisconsin's famous crops. There was a daily parade through the grounds that I was always part of. It was so thrilling to sit on a wagon behind a team of horses and ride through the whole fairgrounds to smile, wave and greet people.
>
> I felt fortunate and secretly thrilled to meet the grandstand performers. My role was to go backstage and present them a Wisconsin cheese gift box. (It was four wedges of cheddar in the shape of a "W"). I was able to meet and talk to Peter Frampton and Barbara Mandrell.[15]

Shirley Baumann, a former 4-H agent in Kewaunee County, recalled when she took a group of county 4-H members and their exhibits to the state fair around 1978. Several of the 4-H members showed chickens, and others showed rabbits. Not beyond trying to fool some of the city folks attending the fair, the 4-H'ers put some of the chicken eggs in with the rabbits. "They had a great time explaining to fairgoers that yes, indeed, rabbits lay eggs. Everyone knows about the Easter Bunny, don't they?"[16]

Nyla Musser, longtime Family Living agent in Jackson County, recalled a story from the days when she spent many hours working at the fair. One year, someone decided to create hold a milking contest in front of the grandstand, with the county Extension staff consisting of Nyla, county agricultural agent Eugene Savage, county 4-H agent Darrel Apps, and one 4-H member as contestants. Musser said, "The contest put the agents up against one another and brought all of the 4-H members together as well as the UW Extension staff. I remember winning the contest while milking one of Fred Mosley's Guernsey cows. The other agents laughed and said I must have been lucky to have a cow with a lot of milk. I argued that it was because I grew up on a Guernsey dairy farm and was an expert at milking cows by hand."[17]

## ROMANCE AT THE FAIR

Maybe it's the sparkling neon, the close quarters on the Ferris wheel, or just the feeling of excitement in the air, but a surprisingly common thread among fair reminiscences are stories of people who found love—or even a future spouse— at the fair.

Vickie Schwann shared her story of getting to know her future husband at the 1982 Manitowoc County Fair.

My husband says he fell in love with me at the county fair. I'm not quite sure when I fell in love with him, but I know it wasn't at the fair. I was too busy to think about falling in love. I'm just thankful the fellow who is now my husband kept his interest in me. I had many projects at the fair: sewing, foods, photography, home furnishings, cultural arts, child development plus poultry and rabbits. All of this with 4-H. I also showed sheep with FFA.

A couple buys snacks at the Centennial Exposition, 1948

At the fair in 1982, I was fitting my sheep when a young child came to pet it and ask me questions. A newspaper reporter from the *Manitowoc Herald Times Reporter* happened to see it, snapped a photo, and put it in the paper. A farmer, Gerald Schwann, saw the photo and asked his son, Mark, if he knew this girl. Mark said that he did, as they had met earlier that year at an FFA speaking contest and got to know each other during speaking contest meets. They put the clipping on the refrigerator. Mark had graduated from high school earlier that year, so this was to be his final year showing steers at the fair as an FFA member.

That 1982 fair was a busy one for me. In addition to my several entries, I had other responsibilities as well. Our Valders FFA chapter sponsored the Agriculture Olympics, and as the current president of the FFA, I was involved with that. Our FHA [Future Homemakers Association] chapter had a booth at the fair, and I was in charge of it. Plus, there was the clothing style revue. The responsibilities never seemed to end, that is until late Sunday afternoon. As the oldest in my family, I planned to stay at the fair so that when the fair management released the animals at 6:00 p.m., I could load the poultry and rabbits and load my market sheep for its buyer. I had nothing to do until 6:00 p.m., but who should show up but Mark. We had a long visit. But then it was 6:00 and I was once more busy. As he was still sticking around, I suggested he could help me carry boxes to my car, which he did.

When everything was loaded, Mark said he was interested in going to the Air Supply concert at the fair and asked would I like to go along. I let my mom know that I wouldn't be home as early as planned. Finally, after the concert was over, it was almost midnight, and the fair was shutting down. Mark walked me back to my car. I thought we would say goodbye—and who knows when we might see each other again. Instead, he asked me out on Friday night. Then he bent over and stole a kiss, right there in front of the pig barn at the Manitowoc County Fair. We married on September 8, 1984. We have four children; today they are all married as well."[18]

Colleen Kottke, editor of the *Wisconsin State Farmer*, has these memories of how she met her spouse:

Like most kids who grew up on the fringe of the agricultural community, my association with the county fair consisted of a trip or two down the Midway with my parents. That all changed when a friend invited me along to a 4-H hayride at the Kottke farm four miles down the road from us. Little did I know that I would come face to face with my life partner that night.

As a "late to the party 4-H member," I made up for lost time by enrolling in countless projects. As the ribbons were doled out, I realized that quantity didn't always add up to quality. But those projects allowed me to delve into areas that would later bring me much joy in life: gardening, flowers, photography, art and music.

One "unofficial" project brought me the most happiness, and that was the general leader's son. Dating a farmer opened up a whole new avenue of experiences at the fairgrounds. Who needed the midway when there were livestock shows and auctions down at the other end? I had discovered a vibrant agricultural community of fellowship among farm people.

After we wed, Glen and I continued in the tradition of his family by becoming 4-H leaders and parents of four 4-H members of our own. Getting ready for the county fair took on a whole new sense of urgency when trying to motivate little procrastinators in getting fair projects ready on time. As the years went by and the kids grew older, it was a pleasure to stand back and watch and listen as they conversed with the judge, proudly (and knowledgeably) explaining the details of their projects.

My mother-in-law has always teased me that my husband, Glen, was my best fair project, and in a way that's true. Had we not met on that hay wagon over forty years ago, look at all the fun I would have missed at the county fair![19]

Sharon and Michael Marx of Ringle, Wisconsin, met on the midway at the Wisconsin Valley Fair in August 1981 and married the next November. Today they operate the dairy and beef farm where Michael grew up. Sharon said, "We both are very much involved with the very same 'fair' where we first met. He has been on the fair board as a director since November 2011. I am the 'fair photographer.' We love the fair and all it represents."[20]

According to Gay Ruby of Pewaukee, her love story began at the Wisconsin State Fair in 1970, where she was the Fairest of the Fair and future husband Jake was the son of the draft horse superintendent. Gay lived in the Administration Building with a chaperone during the fair. As she recalled,

> Every morning, our first stop was the Flower Building for a fresh corsage. Every day, I greeted fairgoers and handed out prize ribbons. Every afternoon, the various fair "queens" rode in the afternoon parade, seated on the benches of wagons pulled by draft horses.
>
> The first time I saw Jake was when he and his father drove their six-horse hitch into the arena. I was smitten and was excited when a couple of days later I rode on the Ruby Realty wagon with him!
>
> After the fair, Jake wanted to ask me out, so he called the fair office and told them I had left my gloves on the wagon and he needed my telephone number so he could return them. They gave him my number and our romance began. He also dated another fair queen during the same time period, but by Christmas 1970, we were committed to each other.
>
> We married in 1973 . . . had two children . . . spent eight years in California and Washington State where Jake managed fairs . . . and we now live in the town of Delafield, savoring our three grandchildren and our memories of how and where our love began. Truly was a magical way to meet someone and fall in love![21]

# 16

# THE VALUE AND LEGACY OF FAIRS

As times have changed, fairs have changed as well. Some once-popular fairs, such as those in the communities of Stanley and New London, didn't last. But those that have persisted—some for well more than a century—have adapted to changing times by offering new activities and entertainment to keep audiences coming. In fact, fairs have always been a place where people could see and try things they had never experienced before, from innovations in household and farming equipment to the first airplane rides.

Requiring the efforts of many dedicated, passionate people to make them happen, some fairs have been done in by disagreements over location selection, funding sources, and property maintenance. With rising costs and dropping attendance, some have had to find new sources of income, such as renting out fairgrounds or buildings for other events throughout the year.

Financial challenges have always loomed, caused by everything from bad weather to wars, recessions, depressions, and disease epidemics. Population decline in some counties has resulted in fewer exhibitors and fewer visitors. But as one former fair board member said, "We are hanging on." With a slim percentage of the US population living on farms, some might call county fairs a relic of the past. Why is it important for them to continue?

The primary goal of Wisconsin's first fairs was the improvement of agriculture. At that time, the majority of the population lived on farms. It was a time before there were agricultural colleges, county agents, and university agricultural research stations, a time before radio provided information for farmers, a time when few people even had telephones. Farmsteads were often a

Onlookers watch demonstrations of new farm equipment, including the Farmall F-12 tractor, at the Wisconsin State Fair, 1935.
WHI IMAGE ID 66464

half mile or more apart, and transportation consisted of a long journey in a cart pulled by oxen or perhaps a horse-drawn buggy. Yet farmers knew their neighbors and willingly shared their farming knowledge.

Agricultural societies recognized that hosting a fair was an organized way to bring country people to together to learn from one another. If a farmer planted a new variety of oats or discovered a plow that worked well in stony ground, he was usually more than willing to share that information. An element of competition didn't hurt, either. Country people gathered to learn who had the best corn, best hog, best draft horse or cow. By exhibiting their farm produce and livestock, and having it judged and ranked, farmers could see how their efforts and methods stacked up to others.

A stunt car act thrills the crowd at the Dane County Fair, 1930.
WHI IMAGE ID 20149

From these humble beginnings, fairs became a community gathering place and social experience. Some folks who lived on opposite ends of the county saw one another only at the annual fair. Stories were shared and memories recalled. Fairs soon added entertainment for rural people who, beyond their church gatherings and country school events, had few such opportunities. From the early days, when horse racing and then a modest carnival were the most popular draws, to today's fairs featuring car races, *American Idol*–style talent shows, giant roller coasters, and big-name artists in the grandstand, fairs bring spark and excitement to the lives of hardworking farm people.

Kari Ruf, onetime member of the Fayette Go-Getters 4-H and Darlington FFA and now the manager of the Lafayette County Fair, credits fairs with bringing "farmers, community members, businesses, and people of all ages to one place where they can eat, learn, and enjoy the world around them. . . . From the entertainment to education in the barns and floral hall, there is something for everyone. The purpose of the fairs today is one of summertime exploration and enjoyment in an otherwise nonstop swirl we call life."[1]

Youngsters learn about bugs at a UW Extension booth at the state fair.
USED WITH PERMISSION BY UW–MADISON DIVISION OF EXTENSION

Sauk County Fair Manager Liz Cook said that fairs provide "a chance to have valuable time together as friends and families build relationships. . . . As I travel to many fairs, the most memorable ones have a definite sense of community, and can share that with their guests."[2]

In the early days of fairs, pretty much everyone involved lived on farms. Today, the number of farmers in the United States has dwindled to less than 2 percent of the population, and fairs draw visitors from city and country alike. Kellie Boone, executive director of the Washington County Fair Park and Conference Center, explained, "County fairs aren't just for rural farmers—fairs have got a lot more to offer than carnival rides and a rooster crowing contest. [Fairs] provide jobs, support local businesses and other local nonprofits, build relationships, and provide education for agricultural advocacy. The fair is a place to start traditions, make memories, and capture moments. Because of this, county fairs are also an incredible opportunity for companies and organizations to extend their brand reach and connect with a diverse target audience of potential new customers."[3]

Just as they always have, fairs play a vital education role. Now that fewer and fewer people grow up with a farming background, fairs provide important hands-on experiences with farming and its relevance in people's lives. As Beth Dippel, executive director of the Sheboygan County Historical Research Center, explained, "As farming changes, a county fair remains a place for nonagriculture people to reconnect with the source of their food."[4] Denise Zirbel, Kenosha County fair manager, agreed, noting, "I believe the value of a county fair is that it provides an opportunity for agricultural education and information to be conveyed to an ever-increasing urban population in a fun, family environment."[5]

The education of young people in particular has been a focus of fairs since the passage of the Smith-Lever Act in 1914, and the creation of the Cooperative Extension Service shortly thereafter, led to youth being allowed to exhibit at fairs through 4-H and Future Farmers of America clubs. Participating in a county or state fair has now imparted valuable lessons—about farming and about life—to generations of participants. Bonnie Schmitz, a former 4-H'er whose two sons raised pygmy goats for their own 4-H projects, explained that her boys "learned more than animal caretaking. They learned how to deal with people, working at the food stand, sometimes serving customers, and working back in the kitchen with the hot, oily, sticky atmosphere. Sometimes they worked in the petting zoo helping kids learn to love animals. And sometimes they escaped and got to have fun with the rides and hanging out with friends."[6]

Debbie Crave, now vice president of Crave Brothers Farmstead Cheese, grew up in Beloit and was a ten-year member of the Turtle 4-H Club in Rock County. She described her fair activities as a way to "truly 'learn by doing'—the 4-H slogan. . . . I remember one time I sewed the legs of my pants together by accident, instead of sewing the pant leg seam." She continued,

> It took forever to pull all those stitches out and start over. I think I always did one thing wrong before I did two things right. . . . I sewed pillows and wall hangings, a blazer, vest, and skirt! I knitted slippers and hats, and I baked breads and cakes and cookies. But I think my best project was flowers. I loved flower arranging. My mother guided me and helped me learn the best flowers to grow like zinnias and baby's breath, how to harden and prepare flowers for arranging, and how to put together a beautiful centerpiece. After several years of practicing and planting, it all came together for me. I received three merit awards

The lessons learned from raising, preparing, and showing an animal are varied and impossible to measure.
PHOTO BY STEVE APPS

on my flower arrangements at the county fair my last year in 4-H! The merit award was like a grand champion ribbon![7]

Megan Busse, a third-generation 4-H'er who exhibited at the Kenosha County Fair, recalled one lesson she learned from a judge that has never left her:

One year, I made a quick bread for the first time—and I burned the living daylights out of it. The top and sides were crispy black and the middle was raw. I told my mother that I wasn't bringing it to the fair. She informed me that I was bringing it to fair and that I was going to ask the judge what I did wrong. (Kenosha has face-to-face youth judging, which I've found to be a fantastic learning experience). So I set off to the fair with my raw, burnt banana bread. I learned from the judge that I should cover it with foil until the last few minutes of baking. I got a third place ribbon and a life lesson. And I haven't burned a loaf since![8]

Wisconsin Public Radio host Larry Meiller belonged to the Hope 4-H Club and took individual projects to the Stoughton and Dane County Fairs. He credits fairs with teaching him not only gardening, leather craft, and cooking skills but also "how to work with others, how to imagine and build an exhibit, how to express myself in front of a group." As he noted, "[T]he skills I learned I have used my entire life."[9]

Timothy Casucci, former 4-H member in Rock County and today a graphic designer in Madison, cited similar valuable skills learned from creating projects for exhibiting at the Rock County Fair:

> I gained the ability to decide what a project was going to be, how to plan and create it. . . . I learned how to listen to instructions and suggestions and apply them to reach the result I wanted. I learned how to stick with a project and meet a deadline and then put myself out there for constructive criticism and listen and learn from doing it. I learned how to improve on what I had done even if a project won a blue ribbon. This knowledge is repeated constantly today with my creation and presentation of visual work as a graphic designer. I learned to be humble in winning and to learn from lesser results.[10]

Rick Daluge, assistant dean emeritus and former director of the Farm Short Course at the University of Wisconsin College of Agricultural and Life Sciences, joined 4-H at age ten in Rock County and participated for nine years. He recalled one important life skill that kids for generations have learned on the midway: spending time at the fair "taught me how to budget my money—twenty dollars was expected to feed me at the fair for five days!"[11] Timothy Casucci echoed this sentiment, recounting how his fair experiences taught him to "manage my meager pocket money. If I threw away all my money on the midway, I couldn't have a cheeseburger and a coke when I was hungry."[12]

In some cases the lessons learned through the fair experience were painful, even when they were a fundamental part of farming life. Betty Lassa-Blauvelt shared the story of her twelve-year-old daughter Theresa's heartbreak after raising a calf as a 4-H project for the Central Wisconsin State Fair. "Theresa fell in love with him at first sight," she recalled. "He was a seventy-pound bundle of mouse-colored fur, and she named him Smokey. She spent all of her free time sitting curled up with him talking, petting and loving him.

For some fairgoers, the sights, sounds, and flavors of the fair are worth every hard-earned penny.
WHI IMAGE ID 87599

During the spring and summer she walked Smokey all around the farm and even up the steps into the house. Smokey was never without food in his pan or eating out of someone's hand."

Then the day came to haul the animals to the fairgrounds. "For Sale signs were hung on the pens, and Theresa and Smokey settled in for the night," Lassa-Blauvelt remembered. "For five days, the two of them were inseparable. Smokey was very well behaved in the show ring and obeyed Theresa's every command. He won a blue ribbon and received much attention and praise."

A few days later, Theresa ran up to her mother, sobbing her heart out. "I jumped out of the truck and ran over to her. Kneeling down in front of her, I said, 'What's the matter? What happened?' In between heart-wrenching sobs, she blurted out, 'I----sold----Smokey!' With the help of her brothers, we learned the details of the sale.

"The excitement and enthusiasm of competition [had] blurred the fact that the purpose of raising these fine animals was to sell them. The impact hit

Cattle judging at the state fair, circa 1960
WHI IMAGE ID 26225

Theresa when she realized Smokey would not be going home with her." A short time later, Smokey's buyers pulled up in their cattle trailer and introduced themselves. "They soothed Theresa's broken heart by assuring her that they would take very good care of Smokey. They planned to use him to sire more calves just like himself."[13]

Many people attribute skills gained through their fair experiences with opening doors to a job or future career path. Kari Ruf recalled that she started working at the fair at age fifteen. "That turned into a first place FFA State Proficiency award for Agriculture Communications and [was] where I learned my passion for sharing the agriculture story. I now work full time in agriculture communications. I never left the fair, either. Now, seventeen years later, I still spend my summers there."[14]

Bambi Butzlaff Voss was a 4-H member from ages nine to nineteen in the 1970s and exhibited every year at the Dodge County Fair. She recalled,

> I lived for fair days and always entered beef cattle. I was able to sell them at the meat animal auction to pay for college. One of my most memorable stories was going to the radio tent when the local station was broadcasting live. . . I was sixteen at the time. After the interview, the announcer asked if I ever thought of going into radio work. I didn't think I could, but he explained that if I was willing to learn, I could be a radio announcer or DJ. Well, after several months of training with no pay, I finally had my own paid shift. I did radio work until I was twenty-one years old at WBEV/WXRO in Beaver Dam.[15]

Fran O'Leary, editor of the *Wisconsin Agriculturist* and former 4-H project leader and president of the Fond du Lac County 4-H Leaders Board of Directors, recounted, "Our four sons showed 4-H projects, including dairy cattle, at the Fond du Lac County Fair for twenty-six consecutive years from 1987 to 2013." All four now work in agriculture. "They were all active in 4-H," she noted, "showing dairy cattle and participating in Dairy Bowl and dairy judging. They were also active in FFA and the Junior Holstein Association. I credit this involvement with helping them decide to go to college, graduate, get jobs, and become the successful young adults they are today. Their favorite activity was always the county fair! It was as big a deal to them as Christmas—they loved every minute of it."[16]

PHOTO BY STEVE APPS

Like Fran O'Leary, other agriculture leaders point to fairs as important training ground for essential life skills. According to Greg Blonde, Waupaca County agriculture agent, these lessons include "hard work, patience, perseverance, good sportsmanship, communication, teamwork, confidence, humility, and friendship."[17] Jim Massey, the retired editor of *The Country Today*, has witnessed many farm kids leading their steers up and down country roads, getting them ready for the fair. "Those kids aren't sitting in front of a TV or playing a video game on a handheld device," he said. "They are learning self-discipline and the work ethic that you can only get by being responsible for a project. . . . The majority of the kids bringing animals to the fair take pride in their animals and how those animals perform in the show-ring. That does not come without work and sacrifice."[18]

The year 2020 will likely be seen as the worst year ever for fairs. Many county fairs and the Wisconsin State Fair were forced to cancel due to the COVID-19 pandemic, as for much of the year almost all public gatherings were cancelled, replaced with "virtual" community events, church services, and school lessons conducted online. But if the history of fairs can be considered a predictor of the future, fairs will persevere.

Fairs continue to meet their original mission of improving and educating about agricultural practices, but they provide participants far more than that. As a writer for the *Fond du Lac County Reporter* wrote, the purpose of fairs is not only to educate but "to help people learn about life and what is good, to find out what is profitable and what is enjoyable, and to learn how to adjust better to change, how to be better people, how to be responsible and better citizens, and how to be more self-sufficient."[19] And as *Agri-View* editor Julie Belschner put it, "County fairs are a reflection of the heart of America—farmers. I hope one hundred years from now they will still connect children to the roots of our nation." May we all continue to attend them, support them, and appreciate their value in our lives and our history.[20]

# NOTES

## CHAPTER 1

1. *Merriam-Webster*, s.v. "feria (*n.*)," www.merriam-webster.com/dictionary/feria.

2. *Encyclopaedia Brittanica Online*, s.v. "Fair," www.britannica.com/topic/fair.

3. International Association of Fairs and Expositions, "History of Fairs," www.fairsandexpos.com/eweb/DynamicPage.aspx?Site=iafe&WebCode=History.

4. *Encyclopaedia Brittanica Online*, s.v. "Fair."

5. Durham, CT, Patch, "A Rich History: American Agricultural Fairs," https://patch.com/connecticut/durham/a-rich-history-american-agricultural-fairs.

6. Philadelphia Society for Promoting Agriculture, "Overview," https://pspaonline.com/history/overview.

7. Ned Oliver, "First Agricultural Fair Revisted," *Berkshire Eagle*, November 3, 2011.

8. Personal correspondence from Tim Casucci, July 8, 2019.

9. Russell Gasch, *The Calumet County Fair: 1856 to 1988* (Chilton, WI: Calumet County Fair, 1988).

10. Charles D. Byrne, "Present County Fairs Founded on Primitive Early Exhibits," *Wisconsin State Journal*, Sunday, September 10, 1922.

11. Laws of Wisconsin, 1856 Legislature, Act 74, Chapter 74, Sections 1, 2, 3 & 6, May 14, 1856. https://docs.legis.wisconsin.gov/1856/related/acts/74.pdf.

12. Laws of Wisconsin, 1856 Legislature, Act 74.

13. Laws of Wisconsin, 1856 Legislature, Act 74.

14. Joseph Schafer, *A History of Agriculture in Wisconsin* (Madison, WI: State Historical Society of Wisconsin, 1922), p. 113.

15. Byrne, "Present County Fairs."

16. Byrne, "Present County Fairs."

17. Robert C. Nesbit, *The History of Wisconsin: Volume III: Urbanization and Industrialization, 1873–1893* (Madison, WI: State Historical Society of Wisconsin, 1985), pp. 23–25.

## CHAPTER 2

1. Jerry Apps, *Wisconsin Agriculture: A History* (Madison, WI: Wisconsin Historical Society Press, 2015), p. 80.
2. Apps, *Wisconsin Agriculture*, pp. 80–84.
3. Apps, *Wisconsin Agriculture*, p. 120.
4. Apps, *Wisconsin Agriculture*, pp. 102–107.
5. Personal correspondence from Nancy Franz, May 19, 2019.
6. Personal correspondence from Guy Dutcher, May 17, 2019.
7. Personal correspondence from Barbara Rogan, July 12, 2019.
8. Sherry Kelley, "Past Fair Secretary Van Loon Looks Forward to 140th Waushara County Fair," *Waushara Argus*, August 2015.
9. Personal correspondence from Nancy Franz, May 19, 2019.
10. Abigail Martin, "Volunteers: The Hands That Make the Fair Go Round," *Wisconsin Agriculturist*, August 2019.
11. Memorandum of Understanding between Lincoln County (WI) 4-H Leaders' Association, Inc., and Lincoln County (WI) Fair Association, 2012.

## CHAPTER 3

1. "Green County Fair History," www.greencountyfair.net/pageserver/history.
2. E. R. McIntyre, *Fifty Years of Cooperative Extension* (Madison, WI: Wisconsin Cooperative Extension Service, 1962), p. 189.
3. Jerry Apps, *The People Came First* (Madison, WI: University of Wisconsin Extension, 2002), p. 38.
4. Apps, *The People Came First*, p. 39.
5. Apps, *The People Came First*, p. 51.
6. Apps, *The People Came First*, p. 51.
7. Floyd Doering, David R. Laatsch, and Brenda R. Scheel, *100 Years of Strengthening Agricultural Education Since 1917: The Smith Hughes Act* (Madison, WI: Wisconsin Association of Agricultural Educators, 2017), p. 5.
8. Doering, Laatsch, and Scheel, *100 Years*, p. 8.
9. *Premium Book*, Clark County Fair, Neillsville, WI, 2019, from the author's collection.
10. *Premium Book*, Clark County Fair.
11. Personal correspondence from Joan Palmer, August 27 and September 10, 2019.
12. Personal correspondence from Cathy and Tim Wiesbrook, June 12, 2019.

## CHAPTER 4

1. Steve Waller, "Danish Judging System," www.annettfarms.com/html/danish_judging__system.html.
2. Personal correspondence from Linda Kustka, September 6, 2019.
3. Ila Sanders, "Blue-Ribbon Judgment," *Our Wisconsin*, August/September 2016.
4. Personal correspondence from Nancy Franz, May 19, 2019.
5. Interview with Pat Ritchie, August 16, 2019, at the Waushara County Fair.
6. Interview with Dale Simonson, August 18, 2019, at the Waushara County Fair.
7. Personal correspondence from Ronna Ballmer, June 4, 2019.
8. Personal correspondence from Kassie Schepp, May 14, 2019.
9. Personal correspondence from Jim Massey, October 8, 2019.

PHOTO BY STEVE APPS

## CHAPTER 5

1. Personal correspondence from Cyndy Hubbard, July 2, 2019.
2. Personal correspondence from Cyndy Hubbard.
3. Personal correspondence from Cyndy Hubbard, April 16, 2021.
4. Personal correspondence from Cyndy Hubbard, July 2, 2019.
5. Tom Weso, *Good Seeds: A Menominee Food Memoir* (Madison, WI: Wisconsin Historical Society Press, 2016), pp. 98–100.
6. Personal correspondence from Paul Wollangk, July 2, 2019.
7. Personal correspondence from Paul Wollangk.
8. Personal correspondence from Tim Casucci, July 8, 2019.
9. "History of Cotton Candy," www.candyhistory.net/candy-origin/cotton-candy-history.
10. "History of Cotton Candy."
11. OnMilwaukee.com, "The Wisconsin State Fair Cream Puff," https://onmilwaukee.com/seasonal/festivals/articles/wisconsin-state-fair-classics-cream-puff.html; OnMilwaukee.com, "A Few Facts about the State Fair Cream Puffs," https://onmilwaukee.com/seasonal/festivals/articles/creampufffacts15.html.
12. Gold Medal, "Where Did Funnel Cakes Come From?" www.gmpopcorn.com/resources/blog/where-did-funnel-cakes-come-from.
13. Wisconsin State Fair, "Foods On-a-Stick," https://wistatefair.com/fair/foods-on-a-stick.

## CHAPTER 6

1. Conklin Shows, "Definitions and Brief History of Carnivals and Midways," https://conko.com/history/stories/carnivals-calgary-stampede/history-carnivals-midways.html.
2. Conklin Shows, "Definitions and Brief History."
3. Doc's Midway Cookhouse, "Carnival History in America," www.docsmidwaycookhouse.com/carnival-history.
4. Interview with Amy Olson, July 22, 2019.
5. Lyn Jerde, "New Carnival Company's Owner Has Long History with Columbia County Fair," *Portage Daily Register*, July 25, 2018.
6. Personal correspondence from Julie Belschner, October 12, 2019.
7. Personal correspondence from Julie Belschner.
8. Jamie Malanowski, "The Brief History of the Ferris Wheel," *Smithsonian Magazine*, June 2015.
9. Malanowski, "Brief History."
10. Malanowski, "Brief History."

11. International Independent Showmen's Museum, "History of the Merry-Go-Round," http://showmensmuseum.org/vintage-carnival-rides/history-of-the-merry-go-round.

12. International Independent Showmen's Museum, "History of the Merry-Go-Round."

13. Curt Brown, "Minnesota History: Tilt-A-Whirl Gives Fairbault, Minn., a Historic Spin," *Star Tribune*, April 2, 2015.

14. Personal correspondence from Tim Casucci, July 8, 2019.

15. International Independent Showmen's Museum, "The Sideshow Exhibit." http://showmenmuseum.org/the-amazing-sideshows.

16. Personal correspondence from LaVonne Wier, July 5, 2019.

17. AARP, "7 Rigged Carnival Games," www.aarp.org/money/scams-fraud/info-07-2012/rigged-carnival-games.html.

18. AARP, "7 Rigged Carnival Games."

19. AARP, "7 Rigged Carnival Games."

20. Northern Wisconsin Agricultural and Mechanical Association, *Transactions of the Northern Wisconsin Agricultural and Mechanical Association, for the Years 1870, 1871, 1872 and 1873,* vol. 1 (1874), Third Annual Fair, pp. 65–66.

21. Interview with Amy Olson, July 22, 2019.

## CHAPTER 7

1. E. E. Jones, "A History of Columbia County, Wisconsin," 1914, published by *Agri-View* at www.agupdate.com May 2, 2019.

2. Columbia County fair history compiled from E. E. Jones, "A History of Columbia County, Wisconsin," 1914, published by *Agri-View* at www.agupdate.com May 2, 2019.

3. Dane County fair history compiled from Dane County Fair, "Historical Highlights," www.danecountyfair.com/pages/History.php; Alliant Energy Center, "Alliant Energy Center History," www.alliantenergycenter.com/About-Us/History#.XkMBMW5FyM8.

4. Dodge County fair history compiled from Diane Graff, "First Dodge County Fair Had Only One Building," *Watertown Daily Times*, August 18, 2012; Dodge County Fairgrounds, "Dodge County Fair," www.dodgecountyfairgrounds.com/dodge-county-fair.

5. Green County fair history compiled from Green County Fair, "Green County Fair History," http://greencountyfair.net/pageserver/history.

6. Iowa County fair history compiled from *2019 Iowa County Junior Class Fair Book,* Mineral Point, WI: Iowa County Fair Board, 2019; Iowa County Fair, "Our istory, What We're About," https://iowacountyfair.org/our-history.

7. Hoard Museum, "Jefferson County Fair," http://hoardmuseum.org/jefferson -county-fair.

8. Jefferson County fair history compiled from Hoard Museum, "Jefferson County Fair," http://hoardmuseum.org/jefferson-county-fair; Jefferson County Fair, www.jcfairpark.com/p/fair.

9. Lafayette County fair history compiled from personal correspondence from Kari Ruf, Lafayette County Fair Manager, February 10, 2020; "Lafayette Southwest Wisconsin Ag Innovation Center, Request for Proposal, 2018," Darlington, Wisconsin.

10. Lodi Agricultural Fair history compiled from Lodi Agricultural Fair Board, "History of the Lodi Fair," www.lodiagfair.com/history.html.

11. Rock County fair history compiled from Ruth Ann Montgomery, "Evansville Fairgrounds," http://evansvillehistory.net/fairgrounds.html; Carol Lohry, Scott Shaffer, and Randal Waller, "History of County 4-H Fair," in *City on the Rock River* (Janesville, WI: Janesville Historic Commission, 1998), p. 180; *50-Year History of the Rock County 4-H Fair* (Janesville, WI: Rock County 4-H Fair, 1979).

12. Sauk County fair history compiled from Sauk County Fair, "Sauk County Fair History," https://saukcountyfair.com/fair-history; personal correspondence from Liz Cook, secretary/manager, Sauk County Agricultural Society, February 14, 2020.

13. Stoughton Fair information compiled from personal correspondence from Rob White, September 12, 2019.

14. Walworth County fair history compiled from Ginny Hall, *Elkhorn History*, published by Lake Geneva Public Library, 2019; Walworth County Fair, www.walworthcountyfair.com.

## CHAPTER 8

1. Katie Tabeling, "1920 Fair Poster Sees New Life," *Kenosha News*, August 20, 2015.

2. Kenosha County fair history compiled from Roger F. Sherman, "History of Kenosha County Fair," 2012, unpublished; personal correspondence from Denise Zirbel, Kenosha County Fair manager, February 12, 2020.

3. Ozaukee County fair history compiled from Ozaukee County Fair, "History of Ozaukee County Fair," https://ozaukeecountyfair.com.history; Madeline Heim, "Ozaukee County Fair's Affordability Built on Backs of Hardworking Volunteers," *Milwaukee Journal Sentinel*, August 2, 2016.

4. Racine County fair history compiled from Burlington Historical Society, "Burlington Hosted Racine County Fair for 20-plus years," www.burlington history.org/burlington-hosted-racine-county-fair-20-plus-years.

5. Sheboygan County fair history compiled from "History of Association Which Has Given County Best Fair in the State," *Sheboygan Telegram*, August 14, 1922; Beth Dippel, "Sheboygan County Fair Marks 166th Year After Searching for a Home in Early Years," *Sheboygan Press*, September 1, 2017; personal correspondence from Beth Dippel, Sheboygan County Historical Research Center, February 15, 2020.

6. Washington County fair history compiled from Washington County Fair Park and Conference Center, "History of the Washington County Fair Park," www.wcfairpark.com/about; Judy Etta, "Celebrating 50 Years of the Livestock Auction at Washington County," *Washington County Insider*, July 22, 2019.

7. "Waukesha County, Wisconsin Geneaology," www.familysearch.org/wiki/en/Waukesha_County,_Wisconsin_Genealogy.

8. Waukesha County fair history compiled from Waukesha County Fair, www.waukeshacountyfair.com.

PHOTO BY STEVE APPS

## CHAPTER 9

1. Buffalo County Fair, "Buffalo County Agricultural Society Fair Founders," www .buffalocountyfairwi.com.

2. Pepin/Buffalo Counties fair history compiled from Sara L. Tischauser, "Pepin County Fair to Merge with Buffalo County Fair," Cannon Falls, MN, *Republican Eagle*, December 20, 2017; www.rivertowns.net/news/4376468-pepin -county-fair-merge-buffalo-county-fair; Sarah Winkelman, "Pepin County Fair Merges with Buffalo County Fair," WEAU News, www.weau.com/content/ news/Pepin-County-Fair-merges-with-Buffalo-County-Fair-490033181.html.

3. Crawford County fair history compiled from Crawford County Agricultural Society, "Agriculture and the Agricultural Society," www.usgenweb.info/ wicrawford/books/chap19.htm.

4. Grant County fair history compiled from personal correspondence from Amy Olson, Grant County Fairgrounds and Operations Director, December 11, 2019.

5. Jackson County fair history compiled from "A History of the Jackson County Fair," Jackson County Historical Society, Black River Falls, WI, 2008.

6. La Crosse County fair history compiled from La Crosse County Agricultural Society, www.lacrosseinterstatefair.com/about_us; Emily Pyrek, "Hometown History: The La Crosse Interstate Fair," *La Crosse Tribune*, July 11, 2016.

7. "Monroe County Fair Has a Long History," Tomah *Monitor-Herald*, July 27, 2009.

8. Monroe County Fair, "Learn-N-Earn Activities," www.monroecountyfairwi.com.

9. Monroe County fair history compiled from "Monroe County Fair Has a Long History," Tomah *Monitor-Herald*, July 27, 2009; personal correspondence from Shae Fox, February 28, 2020; Monroe County Fair, www.monroecounty fairwi.com.

10. Richland County fair history compiled from Richland County Fairgrounds, "Richland County Fair Sesquicentennial," https://fair.co.richland.wi.us/fair/ committe-member/history.

11. Trempealeau County fair history compiled from *Trempealeau County Fair: 125th Year* (Galesville, WI: Trempealeau County Agricultural Society, 1983); Trempealeau County Fair, www.trempealeaucountyfair.com.

12. Vernon County fair history compiled from Vernon County Fair, "History of the Fair," www.vernoncountyfair.com/history.htm.

## CHAPTER 10

1. Adams County fair history compiled from Adams County Library, "The Adams County Fair," www.adamscountylibrary.info/files/localhistory/past_present/images/00000010.pdf; www.adamscountyfairwi.com/schedule-1.

2. Central Wisconsin State Fair history compiled from Breanna Butler, "History of the Central Wisconsin State Fair," Explore Marshfield, https://exploremarshfield.com/history-central-wisconsin-state-fair; Kris Rued-Clark, *Round Barn Tales* (Marshfield, WI: Central Wisconsin State Fair Association, 2006).

3. University of Wisconsin Division of Extension, "Extension Green Lake County," https://greenlake.extension.wisc.edu/fair.

4. Green Lake County fair history compiled from "Green Lake County Fair Silver Anniversary," Agriculture Committee, Green Lake County Board, Green Lake, Wisconsin, 1963; personal correspondence from Kim Zills, December 12, 2019; University of Wisconsin Division of Extension, "Extension Green Lake County," https://greenlake.extension.wisc.edu/fair; personal correspondence from Jerry Disterhaft, Green Lake County, February 26, 2020.

5. Juneau County Fair, "About Us," www.juneaucountyfair.com/aboutus.html.

6. Juneau County fair history compiled from Juneau County Fair, "About Us," www.juneaucountyfair.com/aboutus.html; D. Paradise, "Junior County Fair Celebrates 150 Years," *Juneau County Star-Times*, August 7, 2015; J. Cuevas, "Fair History Remembered in Book," *Juneau County Star-Times*, Sept 1, 2015; Christopher Jardine, "Mauston Hosting 154th Juneau County Fair," *Juneau County Star-Times*, August 8, 2019.

7. Marquette County fair history compiled from Kathleen McGwin, *Recipe for Community* (Westfield, WI: Marquette County Historical Society, 2012), pp. 166–168; personal correspondence from Kathleen McGwin, February 15, 2020; personal correspondence from Dawn (Polcyn) Peterson, February 4, 2020.

8. New London Fair history compiled from Melinda Roberts, "Marker 559, New London Fairground," www.hmdb.org/m.asp?m=167373.

9. Portage County fair history compiled from The Portage County Fair of Amherst, WI, "About," http://amherstfair.com/about-2; Portage County Fair, "Portage County Fair, Rosholt," https://rosholtfair.com/history.

10. Waupaca County fair history compiled from Frank Haffner, "History of the Waupaca County Fair," https://waupacacountyfair.org/wp-content/uploads/2016/02/wcf-history.pdf; personal correspondence from Waupaca County Agriculture Agent Greg Blonde, February 17, 2020.

11. Waushara County fair history compiled from personal correspondence from Mary Kunasch, senior publisher, *Waushara Argus/Central WI Resorter*, May 13, 2019; personal correspondence from Dee Dee Jakubowski, Waushara County Historical Society, August 18, 2019; Phil Poullette, "100 Years of Fair Celebrations," *Waushara Argus*, August 14, 1975.

## CHAPTER 11

1. Alto Fair history compiled from Alto 4-H and Farm Bureau Fair, "73rd Annual 4-H Farm Bureau Alto Fair," altofair.com/schedule.html; Mary Bergin, "Alto Fair: Smallest in Wisconsin, Big Respect for Tradition," http://roadstraveled .com/alto-fair-smallest-in-wisconsin-big-respect-for-tradition.

2. Brown County fair history compiled from material from Mary Jane Herber and Dennis Jacobs, Brown County Library Local History and Genealogy Department, Green Bay, WI; Brown County Fair, www.browncountyfair.com.

3. Calumet County fair history compiled from Calumet County Fair, www.calumet-countyfair.com and www.calumetcountyfair.com/fair_history.html; Russell Gasch, *The Calumet County Fair: 1856 to 1988* (Chilton, WI: Calumet County Fair, 1988); Renee Gasch, *Calumet County Fair History* (Brillion, WI: Zander Press, 2006); personal correspondence from Clara Hendrich, March 27, 2020.

4. Hjalmar Holand, *History of Door County: The County Beautiful*. Chicago: S. J. Clarke Publishing, 1917.

5. Door County fair history compiled from Destination Door County, "Door County Fair," www.doorcounty.com/business-directory/door-county-fair; Robert Johnson, "Traveling Back: County Fair Success Due to More than Simple Competition," *Green Bay Press Gazette*, August 2, 2019; "Eight Things to Know for the 150th Annual Door County Fair," *Green Bay Press Gazette*, July 25, 2021.

6. Tina Kohlman, "Fond du Lac County Fair Has Rich History," *Fond du Lac County Reporter*, July 18, 2015.

7. Fond du Lac County fair history compiled from personal correspondence from Tina Kohlman, February 17, 2020; "Fond du Lac County Fairgrounds," www .fdlco.wi.gov/departments/departments-f-m/fairgrounds.

8. Kendra Meinert, "Big Concerts Big Part of Kewaunee Fair's 100 years," *Green Bay Press Gazette,* July 20, 2017

9. Kewaukee County fair history compiled from "County Fair 60 Years Old," *Kewaunee Enterprise*, August 19, 1932; Kendra Meinert, "Big Concerts Big Part of Kewaunee Fair's 100 years," *Green Bay Press Gazette*, July 20, 2017; "About," Kewaukee County Fair, Facebook, www.facebook.com/pages/category/ Performance---Event-Venue/Kewaunee-County-Fair-1439430882936888.

10. Robert M. Dessureau, *History of Langlade County, Wisconsin* (Antigo, WI: Berner Brothers Publishing Company, 1922), pp. 90–91.

11. Langlade County fair history compiled from Langlade County Fair, www.langladecountyfair.net/p/about.

12. Manitowoc County Historical Society, "William Rahr and the 1906 County Fair," www.manitowoccountyhistory.org/stories/2017/8/16/william-rahr-and -the-country-fair.

13. Manitowoc County fair history compiled from Manitowoc County Historical Society, "William Rahr and the 1906 County Fair," www.manitowoccounty history.org/stories/2017/8/16/william-rahr-and-the-country-fair; Manitowoc County Fair Brew Competition, https://manitowoccountyexpo.brewcomp.com.

14. Marinette County fair history compiled from "History of the Fair," news release to the *Marinette Eagle Star*, April 29, 1981, submitted by Nancy Servais, head secretary, UW–Madison Extension Marinette County, April 8, 2020;

PHOTO BY STEVE APPS

"Marinette County Fair," www.marinettecountyfair.com; "Wausaukee History," www.wausaukee.com/assets/wausaukee-wi-history-page-5.pdf.

15. Oconto County fair history compiled from Oconto County Fair, www.oconto countyfair.org; William Benjamin Henry, "The History of Oconto County" (bachelor of arts thesis, University of Wisconsin–Madison, 1921).

16. "Seymour's First Fair an Unprecedented Triumph," *Appleton Post*, October 15, 1885.

17. Outagamie County fair history compiled from "Seymour's First Fair an Unprecedented Triumph," *Appleton Post*, October 15, 1885; personal correspondence from William Collar, September 10, 2019.

18. Shawano County fair history compiled from personal correspondence from Jesse Borien, curator, Shawano County Historical Society, January 30, 2020.

19. Richard J. Harney, *History of Winnebago County, Wisconsin, and Early History of the Northwest* (Oshkosh, WI: Hicks Book Printers, 1880), pp. 130–131.

20. *Transactions: Northern Wisconsin Agricultural and Mechanics Association*, Oshkosh, WI, January 1, 1873.

21. *Transactions: Northern Wisconsin Agricultural and Mechanics Association*, Oshkosh, WI, January 1, 1874.

22. *Transactions*, January 1, 1874.

23. Winnebago County fair history compiled from Harlan Hirschy, *The Winnebago County Fair: 150 Years Old in 2005* (Oshkosh, WI: Winnebago Fair Association, 2005), p. 5; *Proceedings of the Board of Supervisors of Winnebago County*, Oshkosh, WI, March 1911; untitled article in *Oshkosh Daily Northwestern*, September 7, 1965; Winnebago County, "Sunnyview Expo Center," www .co.winnebago.wi.us/sites/default/files/uploaded-files/expo_booklet_0.pdf; Winnebago County Fair, https://winnebagocountyfaironline.com.

## CHAPTER 12

1. Family Search wiki, "Ashland County, Wisconsin, Genealogy," www.family search.org/wiki/en/Ashland_County,_Wisconsin_Genealogy.

2. Ashland County fair history compiled from Ashland County Fair, www.ashland cofair.org; "Historic Ashland: There's a Lot of History behind the Ashland County Fair," Ashland *Times-Gazette*, September 17, 2011, www.times-gazette .com/article/20110917/NEWS/309179573.

3. "Annual Report of the Bayfield Agricultural Agent, Washburn, 1939," http://digi coll.library.wisc.edu/cgi-bin/WI/WI-idx?type=browse&scope=WI.BayfiCoAA.

4. Bayfield County fair history compiled from Bayfield County, Wisconsin, Podcast Episode 24: "Local Fare and the Bayfield County Fair," bayfieldcounty.org;

Wisconsin State Agricultural Society, *Transactions of the Wisconsin State Agricultural Society Together with Short-Hand Report of Annual Convention*, vol. 34 (Madison, WI: Democrat Printing Company, State Printers, 1896), http://digital.library.wisc.edu/1711.dl/WI.WSASv34; "Bayfield County Fair," www.bayfieldcounty.org/244/Bayfield-County-Fair.

5. Clark County fair history compiled from Wisconsin Department of Tourism, "Clark County Fair," www.travelwisconsin.com/events/fairs-festivals/clark-county-fair-42623; personal correspondence from Natalie K. Erpenbach, Administrator, 1897 Clark County Jail Museum, Inc., October 10, 2019, and October 26, 2019; *Clark County Fair Centennial: 1872–1972* (Neillsville, WI: Clark County Fair Board, Centennial Committee, 1972); "2020 Clark County Fair Cancelled," centralwisconsinnews.com, June 16, 2020.

6. Douglas County fair history compiled from interview with Pat Luostari, March 16, 2020; Head of the Lakes Fairgrounds, http://headofthelakesfairgrounds.com.

7. Florence County fair history compiled from Florence County GenWeb Project, https://sites.rootsweb.com/~wifloren; www.florencecountyfair.com.

8. Forest County fair history compiled from Wisconsin Department of Tourism, "Forest County Fair," www.travelwisconsin.com/events/fairs-festivals/forest-county-fair-42514.

9. Interview with Eugene Luoma, February 4, 2020.

10. Iron County fair history compiled from Iron County Fair, http://ironcountyfair.net; interview with Eugene Luoma, Saxon, February 4, 2020.

11. Lincoln County fair history compiled from *Lincoln County 4-H Free Fair Centennial:1888–1988* (Merrill, WI: UW Extension, 1988); Lincoln County Fair Association, lincolncofair.com.

12. Oneida County fair history compiled from personal correspondence from fair board member and historian Kerry Bloedorn, February 23, 2020; Kris Gilbertson, "Once One of the Best, Fair is No More," *Rhinelander Daily News*, August 28, 1978; Michael Skubal, "Oneida County Fair," *Rhinelander Daily News*, July 31, August 1, 2010; Oconto County Fair, www.ocfairwi.com.

13. Price County fair history compiled from personal correspondence from Peter Dahlie, chairman, Price County Fair Board, December 2, 2019.

14. Henry Gannett, *The Origin of Certain Place Names in the United States* (Washington, DC: Government Printing Office, 1905), p. 135.

15. Katharine Woodrow Dresden, "History of Rusk County, Wisconsin" (master of arts thesis, University of Wisconsin–Madison, 1931). p. 53.

16. Rusk County fair history compiled from Katharine Woodrow Dresden, "History of Rusk County, Wisconsin"; Rusk County Jr. Fair, www.ruskcountyjrfair.com.

17. Sawyer County Historical Society and Museum, www.sawyercountyhist.org/sawyer-county.

18. Lake-Link, Inc., "Sawyer County Lakes," www.lake-link.com/wisconsin-lakes/sawyer-county/782/.

19. Sawyer County fair history compiled from Sawyer County Fair, www.sawyer countyfair.org; Hayward Area Chamber of Commerce, https://hayward areachamber.com/events.

20. Taylor County, "Taylor County Courthouse History," www.co.taylor.wi.us/your-government/history; Gordon Ruesch and Stephen Lars Kalmon, eds., *Our Home—Taylor County Wisconsin—A Topical History of Our Roots* (Medford, WI: Taylor County History Project, 2014).

21. Taylor County fair history compiled from Taylor County Fair, http://witaylor countyfair.com.

22. Vilas County fair history compiled from Vilas County Fair, "History of Fairs," https://vilascountyfair.com/general-information/history-of-fairs.

23. Wisconsin Valley Fair history compiled from Wisconsin Valley Fair, "History," www.wisconsinvalleyfair.com/p/about/285; personal correspondence from Diane Lotter, Sponsorship and Marketing, Wisconsin Valley Fair, February 2, 2020.

## CHAPTER 13

1. Barron County fair history compiled from Barron County Fair, www.barron countyfair.com.

2. University of Wisconsin–River Falls, "Brief History of Burnett County, Wisconsin," www.uwrf.edu/AreaResearchCenter/BurnettHistory.cfm.

3. Burnett County fair history compiled from Burnett County Agricultural Society Fair, www.burnettcoagfair.com; Central Burnett County Fair, https://cbcfair.org.

4. Dunn County fair history compiled from Dunn County Fair, "Dunn County Fair History," https://dunncountyfair.org.

5. Eau Claire County fair history compiled from personal communication from Debbie Kitchen, fair coordinator, March 5, 2020; Eau Claire County Fair, "Fair History," http://eauclairecountyfair.com/fair-history.html.

6. Dan Lyksett, "Northern Wisconsin State Fair: Fair Bit of History," Eau Claire *Leader-Telegram*, July 8, 2015.

7. Chippewa County fair history compiled from Dan Lyksett, "Northern Wisconsin State Fair: Fair Bit of History," Eau Claire *Leader-Telegram*, July 8, 2015;

PHOTO BY STEVE APPS

Chippewa County Tourism Council, "Northern Wisconsin State Fair," http://chippewacounty.com/business/eat/northern-wisconsin-state-fair; Northern Wisconsin State Fairgrounds Association, "Northern Wisconsin State Fair," www.nwsfa.com/events/2020/northern-wisconsin-state-fair.

8. Pierce County fair history compiled from Pierce County Historical Association, "1850–1890," https://piercecountyhistorical.org/county-history/1850-1900; Wisconsin Department of Tourism, "Pierce County Fair," www.travelwisconsin .com/events/fairs-festivals/pierce-county-fair-43978; personal correspondence from Ann M. Webb, Pierce County Fair manager, March 17, 2020.

9. Polk County fair history compiled from personal correspondence from Russ Hanson, March 23, 2020, which included notes from local historian Earl Sanford; E. E. Husband, "Echoes from the Past," *Polk County Press*, 1953; Polk County Fair, https://polkcountyfair.com/about.

10. Ad in the *Stanley Republican*, September 11, 1914.

11. Stanley Fair history compiled from *Stanley: Our Town, 1881–1981* (Stanley, WI: Stanley Historical Society, 1981), pp. 189–191.

12. St. Croix County fair history compiled from St. Croix County Fair, "Over 125 Years of St. Croix County History," http://stcroixcofair.com/fairgrounds-history; Wisconsin Department of Tourism, "St. Croix County Fair," www.travelwisconsin.com/events/fairs-festivals/st-croix-county-fair-43979.

13. Washburn County fair history compiled from personal correspondence from Linda Degner, January 28, 2020, and February 20, 2020. Linda drew from the *Washburn County Register*, *Spooner Advocate*, *The Country Today*, and Washburn County Fair Board minutes.

## CHAPTER 14

1. Richard N. Current, *The History of Wisconsin, Volume II: The Civil War Era, 1848–1873* (Madison, WI: State Historical Society of Wisconsin, 1976), pp. 92–93.

2. Jerry Zimmerman, *150 Years of the Wisconsin State Fair: 1851–2001* (West Allis, WI: Wisconsin State Fair Park, 2001).

3. *Transactions of the Wisconsin State Agricultural Society* (Madison, WI: Beriah Brown, State Printer, 1852), pp. 13–16.

4. *Transactions*, p. 16; Joseph Schafer, *A History of Agriculture in Wisconsin* (Madison, WI: State Historical Society of Wisconsin, 1922), p. 113.

5. Personal correspondence from Jenna Jorgenson, Competitive Exhibits, Wisconsin State Fair, February 3, 2020.

6. Wisconsin Historical Society, "Wisconsin State Fair, Image Gallery Essay," www.wisconsinhistory.org/org/Records/Article/CS3963; Wisconsin Public Radio, "A Look Back at the History of the Wisconsin State Fair," www.wpr.org/look-back-history-wisconsin-state-fair.

7. US Department of Agriculture, National Agricultural Library, "Lincoln's Milwaukee Speech," www.nal.usda.gov/lincolns-milwaukee-speech.

8. Zimmerman, *150 Years of the Wisconsin State Fair*; "History of the Wisconsin State Fair," WISN 12 News, June 30, 2009, www.wisn.com/article/history-of-the-wisconsin-state-fair/6294484.

9. Zimmerman, *150 Years of the Wisconsin State Fair*.

10. Zimmerman, *150 Years of the Wisconsin State Fair*.

11. Wisconsin State Fair, "History of the Milwaukee Mile," http://wistatefair.com/wsfp/wp-content/uploads/2013/02/Milwaukee-Mile-History.pdf.

12. Zimmerman, *150 Years of the Wisconsin State Fair*; University of Wisconsin Division of Extension, "Timeline of Wisconsin 4-H History," https://blogs.extension.wisc.edu/4hcentennial/history.

13. *The Wisconsin Century Book* (Milwaukee, WI: Wisconsin Centennial Exposition, 1948).

14. *The Wisconsin Century Book*, pp. 5, 88–89.

15. Chris Foran, "In 1968, the Wisconsin State Fair Made Grandstand Shows Free—With Mixed Results," *Milwaukee Journal Sentinel*, August 7, 2018.

16. Foran, "In 1968."

17. Blaine Schultz, "Wisconsin State Fair: A Brief History," *Shepherd Express*, July 18, 2019, https://shepherdexpress.com/arts-and-entertainment/ae-feature/wisconsin-state-fair-a-brief-history.

18. Personal correspondence from Kristi Chuckel, Director of Public Affairs, Wisconsin State Fair Park, February 20, 2020.

PHOTO BY STEVE APPS

19. Matt Muller, "Here's the Menu for the Final Week of the State Fair Drive-thru," onmilwaukee.com, August 12, 2020, https://onmilwaukee.com/articles/state-fair-drive-thru-menus.

## CHAPTER 15

1. Personal correspondence from Pam Jahnke, September 20, 2019.

2. Tom Weso, *Good Seeds: A Menominee Food Memoir* (Madison, WI: Wisconsin Historical Society Press, 2016), pp. 98–100.

3. Personal correspondence from Kassie Schepp, May 14, 2019.

4. Personal correspondence from Julie Belschner, October 12, 2019.

5. Personal correspondence from Betty Lassa-Blauvelt, September 1, 2019.

6. Personal correspondence from Pam Jahnke.

7. Personal correspondence from Phyllis Sonsalla, October 10, 2019.

8. Personal correspondence from Cheryl Ehrke, June 30, 2019.

9. Personal correspondence from Martin J. Wolf and Diana Wolf Braza, June 26, 2019.

10. Personal correspondence from Lynda Ketelboeter, May 20, 2019.

11. Personal correspondence from Larry Meiller, October 14, 2019.

12. Personal correspondence from Linda Kustka, September 6, 2019.

13. Personal correspondence from Linda Kustka.

14. Personal correspondence from Melanie Miller, June 12, 2019.

15. Personal correspondence from Debbie Crave, July 11, 2019.

16. Personal correspondence from Shirley Baumann, April 30, 2019.

17. Personal correspondence from Nyla Musser, October 6, 2019.

18. Personal correspondence from Vickie Schwann, November 18, 2019, and phone interview November 21, 2019.

19. Personal correspondence from Colleen Kottke, October 10, 2019.

20. Personal correspondence from Sharon Marx, June 24, 2019.

21. Personal correspondence from Gay Ruby, May 21, 2019.

## CHAPTER 16

1. Personal correspondence from Kari Ruf, February 5, 2020.

2. Personal correspondence from Liz Cook, February 12, 2020.

3. Personal correspondence from Kellie Boone, February 14, 2020.

4. Personal correspondence from Beth Dippel, February 16, 2020.

5. Personal correspondence from Denise Zirbel, December 4, 2019.

6. Personal correspondence from Bonnie Schmitz, October 15, 2019.

7. Personal correspondence from Debbie Crave, July 11, 2019.

8. Personal correspondence from Megan Busse, July 1, 2019.

9. Personal correspondence from Larry Meiller, October 14, 2019.

10. Personal correspondence from Timothy Casucci, November 29, 2019.

11. Personal correspondence from Rick Daluge, July 28, 2019.

12. Personal correspondence from Timothy Casucci, November 29, 2019.

13. Personal correspondence from Betty Lassa-Blauvelt, September 3, 2019.

14. Personal correspondence from Kari Ruf, February 5, 2020.

15. Personal correspondence from Bambi Butzlaff Voss, June 4, 2019.

16. Personal correspondence from Fran O'Leary, October 17, 2019.

17. Personal correspondence from Greg Blonde, February 27, 2020.

18. Personal correspondence from Jim Massey, November 8, 2019.

19. Tina Kohlman, "Fond du Lac County Fair Has Rich History," *Fond du lac County Reporter*, July 18, 2015.

20. Personal correspondence from Julie Belschner, October 12, 2019.

PHOTO BY STEVE APPS

# SELECTED BIBLIOGRAPHY

For a complete list of Wisconsin fairs, including planned dates and links to individual fairs' websites, visit www.wifairs.com.

## BOOKS

Apps, Jerry. *The People Came First*. Madison, WI: University of Wisconsin–Extension, 2002.

Apps, Jerry. *Wisconsin Agriculture: A History*. Madison, WI: The Wisconsin Historical Society Press, 2015.

Current, Richard N. *The History of Wisconsin, Volume II: The Civil War Era, 1848–1873*. Madison, WI: The State Historical Society of Wisconsin, 1976.

Dessureau, Robert M. *History of Langlade County, Wisconsin*. Antigo, WI: Berner Brothers Publishing Company, 1922.

Doering, Floyd, David R. Laatsch, and Brenda R. Scheel. *100 Years of Strengthening Agricultural Education Since 1917: The Smith Hughes Act*. Madison, WI: Wisconsin Association of Agricultural Educators, 2017.

Harney, Richard J. *History of Winnebago County, Wisconsin, and Early History of the Northwest*. Oshkosh, WI: Hicks Book Printers, 1880.

Holand, Hjalmar. *History of Door County: The County Beautiful*. Chicago: S. J. Clarke Publishing, 1917

McGwin, Kathleen. *Recipe for Community*. Montello, WI: Marquette County Historical Society, 2012.

McIntyre, E. R. *Fifty Years of Cooperative Extension*. Madison, WI: Wisconsin Cooperative Extension, 1962.

Nesbit, Robert C. *The History of Wisconsin: Volume III: Urbanization and Industrialization, 1873–1893*. Madison, WI: The State Historical Society of Wisconsin, 1985.

Reck, Franklin M. *The 4-H Story: A History of 4-H Club Work.* Ames, Iowa: The Iowa State College Press, 1951.

Schaefer, Joseph. *A History of Agriculture in Wisconsin.* Madison, WI: State Historical Society of Wisconsin, 1922.

*Stanley: Our Town, 1881–1981.* Stanley, WI: Stanley Historical Society, 1981.

Weso, Tom. *Good Seeds: A Menominee Food Memoir.* Madison, WI: Wisconsin Historical Society Press, 2016.

*The Wisconsin Century Book.* Milwaukee, WI: Wisconsin Centennial Exposition, 1948.

Zimmerman, Jerry. *150 Years of the Wisconsin State Fair: 1851–2001.* West Allis, WI: Wisconsin State Fair Park, 2001.

## PERIODICALS

*Appleton Post* (Appleton, Wisconsin), Thursday, October 15, 1885.

Brown, Curt. "Minnesota History: Tilt-A-Whirl gives Fairbault, Minn., a Historic Spin." *Star Tribune,* April 2, 2015.

Byrne, Charles D. "Present County Fairs Founded on Primitive Early Exhibits." *Wisconsin State Journal,* Sunday, September 10, 1922.

Dippel, Beth. "Sheboygan County Fair Marks 166th Year After Searching for a Home in Early Years." *Sheboygan Press,* September 1, 2017.

Etta, Judy. "Celebrating 50 Years of the Livestock Auction at Washington County." *Washington County Insider,* July 22, 2019.

"Fair History Remembered in Book." *Juneau County Star-Times,* September 1, 2015.

Gilbertson, Kris. "Once One of the Best, Fair Is No More." *Rhinelander Daily News,* August 28, 1978.

Graff, Diane. "First Dodge County Fair Had Only One Building." *Watertown Daily Times,* August 18, 2012.

Heim, Madeline. "Ozaukee County Fair's Affordability Built on Backs of Hard-working Volunteers." *Milwaukee Journal Sentinel,* August 2, 2016.

"History of Association Which Has Given County Best Fair in the State." *Sheboygan Telegram,* August 14, 1922.

Husband, E. E. "Echoes from the Past." *Polk County Press,* 1953.

"In 1968, the Wisconsin State Fair Made Grandstand Shows Free—With Mixed Results." *Milwaukee Journal Sentinel,* August 7, 2018.

Jardine, Christopher. "Mauston Hosting 154th Juneau County Fair." *Juneau County Star-Times,* August 8, 2019.

Johnson, Robert. "Traveling Back: County Fair Success Due to More Than Simple Competition." *Green Bay Press Gazette,* August 2, 2019.

"Junior County Fair Celebrates 150 years." *Juneau County Star-Times,* August 7, 2015.

Kelley, Sherry. "Past Fair Secretary Van Loon Looks Forward to 140th Waushara County Fair." *Waushara Argus,* August, 2015.

Kohlman, Tina. "Fond du Lac County Fair Has Rich History." *Fond du Lac County Reporter,* July 18, 2015.

Lyksett, Dan. "Northern Wisconsin State Fair: Fair Bit of History." Eau Claire *Leader-Telegram,* July 8, 2015.

Malanowski, Jamie. "The Brief History of the Ferris Wheel." *Smithsonian Magazine,* June 2015.

Martin, Abigail. "Volunteers: The Hands That Make the Fair Go Round." *Wisconsin Agriculturist,* August 2019.

Meinert, Kendra. "Big Concerts Big Part of Kewaunee Fair's 100 Years." Green Bay Press Gazette, July 20, 2017.

"Monroe County Fair Has a Long History," Tomah *Monitor-Herald,* July 27, 2009.

O'Leary, Fran. "Let's Go to the Fair." *Wisconsin Agriculturist,* July 2019.

Oliver, Ned. "First Agricultural Fair Revisted." *Berkshire Eagle,* November 3, 2011.

*Oshkosh Daily Northwestern,* September 7, 1965.

Poullette, Phil. "100 Years of Fair Celebrations." *Waushara Argus,* August 14, 1975.

Pyrek, Emily. "Hometown History: The La Crosse Interstate Fair." *La Crosse Tribune,* July 11, 2016.

Skubal, Michael. "Oneida County Fair." *The* [Rhinelander, Wisconsin] *Daily News,* July 31, August 1, 2010.

*Stanley Republican* [Stanley, Wisconsin], Friday, September 11, 1914.

Tabeling, Katie. "1920 Fair Poster Sees New Life." *Kenosha News,* August 20, 2015.

## PAMPHLETS AND BULLETINS

*50-Year History of the Rock County 4-H Fair*. Janesville, WI: Rock County 4-H Fair, 1979.

Gannett, Henry. *The Origin of Certain Place Names in the United States.* Washington, DC: Government Printing Office, 1905.

Gasch, Renee. *Calumet County Fair History.* Brillion, WI: Zander Press, 2006.

Gasch, Russell. *The Calumet County Fair: 1856 to 1988.* Chilton, WI: Calumet County Fair, 1988.

Hall, Ginny. *Elkhorn History.* Lake Geneva Public Library, 2019.

Harney, Richard J. *History of Winnebago County, Wisconsin, and Early History of the Northwest.* Oshkosh, WI: Hicks Book Printers, 1880.

Hirschy, Harlan. *The Winnebago County Fair: 150 Years Old in 2005.* Oshkosh, WI: Winnebago Fair Association, 2005.

PHOTO BY STEVE APPS

*Lincoln County 4-H Free Fair Centennial:1888–1988*. Merrill, WI: UW Extension, August 1, 1988.

Lohry, Carol, Scott Shaffer, and Randal Waller. "History of County 4-H Fair. In *City on the Rock River*. Janesville, WI: Janesville Historic Commission, 1998.

Rued-Clark, Kris. *Round Barn Tales*, Marshfield, WI: Central Wisconsin State Fair Association, 2006.

Ruesch, Gordon, and Stephen Lars Kalmon, eds. *Our Home—Taylor County Wisconsin—A Topical History of Our Roots*. Medford, WI: Taylor County History Project, 2014.

Sherman, Roger F. "History of Kenosha County Fair," 2012. Unpublished.

*The Wisconsin Century Book.* Milwaukee, WI: Wisconsin Centennial Exposition, 1948.

*Trempealeau County Fair: 125th Year.* Galesville, WI: Trempealeau County Agricultural Society, 1983.

*2019 Iowa County Junior Class Fair Book.* Mineral Point, WI: Iowa County Fair Board, 2019.

Zimmerman, Jerry. *150 Years of the Wisconsin State Fair: 1851–2001.* West Allis, WI: Wisconsin State Fair Park, 2001.

## REPORTS AND THESES

*Clark County Fair Centennial: 1872–1972.* Neillsville, WI: Clark County Fair Board, Centennial Committee, 1972.

Dresden, Katharine Woodrow. "History of Rusk County, Wisconsin." Master of arts thesis, University of Wisconsin–Madison, 1931.

Henry, William Benjamin. "The History of Oconto County." Bachelor of arts thesis, University of Wisconsin–Madison, 1921.

Northern Wisconsin Agricultural and Mechanical Association. *Transactions of the Northern Wisconsin Agricultural and Mechanical Association, for the Years 1870, 1871, 1872 and 1873.* Vol. 1 (1874), Third Annual Fair.

*Proceedings of the Board of Supervisors of Winnebago County.* Oshkosh, WI, March 1911.

*Transactions of the Wisconsin State Agricultural Society.* Madison, WI: Beriah Brown, State Printer, 1852.

*Transactions: Northern Wisconsin Agricultural and Mechanics Association.* Oshkosh, WI, January 1873.

*Transactions: Northern Wisconsin Agricultural and Mechanics Association.* Oshkosh, WI, January 1, 1874.

# ACKNOWLEDGMENTS

**M**any people helped me with this project by contributing historical information, photos, and stories of their experiences with Wisconsin fairs. If I have failed to mention anyone's name, I apologize. Thank you to Stacey Ambort, Jane H. Anklam, Monica Augustine, Roma Ballmer, Shirley Baumann, Julie Belschner, Jody Bezio, Kellie Boone, Betty Lassa-Blauvelt, Kerry Bloedorn, Greg Blonde, Jesse Borien, Diana Wolf Braza, Timothy D. Casucci, Kristin Chuckel, William Collar, Steve Corrigan, Debbie Crave, Rick Daluge, Beth Dippel, Linda Degner, Randy Domer, Guy Dutcher, Cheryl Ehrke, Natalie Erpenback, Douglas Finn, Shae Fox, Nancy Franz, Russ Hanson, Mary Jane Heber, Clara Hedrich, Cyndy Hubbard, Dennis Jacobs, Pam Jahnke, Dee Dee Jakubowski, Jenna Jorgenson, Linda Ketelboeter, Debbie Kitchen, Judy Knudsen, Colleen Kottke, Mary Kunasch, Linda Kustka, Diane Lotter, Fran O'Leary, Eugene Luoma, Pat Luostari, Larry Luostari, Jim Massey, Larry Meiller, Melanie Miller, Sharon Marx, Nyla Musser, Amy Olson, Clarence Olson, Morgan Paavola, Joan Palmer, Dawn Polcyn Peterson, Pat Ritchie, Barbara Rogan, Gay Ruby, Kari Ruf, Ila Sanders, Kassie Schepp, Bonnie Schmitz, Vickie Schwann, Nancy Servais, Dale Simonson, Phyllis Sonsalia, Sandra Stuttgen, Bambi Butzlaff Voss, Ann Webb, Rob White, LaVonne Wier, Cathy and Tim Wiesbrook, Martin J. Wolf, Paul Wollangk, Kim Zills, and Denise Zirbel. (Contributions have been lightly edited for consistency and space considerations.)

Once again, thanks to my wife, Ruth, who reads all my material from the very beginning of a project to its completion. Kate Thompson, director of the Wisconsin Historical Society Press, has edited many of my books and continues to help make them readable. Finally, a big thank you to Kristin Gilpatrick, Wisconsin Historical Society Press sales and marketing manager. She and her crew work tirelessly to let the world know about my books.

# INDEX

EXHIBITOR -704-031?

Department: 7
Class: AA
Lot: 4
POULTRY
ALL FEATHERED LEGS
Young Female

EXHIBITOR
(FOLD ON THIS SCORE)
**Emma Hamilton**
Russell Flats 4-H Club
Westfield, WI

CLAIM CHECK
EXHIBITOR -704-03122
7-AA-4 Young Female
**Emma Hamilton**                    6369

FIRST
PREMIUM

MARQUETTE
COUNTY
FAIR

WESTFIELD
WISCONSIN

made by
FAIR PUBLISHING H
Norwalk, OH 448
Phone - 800-824-3

DATE
CLASS
PRIZE
WON BY

2014

MARQUETTE
COUNTY
FAIR
JUNIOR

POULTRY

# ABOUT THE AUTHOR

Jerry Apps was born and raised on a central Wisconsin farm. He is a former county extension agent and professor emeritus for the College of Agriculture and Life Sciences at the University of Wisconsin–Madison. As a 4-H member, Jerry exhibited cattle and other projects at county fairs for ten years; he also served as a county fair judge for ten years. Today he works as a rural historian, full-time writer, and creative writing instructor. Jerry has received the Major Achievement Award from the Council for Wisconsin Writers and the Distinguished Service Award from the UW–Madison College of Agricultural and Life Sciences, and he was elected a Fellow in the Wisconsin Academy of Sciences, Arts and Letters in 2012.

PHOTO BY STEVE APPS

Jerry is the author of more than fifty fiction, nonfiction, and children's books with topics ranging from barns, one-room schools, cranberries, cucumbers, cheese factories, and the humor of mid-America to farming with horses and the Ringling Brothers circus. He and his wife, Ruth, have three grown children, seven grandchildren, and one great-grandson. They divide their time between their home in Madison and their 120-acre farm, Roshara, in Waushara County.